The most important thing in Al's lif[e] ever got into a conversation with him a[bout]point not to honors or degrees or accomplishments, but to the depth of a person's friendship with Christ. Al loved the Lord, and he wanted to do only what was pleasing to him. He also loved people, and he did his best to share with them the one thing that really mattered in life: the love of God. In his work as a scholar and teacher, Al had that remarkable ability of integrating his love for learning with his desire for God and his concern for others. He was loving husband, father, pastor, elder, and friend to so many people. He was also a groundbreaking Old Testament scholar, researcher, and teacher, with a deep love for God's Word and a desire to share that life-giving Word with his colleagues and students. I am sure that Al would be deeply touched by this collection of essays written in his honor. He would be especially moved, I believe, not so much by the high quality of the contributions (as evidenced throughout), but by the deep bonds of friendship that inspired his colleagues and former students to honor him in this way. My friendship with Al goes back to 1971 when we entered Dartmouth College together as freshmen. I remember him then and think of him now as someone who always counted his blessings, and who generously shared his many gifts and talents with others. This volume demonstrates in no uncertain terms what a truly great blessing Al was to the Christian community revolving around Westminster Theological Seminary, and what a wonderful and inspiring gift he was to the international world of biblical scholarship.

—**Dennis J. Billy,** C.Ss.R., John Cardinal Krol Chair, St. Charles Borromeo Seminary, Wynnewood, Pennsylvania

I cherish very special memories of my work with Al—an innovative, thorough, and knowledgeable scholar, and above all a dear friend. My work with him in the 1980s on the digitization of the Leningrad Codex was pleasant and instructive in all aspects. Subsequently, he slowly became a leader in this field. He was at the forefront of the computerized study of the Hebrew Bible and its grammatical analysis, and without him this field would be different today. This fine collection of studies is a token of appreciation for his work, and will remain an everlasting memory of his activities and personality.

—**Emanuel Tov,** J. L. Magnes Professor Emeritus of Bible, Hebrew University, Jerusalem

"Ah, Mercy!" That word that was ever on Al's lips also well describes the focus of his work and his life. As he was conscious of having received mercy, so he lived it and, like Micah, loved it. And as he read his Hebrew Bible (and his Greek New Testament, too), he saw God's *chesed* everywhere in it. The essays in this volume are a fitting tribute to Al, the lover of mercy, because, as Al himself was always concerned to do (even in the midst of parsing an ambiguous verb), they point beyond technical matters to some of the ways in which the Bible directs us both to love and to live God's mercy. Thanks be to God.

—**Dan McCartney,** Professor of New Testament
Interpretation, Redeemer Seminary, Dallas

Al Groves would surely have opened this volume of scholarly essays eagerly, and on scanning the contents page thought: "Why, I know every one of these contributors personally!"—little thinking that this was the motivation for the entire book. He would have been deeply moved, honored, surprised, grateful, and happy to know he was so much loved.

Al Groves had a special capacity to make people *feel* his care for, and interest in, them—and not only as students or scholars but as whole individuals. At the same time, he could gently question and probe both mind and heart in pastoral concern. Reading these pages with gratitude, he would often, surely, have paused and thought: "Now, we must talk further about this."

It is wonderfully fitting that some of his closest friends, colleagues, teachers, and students here offer their learning and their love to the memory of such a man. This physical reminder of his largeness of heart, his lovability, his ability joyfully to unite faith and learning, makes one feel again how much he meant to those who knew, loved, and learned from him—and how much he is missed.

—**Sinclair B Ferguson,** The First Presbyterian Church, Columbia, South
Carolina; Professor of Systematic Theology, Redeemer Seminary, Dallas

Teaching in a theological climate is a very lonely and sometimes daunting enterprise. Even with the most absorbed and friendly class, you are all alone there in front. What you say will inevitably be passed on—sometimes garbled and distorted. When you read the exams and one student after another gets it all wrong, there is really only one conclusion available: you, with all your preparation and good intentions, have deceived a whole class, and they will go on to deceive the waiting world. It is hard to be fearless and open to learning and willing to teach something new and important. It is easy to be safe and lazy. I think teaching the Old Testament is the hardest. It is so far away from today; is Jesus really there? But at Westminster Theological Seminary it was different. Ray Dillard showed us Jesus in the Old Testament, with integrity and with joy.

Ray was pastoral in his preaching and in his recruitment and leadership of his band of brothers in the Old Testament department. The group he brought together and nurtured was truly a team. But that can't happen, can it? Remember how lonesome it is up in front? Someone has said that if it happens, it's possible. It happened. That had to be unique in Old Testament theological education.

But it wasn't unique; it continued. At Ray's much-too-early death, suddenly the unspectacular Al Groves was there, as pastoral of his brood as Ray had been. He had his own kind of cutting-edge scholarship in the arcane world of the Old Testament text. How could the cellar of a crumbling mansion produce the very best Old Testament text ever—and computerized at that? How could that kind of world-class scholarship come with the pastor's heart, for students and especially for his colleagues? It happened again with Al.

We must speak the truth in love. In a seminary, *truth* means the very best painstaking scholarship. *In love* means with kindness and care for all the students, and especially for colleagues in the hard and sometimes hostile world of evangelical Old Testament scholarship. That was Al Groves. It happened again. Isn't the Lord kind?

—**Clair Davis,** Chaplain and Professor of Church History,
Redeemer Seminary, Dallas

It is a pleasure to commend this tribute to Al Groves, a pioneer of the interface between computers and the study of the Hebrew Bible, whose death was a huge and untimely loss. The collection here reflects Al Groves' particular interests, and testifies to the vigor and creativity of Old Testament studies in the best traditions of Westminster Theological Seminary, as well as to the immense personal and scholarly influence of the honoree.

—**Gordon McConville,** Professor of Old Testament Theology,
University of Gloucestershire

Al's interest in the Hebrew biblical text brought him into contact with the fledgling Center for Computer Analysis of Texts (CCAT) that was attempting to gather computerized texts, especially for the subproject Computer Analysis of Texts for Septuagint Studies. Al worked with the late Jack (John) Abercrombie to correct and adjust the computerized Hebrew text that had been acquired from the University of Michigan (Van Parunak) in cooperation with Claremont Graduate School (Dick Whittaker). In the development of things, further work on this Hebrew material was done in the Netherlands by E. Talstra and his team, with Al contributing on this side of the waters. Al became the person in charge of the Hebrew biblical text developments, at first as an arm of CCAT but soon as an independent project. It was a tremendously valuable development in all ways, and his attention to detail and cooperative spirit were much appreciated by all.

—**Robert A. Kraft,** Berg Professor of Religious Studies,
University of Pennsylvania

For two traits, yea for three, will I remember Al Groves:
For prayers redolent with thanksgiving and praise and short on petitions,
For scholarship alive both to textual ideologies and to Yahweh's mission,
And for an unnatural gift of parsing lunch bills into fair divisions.
For these traits, yea for many more, may the God of Israel be praised!

—**Stephen S. Taylor,** Associate Professor of New Testament,
Biblical Seminary, Hatfield, Pennsylvania

This volume is full of gems, cut from the Scriptures, and skillfully polished by gifted scholars who knew and loved our brother Al Groves. I knew Al for almost thirty years, as classmate and colleague, and these essays are a fitting tribute to the man whose heart was full of love for Christ and for his church. They illustrate all that was true of Al: a concern for academic excellence and theological integrity, allied with a warm heart. The task facing Old Testament scholars is often difficult, but these essays are sparkling with light and color and make us want to dig for ourselves so that we may discover new biblical gems that enable us to be more energetic worshipers of the God of Abraham, Isaac, and Jacob.

—**Stafford Carson,** former moderator of the Presbyterian Church in Ireland and minister of First Presbyterian Church, Portadown, Northern Ireland

Eyes to See,
Ears to Hear

Eyes to See, Ears to Hear

ESSAYS IN MEMORY OF

J. ALAN GROVES

Edited by

Peter Enns, Douglas J. Green,
& Michael B. Kelly

P&R
PUBLISHING
P.O. BOX 817 • PHILLIPSBURG • NEW JERSEY 08865-0817

Printed in the United States of America

Library of Congress Cataloging-in-Publication Data

Eyes to see, ears to hear : essays in memory of J. Alan Groves / edited by Peter Enns, Douglas J. Green & Michael B. Kelly.
     p. cm.
  Includes bibliographical references and index.
  ISBN 978-1-59638-122-3 (pbk.)
  1. Bible. O.T.--Criticism, interpretation, etc. 2. Bible. O.T.--Theology. I. Groves, J. Alan. II. Enns, Peter, 1961- III. Green, Douglas J., 1953- IV. Kelly, Michael B., 1965-
  BS1171.3.E94 2010
  230'.0411--dc22
                              2010016527

To Libbie, Alasdair, Rebeckah, Éowyn, and Alden:
Thank you for sharing so much of your husband and father
with so many.

To Al's students:
May you have "ears to hear and eyes to see Jesus."

Contents

Foreword

MOISÉS SILVA

I SUSPECT I'M NOT UNUSUAL in that I especially admire those qualities in other people that are conspicuously absent in me. It is perhaps for that
reason that, in my estimation, the most striking of Al Groves' many virtues
was his welcoming smile and voice whenever someone stepped into his office
to disturb him. And because he never appeared to have felt disturbed, the
typical visitor, no doubt, felt encouraged—if only at a subconscious level—
to interrupt him as frequently as possible.

The truth is that Al had far more on his plate than I, and perhaps any
of his other colleagues, ever did. But a single human being who might come
to see him was, for him, of far greater importance than the pressing work. It
is possible, I suppose, that a sense of obligation was part of what motivated
Al to treat others the way he did. And yet one was never aware that duty
played a role. He truly valued and appreciated people, and was ever willing
to set aside his own interests and plans for their sake.

Al had served in a pastorate before coming to Westminster Seminary—initially as a student, but eventually joining the faculty. Unlike
some others who have made a comparable transition, however, he did
not set his pastoral heart aside when he became more directly involved in
academia. One might think that the highly specialized and technical nature
of his scholarly interests (such as using computer technology to produce
an electronic text of the Hebrew Bible with every word grammatically

analyzed) would have drawn him into an eremitic existence and greatly limited his contact with students.

Quite the opposite was true. Indeed, most students undoubtedly viewed Al as the pastor-teacher par excellence. And we will never know how many troubled believers, both in seminary and in the local church where he served, were helped by his spiritual advice. On two or three occasions, Al half-jokingly referred to me as his "father-confessor" (I quickly granted him absolution). In reality, and in spite of his younger age, he was far more qualified to play that role.

Beyond that—and in the midst of intense pressures and trials—Al was hardly lacking in joie de vivre. I was privileged to be part of a small group who joined him in traveling to professional meetings year after year, and it quickly became apparent to the rest of us that he was exceptionally well qualified to guide us in choosing good places to eat. None of us could match his range of culinary tastes or his capacity to clean every plate until it was spotless. Moreover, his appreciation for life was just as evident in his enjoyment of literature and film. And no one could be around him very long before becoming aware of the great pride and delight he took in his family.

Yet what ultimately distinguished him above all was his deeply personal commitment to Christ. And while the whole tenor of his life gave testimony to his faith, its genuineness and warmth would become immediately evident to anyone who heard him pray. Al would often ask God, for himself and those present, for "eyes to see and ears to hear." Such a prayer reflects a willingness to recognize the reality of human ignorance, struggle, and doubt in the Christian life, but it also expresses a sense of humble dependence on the One who can grant light, strength, and assurance to all who ask. Al's life reflected that prayer. May we all learn to pray and live as he did.

Preface

"Give us eyes to see Jesus,
  ears to hear,
  and hearts to understand."

Al Groves routinely closed his prayers with those words. In fact, we cannot even read them without hearing his voice pleading them to his heavenly Father. With his body in decline from cancer, he closed his charge to the 2006 graduates of Westminster Theological Seminary with those words—a charge that those hundred or so men and women, and many of us in attendance, will not forget. Al meant that prayer, and that charge. His life was one pointed to the grace of God in Jesus Christ, and lived with the intention of directing those with whom he came in contact to their own need for new eyes, ears, and hearts, coming only as a gift from a loving Father.

THE BIBLICAL THEOLOGIAN

Those words, some may recognize, arise directly from the vision in Isaiah 6:10, where Isaiah's call is framed around this difficult-to-understand biblical picture of the prophetic ministry as one of "hardening." Isaiah undertakes his prophetic ministry lest the people see, hear, and understand. The fact that Al would boldly pray that prayer gives us a window into the deep biblical-theological thinking that captured his approach to Scripture. He boldly offered that prayer, aware of the human propensity to be blind, deaf, and dull, but fully confident that Jesus Christ, by the power of his death and resurrection, offers the gift of new eyes, ears, and hearts to the ever-expanding circle of those who follow him, who find life in the kingdom of God (Acts 28:23–31). Al would think of praying this way only because of his deep convictions about what Jesus Christ had accomplished in the fullness of time.

This foundational interest in the life, death, and resurrection of Jesus Christ as providing the climax to the grand story of Scripture inspired a generation of Al's students. The contributors to this volume were deeply influenced by his careful attention to the Hebrew text, his sensitivity to the historical context in which it was written, and his insistence that the OT be understood as ultimately pointing to its climax in Jesus Christ. Al served as coeditor, with Tremper Longman III, of The Gospel According to the Old Testament series, a theological commentary series devoted to exploring the biblical-theological dimensions of the OT. His untimely death prevented Al from finishing his intended contribution to that series, *The Gospel According to Isaiah*. His remarkable biblical-theological work on Isaiah, seen, for example, in his article "Atonement in Isaiah 53,"[1] and contained in over a decade of students' notes, will have to wait to see the further light of day as many of us pick up his ideas and explore and expand them in other venues. Likewise, Al's publication of longer essays on the Deuteronomistic history and the book of Judges (see the Curriculum Vitae in this volume) are really windows into the depth of his biblical-theological thinking. His students tasted the blessings of his learning and reflection; the wider people of God are the poorer for not having heard more from Al firsthand. But by God's grace, Al's "fingerprints" thoroughly cover his students, who take his insights beyond what he was able to do. It is the prayer of the editors of and contributors to this volume that *Eyes to See, Ears to Hear* will play a role in honoring Al, giving thanks to Jesus Christ for the scholarly, pastoral, and spiritual mentor he was to so many.

The Pioneer and Colaborer

Al's written scholarly output was somewhat limited, because he conceived of his contribution to the academic community as taking place behind the scenes. A consummate team player, Al spent much of his career collaborating with many other scholars to provide electronic data for careful study of the Hebrew Bible. Al took great pleasure in colaboring with others,

1. In Charles E. Hill and Frank A. James, eds., *The Glory of the Atonement* (Downers Grove, IL: InterVarsity Press, 2004), 61–89.

working together to ensure the highest quality output for others to use in research. Much of this work was done in the recesses of a computer center, away from the public eye. As Kirk Lowery, the current President and Senior Research Fellow of the J. Alan Groves Center for Advanced Biblical Research, has commented, Al likened his work to that of an engineer who designs the wings of the airplane so that they don't fall off at thirty-one thousand feet, and not the welder who assembles the steel or the pilot who actually flies the plane. This is a wonderful metaphor to understand this important component of Al's scholarly contribution and his meticulous attention to detail: the background work and data had better be right, before the plane is built, test-flown, and put into service carrying people!

Much of this collaborative work was done in the field of the application of computer technology to the study of the Hebrew Bible, a field in which Al was among the early scholars to recognize the importance of doing sound technological work in order better to understand the Hebrew Bible and the Hebrew language. In this scholarly arena, because of Al's early visionary work, it is not uncommon to hear him referred to as a "pioneer." For several years he served as cochair of the Society of Biblical Literature's "Computer Assisted Research Group," providing leadership to the scholarly biblical studies community during the critical years when computers moved from behemoths that occupied entire rooms to boxes that sat atop office desks. This growing access and increased mobility changed the world of computing drastically over Al's three-decade career; he was at the forefront of the leaders bringing this change to bear on biblical studies.

For example, one of Al's earliest scholarly ventures involved playing a role in the production of an electronic edition of the text of the Hebrew Bible, a project in which he collaborated with scholars from The Hebrew University (Jerusalem), The University of Pennsylvania, and Claremont graduate schools. The end result was an electronic text of the Hebrew Bible as close as possible to the important Hebrew Bible manuscript, the Leningrad Codex. The text ultimately produced through this collaboration, known as the Michigan-Claremont-Westminster (MCW) electronic BHS, is currently maintained by the J. Alan Groves Center for Advanced Biblical Studies, and to this day is used for translations and printed editions of the Hebrew Bible, for example, the Hebrew-English Tanakh (Jewish Publication Society, 1999) and the Reader's Hebrew Bible (Zondervan, 2008). Additionally, the MCW text serves as the Hebrew text for many of the standard Bible programs currently available. This important text exists in its current form in large part because of Al's early labors with other scholars, building on their work and, indeed, even going far beyond them.

In addition to playing a significant role in establishing the MCW text, Al was also highly involved collaboratively with the production of a morphology of the Hebrew Bible. This painstaking task involves labeling every component of every word in the Hebrew Bible according to its grammatical part of speech, and even, at times, its grammatical function. For readers who have not studied Hebrew, imagine going through your English Bible and having your eighth-grade grammar teacher ask you to explain every part of speech, word by word! Painstaking indeed! Those who have studied Hebrew and use Hebrew databases in Bible software are very likely benefiting from Al's work, using data that he had a large part in producing and perfecting.

Al's technical expertise continues to benefit the field of biblical studies to the present time. His tireless labor behind the scenes to provide other scholars with tools and data for their work can also be seen in his role as Consultant in Information Systems to the Biblia Hebraica Quinta project, one of the last projects to which Al was able to contribute. This important project will provide scholars and pastors with a fifth modern edition of the Hebrew Bible. In the introduction to the first released volume, the Editorial Committee comments that the project

> benefited from the flexibility and control of a new computerized production method in which all data to be included in the edition are entered into a database, which can then be converted into a variety of electronic and printed forms. This approach would not have been possible without the guidance and assistance of the project's Consultant in Information Systems, Alan Groves of Westminster Theological Seminary . . .[2]

This preface is intended to give some indication of the important role Alan Groves played in the field of biblical studies, admittedly much of it outside the public eye. We have devoted chapter 12 of this festschrift to a fuller treatment of his groundbreaking work, "The Legacy of J. Alan Groves:

2. General *Introduction and Megilloth*, Biblia Hebraica Quinta, Fascicle 18 (Stuttgart: Deutsche Bibelgesellschaft, 2004), xxv. Several other scholars from around the world fill out that paragraph—another indication of Al's regular and welcomed role as a colaborer with others.

An Oral History." Kirk Lowery, the author of that chapter, concludes his article with these words:

> Professor Groves' death prevented him from accomplishing all that he envisioned. Nevertheless, his vision continues to inspire us. The Hebrew syntax database he spoke of is now nearing completion, and plans are already underway for new possibilities, including other ancient Near Eastern languages and texts. The pyramid, the foundations of which he laid, is growing. Tens of thousands of users of all descriptions are making use of the text and data that he created. Unlike ordinary academic publications, Professor Groves' databases are not static, but are living, growing collections of knowledge and experience in understanding the text and message of the Hebrew Bible. Since Professor Groves' work forms the foundation of the Hebrew Bible digital pyramid of knowledge, it is difficult to overstate the significance and impact of his legacy for the next century of biblical studies.

It is not difficult to conceive of Al's contribution to computing and biblical studies. This festschrift in part wants to honor his scholarly contributions, and it is fitting to do so. The contributors to this volume include Al's former colleagues and students at Westminster Theological Seminary. The colleagues represented are Tremper Longman, Bruce Waltke, Douglas Green, Peter Enns, and Michael Kelly, who (along with the late Raymond Dillard) made up the Old Testament department in the years of Al's service; the current faculty moderator, William Edgar (with whom Al team-taught a course on a Christian approach to film—another of Al's passions); and Kirk Lowery, Al's colaborer and successor as Director (and now President) of the J. Alan Groves Institute for Advanced Biblical Studies.

Because Al's greatest legacy is found in the students he taught and mentored, we chose to include essays from former students from the three decades in which he taught: Green and Enns from the 1980s, Karen Jobes, Kelly, and Adrian Smith (who completed his Th.M. in Old Testament under Al) from the early 1990s, and three younger scholars who were among his final group of students from the late 1990s and early 2000s: Chris Fantuzzo, Brad Gregory, and Sam Boyd.

As our final act of honoring our mentor and colleague in this volume, we have included Al's lecture on the occasion of his inauguration as Professor of Old Testament at Westminster Theological Seminary. Like other essays, this is intended to give a sampling of the type of redemptive-historical Old Testament scholarship that came to flower during Al's time on the faculty at the seminary.

But Al's life and legacy go far beyond scholarly contributions. As Moisés Silva brings out in the Foreword, Al had a profound spiritual impact on those around him. The faculty, students, and staff of the seminary enjoyed Al's profound pastoral attention during his all-too-brief time as Vice President for Academic Affairs in 2005–6. So we also offer these essays to honor Al as a brother in Christ, a mentor to his students, a pastor to his colleagues, and one whose life was pointed to the One who gave him life, and who lived his life in the service of others.

Al's prayer has now been answered. He now sees, hears, and knows fully (1 Cor. 13:12). He has now joined the company of disciples. As our Lord says in Luke 10:23–24 (ESV): "Blessed are the eyes that see what you see! For I tell you that many prophets and kings desired to see what you see, and did not see it, and to hear what you hear, and did not hear it."

And for those of us who wait, labor, and serve, grateful and changed by our friendship with Al, we continue to pray this prayer—for eyes to see, ears to hear, and hearts to understand.

Acknowledgments

OUR SINCERE THANKS, first of all, to Marvin Padgett, Karen Magnuson, and John Hughes. Their enthusiasm, flexibility, and attention to detail helped make this volume into a lasting token of thankfulness to God for the life, friendship, and ministry of Al.

Thanks also to our student colleagues, Steve Bohannon and Rob Kashow, for their work preparing the indexes.

Finally, we wish to thank our wives, Sue, Rosemarie, and Shareen, for their steady and compassionate support even as they too shared in the loss of our close friend and brother.

Peter Enns
Douglas J. Green
Michael B. Kelly

Abbreviations

AB	Anchor Bible
AUSS	*Andrews University Seminary Studies*
BCOTWP	Baker Commentary on the Old Testament Wisdom and Psalms
BDB	*Hebrew and English Lexicon of the Old Testament*
BECNT	Baker Exegetical Commentary on the New Testament
BETL	Bibliotheca Ephemeridum Theologicarum Lovaniensium
BHS	Biblia Hebraica Stuttgartensia
CBQ	*Catholic Biblical Quarterly*
ESV	English Standard Version
HALOT	Ludwig Köhler, Walter Baumgartner, and Johann Jakob Stamm, *The Hebrew and Aramaic Lexicon of the Old Testament*, 4 vols., trans. and ed. under supervision of M. E. J. Richardson (Leiden: Brill, 1994–99)
HTR	*Harvard Theological Review*
HUCA	*Hebrew University College Annual*
IBHS	Bruce K. Waltke and Michael O'Connor, *Introduction to Biblical Hebrew Syntax* (Winona Lake, IN: Eisenbrauns, 1990)
JAOS	*Journal of the American Oriental Society*
JBL	*Journal of Biblical Literature*
JETS	*Journal of the Evangelical Theological Society*
JPS	Jewish Publication Society
JSOT	*Journal of the Society of Old Testament*
JSOTSup	Journal of the Society of Old Testament Supplement
KJV	King James Version

LHBOTS	Library of Hebrew Bible/Old Testament Studies
LNTS	Library of New Testament Studies
LXX	Septuagint
MT	Masoretic Text
NAC	New American Commentary
NASB	New American Standard Bible
NIB	New Interpreter's Bible
NIBC	New International Biblical Commentary
NIBCOT	New International Biblical Commentary on the Old Testament
NICOT	New International Commentary on the Old Testament
NIDOTTE	*New International Dictionary of Old Testament Theology and Exegesis*
NIV	New International Version
NIVAC	NIV Application Commentary
NKJV	New King James Version
NLT	New Living Translation
NRSV	New Revised Standard Version
NSBT	New Studies in Biblical Theology
NT	New Testament
OG	Old Greek
OT	Old Testament
OTL	Old Testament Library
RSV	Revised Standard Version
SBT	Studies in Biblical Theology
SJT	*Scottish Journal of Theology*
TaNaK	Hebrew Bible
TDOT	*Theological Dictionary of the Old Testament*
THAT	Ernst Jenni and Claus Westermann, eds., *Theologisches Handwörterbuch zum Alten Testament*, 2 vols. (München: Chr. Kaiser; Zürich: Theologischer Verlag, 1984)
TLOT	*Theological Lexicon of the Old Testament*
TNIV	Today's New International Version
VT	*Vetus Testamentum*
VTSup	Vetus Testamentum Supplement
WBC	Word Biblical Commentary
WTJ	*Westminster Theological Journal*

Personal Words

A Life Well Lived[1]

SINCLAIR B. FERGUSON

Last Saturday I had the privilege of preaching at a memorial service for Alan Groves, my longtime friend. For fifteen years of our lives, we saw each other almost every working day. He was fifty-four—a scholar and a professor of Hebrew.

The service was memorable. A thousand or more were present, many of them younger men and women; another thousand around the world watched the webcast. His four children and his brothers spoke of him movingly. His colleagues read Scripture in English and Hebrew, and spoke eloquently of his friendship. There were nine tributes and much singing. The service lasted about two hours. I doubt if there were many who wanted it to end sooner.

The stature of our friend grew before our eyes as his full portrait was unveiled and we saw him now whole and complete.

I mention this not so much because the occasion has—obviously—lingered with me, but because three things impressed me.

First, for all his learning (Hebrew scholars are a race apart!), absolutely central to Al's life was the Lord Jesus Christ. You could not be in his presence without realizing that. He simply knew Christ and loved him deeply. The sense of the Lord's presence with him was almost palpable.

---

1. Rev. Ferguson wrote this tribute in *First Things*, the weekly newsletter of The First Presbyterian Church of Columbia, South Carolina, where he is senior minister, in the week after he had preached the homily at Al Groves' memorial service.

Second, Al had a habit of pointing things out. One colleague recollected bike riding behind him on the canal paths of Holland. At every point in the road, our friend, in the lead, would point and say, "It's this way, not that!" or "Look at this!" But the supreme expression of this habit was not physical but spiritual. One and another noted how Al always pointed to Jesus—in speech, in action, in all his personal deportment.

Third, what Al was in public he was—even more so—to his wife and children. His children, from early teens to early twenties, could each say that their dad had loved them to Christ. I watched them participate in the worship; it was evident, even in their heart-bursting loss, that they, too, loved their father's Lord. Yes, they have a long furrow now to plough without him. But Al had shown them Christ. This is his lasting memorial.

We both felt we belonged to a great and glorious brotherhood in which we had grown older together—a seminary faculty can be one of the most privileged places in the world to work. But the abiding impression from Saturday was not Al's accomplishments in that world, but that he had been faithful in the ordinary things that Christians share in common. He had trusted and loved Christ; he had pointed others to Christ; he had loved his wife in Christ and led their children to Christ. Therein resides Al's greatest epitaph.

I made my way back to Columbia with a deep sense that everything else we leave behind becomes dust.

Fading is the worldling's pleasure, all his boasted pomp and show
Solid joys, and lasting treasure, none but Zion's children know.

Jonathan Edwards and Al Groves

SAMUEL T. LOGAN JR.

Al Groves reminds me of Jonathan Edwards. Both men died young, each at the age of fifty-five. Both men died shortly after taking on new academic responsibilities—Jonathan Edwards as President of Princeton College and Al Groves as Vice President of Academic Affairs at Westminster Theological Seminary (one of the institutional heirs of that original Princeton). Both men left behind communities agonizing over "what might have been" if they had lived.

But those are the externals of the two lives. The most significant similarity between them was the content of their lives and theologies. In a word, that content was, and by God's grace continues to be, Jesus.

In the most important of his works, the *Treatise on Religious Affections*, Edwards makes the disturbing but thoroughly biblical claim that what characterizes "truly gracious affections" is their Christocentric focus. Ultimately, Edwards argues, the true Christian gives himself to Jesus not in order to get something *from* Jesus (heaven) but in order to give something *to* Jesus (the praise he deserves). Of course, there are unimaginable and eternal blessings in store for the believing Christian, but whenever the heart is more focused on the blessings than on the blesser, we are "seeking first" something other than the kingdom of God and his righteousness.

Moisés Silva picks up on this theme in his Foreword to the present volume, especially in the last paragraph of that Foreword: "Yet what ultimately distinguished him [Al] above all was his deeply personal commitment to Christ." That is why, to take just one of the examples Moisés provides, people came first for Al. And loving the people whom the Lord had placed in Al's path took precedence over everything else, even those gargantuan piles of work on his desk.

In the midst of a particularly difficult time in my life, Al came to our home and sat talking with Susan and me for hours. The cancer that ultimately killed him had already returned, and his responsibilities at the seminary were huge. But Al came to talk with us and to love us. He did not provide an easy answer (the worst that we feared did eventually happen), but he reminded us, gently but powerfully, of a Savior who loved us even more than he did. And that made all the difference.

But the present volume is intended not just to point back to the life of one Christ-centered man. It is intended to speak about different aspects of God's Word in ways that embody that central thrust of Al's life. Over and over again, these essays bring us back to Jesus. When Tremper Longman considers "when bad things happen to good people," he reminds us in the end that the answer to that conundrum is not to deny it but to affirm that it is resolved when the ultimate wrong is done to the best person and when that best person triumphs in a resurrection that destroys the power of all the "bad things" that have ever existed.

When Doug Green takes us through the Twenty-third Psalm, or Pete Enns mines the riches of Qohelet's theology, or Mike Kelly discusses missional hermeneutics, or Karen Jobes examines apostolic reflections on Isaiah 53, the central figure, over and over again, is Jesus. The genius of all these essays is the way in which they embody what both Edwards and Groves taught and lived—the centrality of the Savior.

Edwards once said, "No light in the understanding is good which does not produce holy affection [for Jesus] in the heart." Jonathan Edwards and Al Groves lived this truth, and by God's grace, the essays in this book will move readers in that same Christocentric direction.

On Bridges, Bytes, and Beaches

EEP TALSTRA

One of the many things that one could say about Alan Groves is that he was remarkably gifted at observing and enjoying life in all its breadth. Given his broad range of interests, how shall I choose which memories to comment on?

To me, Alan was an excellent example of the importance of having trained engineers in the field of biblical theology. He was a genuine crafts-man at building bridges between continents, whether between Europe and the United States or between Christian faith and classical Hebrew morphology. I am convinced that his initial technical training as an engineer helped him to think carefully and precisely, both in the study of OT theology and in doing grammar in bits and bytes. Furthermore, in between all his tasks, Alan was always ready to enjoy the Netherlands' island beaches, as well as beaches in America.

We met for the first time in 1987, in Amsterdam, where Alan contributed a paper to a symposium on the occasion of the tenth anniversary of my research group in Bible and computing.[2] Alan presented the

---

2. Alan Groves, "On Computers and Hebrew Morphology," in E. Talstra, ed., *Computer Assisted Analysis of Biblical Texts. Proceedings of the Workshop Held at the Occasion of the 10th Anniversary of the "Werkgroep Informatica" in Amsterdam, November 5–6, 1987*, Applicatio 7 (Amsterdam: Vrije Universiteit University Press, 1989), 45–86.

research that he and his team had performed since 1983 for the Westminster Hebrew database. Presentationally, his contribution was modest, but as the audience quickly perceived, it was thorough and effective in approach. As an engineer, he was able to bring our digital dreams down to earth and into the realm of real data. He compared his work to that of a "street sweeper" after a parade, his tasks being to clean databases and to make data and their analysis precise and consistent. As he said in that paper, "all of us in computer-aided study of texts are involved in a modern-day Masoretic enterprise."

That meeting became the start of a long-term scholarly cooperation that continued until the last years of Alan's academic work. Alan invited me to visit Philadelphia several times for guest lectures. On three occasions between 1992 and 2002, he and his family spent a semester of sabbatical leave with us in Amsterdam. A tangential effect of these visits continues to this day: my youngest son still speaks Dutch to Libbie on the phone!

These were years of deep friendship between our families and of intense scholarly cooperation. Together, Alan and I studied the Hebrew syntax needed for our common goals: to produce solid databases of the biblical text and to explore the theology of biblical books such as Exodus, Judges, and Kings. Our first common project, in close cooperation with our Swiss German friend Christoph Hardmeier, was the Hebrew database QUEST,[3] its later version called SESB.[4]

Alan made me a member of the Westminster delegation at several Society of Biblical Literature conferences. During the 1991 conference in Kansas City, we took a day off, and Alan drove me into the countryside to visit his grandmother, who lived in a small town in a home for elderly people. After the grand hotels of downtown Kansas City, that was a real and valuable introduction to American daily life.

After this reminiscing, I do not need to make choices: Alan Groves means Hebrew texts and computing, singing hymns together, walking the walls of the ancient city of Jerusalem, and enjoying the beaches of the island of Terschelling. It was a blessing to know this colleague and friend.

3. Eep Talstra, Christoph Hardmeier, and J. Alan Groves, eds., *QUEST: Electronic Concordance Applications for the Hebrew Bible* (Haarlem: Netherlands Bible Society, 1992).

4. Christoph Hardmeier, Eep Talstra, and Alan Groves, *SESB: Stuttgart Electronic Study Bible* (Stuttgart: German Bible Society / Haarlem: Netherlands Bible Society, 2004).

A Tribute to a Friend

ED WELCH

"Nothing has changed."

I wasn't so sure. It seemed to me that everything had changed. With four words—"your cancer is malignant"—Al's parents would lose their oldest son; his wife would become a widow; his four children, far too young to lose a father, would, indeed, lose their father; and what about me? Not that it's all about me, but I would lose a dear friend in just a little more than a year. The cancer was inoperable, and there were no viable treatments. But those were his first words to me. He said them about twenty-five minutes after he had been given his diagnosis and prognosis. "Nothing has changed."

This is what he meant. The hour before he was given his dire and accurate prognosis, Al had been certain that Jesus was the reigning King. His kingdom was initiated with power at his resurrection and ascension; his love was established beyond any doubt when he died for those who held him in contempt; and in his death we have forgiveness of sins, which was the first of an explosion of benefits and promises fulfilled. Nothing can separate us from his love; his reign is guaranteed to prosper. On a more personal note, it also meant that my friend's loving Father would care for his wife and children with a unique affection. These are a few things that Al crammed into "nothing has changed."

All this was true pre-diagnosis; it was true post-diagnosis. Yet everything had changed. There were decisions about joining an experimental treatment group; every day would have plenty of tears and many goodbyes; there were gravesites to select; and Al would have to comfort many friends who were already mourning. But he was certain that "Jesus Christ is the same yesterday and today and forever" (Heb. 13:8 NIV).

Imagine—and Al was a good imaginer—what life would be like if we could quickly say that nothing has changed when we encounter snags, inconveniences, and downright tragedies. Unshakable. Utterly unshakable. Imagine life without the angry outbursts and swoons of despair or the long gaps of faithlessness before we turn back to Jesus. Well, I can imagine them by simply remembering Al. He was my near-daily reminder that we live in the age of the Spirit, and that what was previously impossible becomes normal.

His words of faith didn't appear out of nowhere. There is always a backstory when we actually see the Spirit on the move. Here is some of it. Al read the psalms every day. In the twenty-five years that I knew him, he probably never missed a day. Of course, he read lots of other passages. I think he was a read-the-Bible-through-in-a-year guy. But his diet of the psalms is what especially inspired me. God has determined that much of the growth that his people experience comes from the gradual accumulation of hearing or reading the truth, believing it, and living it. Dramatic insights are great when they come, but they usually add just a hint of color to the gradual and inexorable process of growing in Jesus.

I read Psalm 105 today. (I don't read a psalm without thinking about Al.) I needed my own version of "nothing has changed." The psalm is like many others. I've never heard anyone say that it was his or her favorite psalm. It just happened to be next in the schedule.

> Give thanks to the LORD, call on his name; make known among the nations what he has done. Sing to him, sing praise to him; tell of all his wonderful acts. Glory in his holy name; let the hearts of those who seek the LORD rejoice. Look to the LORD and his strength; seek his face always. (Ps. 105:1–4)

The psalmist leads us in a traditional introduction, but already everything has changed. I am taken up out of my many cares, and my heart is focused on things that are even bigger and more important. Then the psalm recounts OT history, which is the history of God. He directs history, and history reveals him and his endless acts of love and faithfulness.

One of the observations that experts have made about the increase in depression is that it has coincided with an era in which there is nothing bigger than us and our own desires. The family is broken or dispersed; there is no security in our jobs; and there is no *cause célèbre*. We are stuck, therefore, with the meager self, and depression is sure to follow. Psalm 105, in contrast, gives us exactly what we need. It brings us into a bigger story and never lets us back down. How pleasant it is to sit on a perch overlooking the universe and see the plans of God. Somehow, we have been joined to Christ in a way that we are involved with a kingdom that is eternal. Then we get off our temporary resting place and look to be part of this larger agenda. Notice how the entire psalm becomes our rationale for simple, daily obedience:

[God did these things] that they might keep his precepts and observe his laws. Praise the LORD. (Ps. 105:45)

So that's how my friend did it. Al did some big things in his life (at least I thought they were big), but his interests were not in résumés. He preferred humble obedience to the King who loved him. The kingdom advances "forcefully" (Matt. 11:12) in ways that can, at first glance, seem mild-mannered.

It has been more than three years since Al's death, and I am still trying to catch up to him. A psalm a day just might do it.

I went to his grave today.

> J. Alan Groves
> December 17, 1952–February 5, 2007
> In Christ death is swallowed up in victory.

A Letter That Alan Groves Wrote
for His Memorial Service:
God's Unfailing Love Endures Forever

AS I HAVE WALKED through the valley of the shadow of death, I have walked hand in hand with Jesus, the one who has already walked through that valley and come out the other side—alive, raised from the dead. And as I hold his hand and trust him, I too am raised with him, for this was his purpose in walking that path: to raise those who trusted in him. His rod and staff, his cross of suffering have become my comfort. Now as I have died, I come before the God, the King of the universe, and I come in Christ. He chose to suffer and die on the cross in my place, so that on account of him, I might have forgiveness from sin and victory over death. And now I have received the resurrection and eternal life that has been my only hope, past, present, and forever.

I have led a truly blessed life. At a young age, I realized that Jesus was not just a story in a comic book, but that he was real and I could actually know him. I wish I could describe to you what a powerful moment of understanding that was, and I have thought about it many times over the years, marveling over and over at the truth of this central fact. The Lord placed me into the perfect family where I was raised by loving parents with wonderful siblings. God gave me a wonderful wife who has been my joy as we have raised four wonderful children together. The Lord has given me the opportunity to be intimately involved in the lives of so many wonderful brothers and sisters, in our fellowship at college, as a pastor in Vermont, as an elder at New Life Church, and as a professor at Westminster Seminary. Through family and ministry, I have had the privilege of loving and being loved by all of you, and I have been struck again and again by the deposit that each of you has left in my life.

Through all my life, Christ has been constant. Even as I have grown and changed, he is still the one whom I loved that first day. And nothing ever changed in how I came to him; every day of my life the story is the same: I come to God in Christ. His love for me has been steadfast, and he has pursued me through every time I have turned away from him and every time I have returned. The constant prayer of my heart for my own life and the lives of those around me has been that we would see Jesus, and that he would be welcome and present among us.

There may be some here who have never trusted Christ for life, who have never known that he is the answer to the sin and death in our lives. I urge you to consider the claims he made to being the Son of God, to consider that he didn't stay dead and sends a message down through the ages that there is life in him and him alone. His death on a cross, humiliating though it seemed, was his glory, by which he has defeated our true enemies—sin and death. By the ultimate sacrifice he made, he humiliated all powers arrayed against him.

If you struggle with faith, let me encourage you that in the hardest moments I have faced, he has been there. And death has been defeated. I am in Christ, as you are in Christ. So let us live out of the grace we have received. Let us live out of Christ. This means looking daily for him, asking him to open your eyes to him, and embracing what you see. Seek him with all your heart. Love him with all your heart. Love those he loves with all your heart, even to the laying down of your life for him. Jesus, the way, the truth, the life. In no other do we have hope. But in him we have hope that endures forever. We grieve, but we grieve with hope. The hope of a resurrection; the hope of life eternal. Together with Jesus.

For most of my Christian life I have wanted to see Jesus face-to-face, to join in with the heavenly chorus in his presence around his royal throne and declare his praise in new ways. Something else has grown through the years: an abiding sense that this is not for me alone. Being with Jesus by myself is not what he wants, nor is it what I want. To be there with you all, those he loves, and those I have come to love—that is true joy. I have often thought of coming to heaven as Jesus standing at the finish line of a race awaiting those looking for him, trusting in him, pursuing him. But it isn't a race for me to finish first or alone. It has always been a race for us to finish together, arm in arm, having encouraged one another in faith.

He is good. From the beginning, his steadfast love has endured. It endures forever. He is gracious God, slow to anger, abounding in steadfast love. Trust in him with all your heart. For he is faithful.

I

Why Do Bad Things Happen to Good People? A Biblical-Theological Approach

Tremper Longman III

ALONG WITH THE others in this volume, I dedicate this essay to the memory of my dear friend Alan Groves. In his final M.Div. year and my first year as a teacher at Westminster, Al took two courses from me. He, of course, excelled, and Ray Dillard and I asked him to join our department. The three of us enjoyed a close departmental camaraderie, being joined by Bruce Waltke from 1985 to 1991. In 1993, Ray Dillard, mentor to both Al and me, suddenly died at the age of 49. The trauma of his death and the new responsibility we shared for the curriculum brought Al and me closer together. I left for Westmont in 1998 and Al became the chair of the department, leading it with his good grace and wisdom until just before his death.

I rehearse our history not only to remind the reader of Al's impressive teaching career, but also to demonstrate that I knew Al well. He was a man of virtue and godliness. He feared God and avoided evil (Job 1:1, 8). Al also struggled with health issues over many of the years that I knew him, and he died young. Al's life and death raise one of the most pervasive biblical-theological issues addressed in the Bible: retribution. To put it in a phrase

1

made popular by Rabbi Kushner's book: "Why do bad things happen to good people and good things happen to bad people?"[1]

BLESSINGS ON THE RIGHTEOUS; CURSES ON THE WICKED

When one thinks about it, it is amazing how much of the OT is dedicated to the proposition that the godly will be blessed and the ungodly will be cursed. I will begin with the book of Proverbs and branch out from there.

Proverbs

The preface to the book of Proverbs begins by stating the purpose of the book: that its readers "know wisdom and discipline" (1:2).[2] The first nine chapters largely comprise a father's speeches to his son with the hope of keeping him on the path of wisdom and off the path of folly. Wisdom, on one level, is a practical skill of living: knowing how to avoid the pitfalls of life and maximize success. Wisdom entails doing the right thing at the right time and saying the right thing at the right time. Of course, wisdom is more profound than knowing how to navigate life. The preface also famously asserts: "The fear of Yahweh is the beginning of knowledge" (1:7). One cannot even get to square one with wisdom without a relationship with the God of the universe.

Thus, Proverbs divides people into two camps: the wise and the fool. Germane to our topic is the claim that the former will experience the best of life, while the latter will suffer. Consider the following proverbs chosen rather randomly for illustrative purposes:

> There is one who gives freely yet gains more,
> but one who withholds what is due will surely become needy. (11:24)

> A healthy tongue is a tree of life,
> but the one with duplicity produces a broken spirit. (15:4)

Note, too, how Woman Wisdom, the personification of Yahweh's wisdom, describes herself and her gifts in Proverbs 8:18–19:

---

1. Harold S. Kushner, *When Bad Things Happen to Good People* (New York: Anchor, 2004).
2. All quotations of Proverbs in this chapter are taken from Tremper Longman III, *Proverbs*, BCOTWP (Grand Rapids: Baker, 2006).

Wealth and honor are with me,
    enduring riches and righteousness.
My fruit is better than gold, even fine gold,
    my yield than choice silver.

The presumption of these passages and many more in Proverbs is that if one follows the way of wisdom and godliness, that person will be rewarded with the good things in life. On the contrary, following the way of the ungodly fool leads to life's problems.

Deuteronomy

Proverbs is not alone in advocating a connection between godly behavior and material abundance in life. The structure of Deuteronomy shows that behavior and consequences are woven into the very tapestry of the covenant.

Deuteronomy is Moses' final sermon. As Moses stands on the plains of Moab, he addresses the generation born in the wilderness and exhorts them to obey Yahweh when they enter the Promised Land. They should not be like their fathers, disobedient and judged in the wilderness. Moses, in essence, leads the people to reaffirm the commitment to the covenant that God established with them at Mount Sinai (Ex. 19–24). It is not surprising that as a covenant-renewal text, the book has the following pattern:

Introduction: 1:1–5
Historical Review: 1:9–3:27
Law: 4:1–26:19
Rewards and Consequences: 27–28
Witnesses: 30:19–20
Review and Succession: 31:9–13

Interestingly, since the mid-twentieth century, scholars have recognized that these elements follow the pattern of an ancient Near Eastern vassal treaty.[3] In essence, the covenant is a treaty between an all-powerful King, Yahweh, and his vassal people, Israel.

For our purposes, though, we should draw our attention to the connection between the legal section and the chapters devoted to rewards and

3. See K. A. Kitchen, *On the Reliability of the Old Testament* (Grand Rapids: Eerdmans, 2003), 283–94.

consequences. In a word, obedience to the law brings material blessings (abundant crops, large families, success in war; see 28:1–14), while disobedience results in deprivation and defeat (28:15–68). In sum, Deuteronomy, the book that summarizes the Pentateuch, illustrates the nexus between behavior and life consequences. Good things happen to good people; bad things happen to bad people.

The Deuteronomic History

Deuteronomy not only summarizes the Pentateuch, but also casts its long shadow over much of the rest of the OT. The retribution theology of a book such as Joshua shows this perspective. The two longest battle accounts are those connected to the battles at Jericho (Josh. 5:13–6:27) and Ai (Josh. 7–8). Jericho was the most formidable of the Canaanite city-states, legendary for its massive walls and long history. On the other hand, Ai was not much of a settlement. Indeed, its very name means "ruin" in Hebrew. Interestingly, though, Jericho easily falls to the Israelites, while Ai initially defeats the attacking Israelite army. Why? Again, these two accounts illustrate the theology of retribution. Obedience brings victory; disobedience results in failure. Joshua and Israel followed all of the divine warrior's instructions (see Josh. 5:13–15 and chap. 6). Ai records the opposite experience. Ai is able to resist Israel because of the disobedience of one man, Achan, who stole plunder from Jericho in defiance of the rules of *herem*, or holy war (see Josh. 7–8). After the sinner is punished, Ai too falls easily. Retribution theology wins out again.

Another prime example of the way the theology of Deuteronomy shapes the presentation of the history of Israel and Judah in Samuel-Kings can be clearly seen by contrasting it with its synoptic counterpart, Chronicles. Samuel-Kings shows no awareness of the end of the exile, ending its historical presentation with a reference to Jehoiachin's release from prison dated to the year that Evil-Merodach (Amel-Marduk) ascended the throne in Babylon (2 Kings 25:27–30; ca. 562 BC). Thus, the final form of the book seems to have been completed during the exile. From the contents, it appears that Samuel-Kings is presenting an argument for why Judah is in exile. Each of the kings is judged by whether he kept the law of centralization (Deut. 12), for instance. When read against the background of Deuteronomy 17:14–20, Samuel-Kings also makes it clear that the kings of neither Israel nor Judah lived up to the divine standard for the king. Israel also did not listen to the true prophets, but rather the false ones (Deut. 13:1–5; 18:15–22). For that reason the curses of the law go into effect (Deut. 28:15–68). None of these concerns can be seen in Chronicles, a historical project that comes to completion sometime in the postexilic period with its different interests.

For the purposes of this essay, the important point is that Samuel-Kings describes Israel and Judah's fate as a result of their not keeping the law.[4] Why are we in exile? "Because we did not keep the law and so the curses of the covenant came into effect." Thus, as in Deuteronomy, one sees that sin leads to suffering.

The Prophets: The Case of Jeremiah

The prophets were the lawyers of the covenant. When Israel broke the law, God would send in his lawyer to bring a case against it, threatening Israel with the curses of the covenant. Think of Jeremiah: Israel has betrayed the covenant by virtue of its idolatry and many other sins (Jer. 10:1–22; 11:1–17). It would suffer for its transgressions.

Note the specifically legal language found in a prophet such as Jeremiah (e.g., Jer. 2:9; see also Mic. 1:2; 6:1–8). Again, the logic of the prophets is based on the covenant. The people and their leaders have broken the law of the covenant and thus deserve to suffer the curses.

The judgment oracle found in Jeremiah 11:1–8 illustrates the connection between the prophet's message and covenant well. Here God instructs Jeremiah to hear again the "terms of my covenant" (v. 3 NLT), a reference to the laws, specifically of the Mosaic covenant, the one he entered into with his people "when I brought them out of the iron-smelting furnace of Egypt" (v. 4). He told them then to obey him. But they "did not listen or even pay attention" (v. 8). The result, anticipated by a text such as Deuteronomy 27–28, is that the curses of the covenant would come into effect.

The message of Jeremiah 11:1–8 is repeated time and time again in the various judgment oracles of the book. Thus, Jeremiah too, as well as most other prophets, is an example of the doctrine of retribution. God's people have sinned and therefore suffer.

---

4. See Tremper Longman III and Raymond B. Dillard, *An Introduction to the Old Testament* (Grand Rapids: Zondervan, 2006), 163–64, 181–86.

Conclusion

Upon reflection, one marvels at just how much of the OT supports the doctrine of retribution. Our examples above are just selections. While Samuel-Kings' central argument is based on the retribution principle, its counterpart Chronicles also teaches that sin has consequences. The major difference appears to be that the former emphasizes delayed retribution in order to explain the exile, while the latter focuses on stories of immediate retribution to discourage the postexilic community's propensity to rebel.[5] We are left with the question: "Does the Bible support the idea of reward for the righteous and punishment for the wicked?" Are the modern advocates of the prosperity gospel right after all?

THE LIMITS OF WISDOM

To answer that question, we turn now to Job and Ecclesiastes, along with Proverbs, the wisdom books of the OT. It appears that one of the canonical functions of these two books is to serve as a corrective to an overly optimistic connection between behavior and quality of life.

Job

In the light of the biblical teaching above, one might find it difficult to blame Job's three friends for their belief that Job is a sinner. If sin leads to suffering, then isn't suffering a sign that a person is a sinner?

Indeed, before speaking, Eliphaz, Bildad, and Zophar sit for seven days in deep empathy with their friend (Job 2:13). They don't offer their opinion until prodded to do so by Job's lament—or, better, *complaint* (Job 3). Indeed, it is misleading to call Job's words a *lament* because that invites comparison to the psalms of lament. Upon closer reading, we see that Job's impassioned statement is closer to the grumbling tradition found in Numbers (e.g., Num. 20:1–13) than to the psalms. In the latter, the prayer is directed toward God, while the former is addressed to other people about God. God invites the lament, but not the complaint.

---

5. Raymond B. Dillard, "Reward and Punishment in Chronicles: The Theology of Immediate Retribution," *WTJ* 46 (1984): 161–72; Raymond B. Dillard, "The Reign of King Asa (2 Chr 14–16): An Example of the Chronicler's Theological Method," *JETS* 23 (1980): 207–18; Roddy L. Braun, *1 Chronicles*, WBC (Waco, TX: Word, 1986), xxxvii–xxxix.

Thus, again, one can hardly blame the three friends for their defense of the integrity of God.

In the disputation that follows, their argument, repeated over and over again, is as follows. Job suffers; thus, he has sinned. In order for him to be restored to his former blessed state, he needs to repent. A good example of this type of argument may be found in Zophar's first speech:

> If only you would prepare your heart
>   and lift up your hands to him in prayer!
> Get rid of your sins,
>   and leave all iniquity behind you.
> Then your face will brighten with innocence.
>   You will be strong and free of fear. . . .
> But the wicked will be blinded.
>   They will have no escape.
>   Their only hope is death. (Job 11:13–15, 20)[6]

Job's condition is a result of his sin, and thus to be restored Job must repent.

Right from the beginning of the book, though, the reader knows that Job's suffering is not the result of sin. We know this with a level of certainty that none of the book's characters have because we are given access to God's own mind on the matter in the preface to the book. God decides to allow Job to suffer in spite of his piety, which is affirmed in words spoken to the Accuser that could have come straight from the book of Proverbs: "Have you noticed my servant Job? He is the finest man in all the earth. He is blameless [*tam*]—a man of complete integrity [*yasar*]. He fears God [cf. Prov. 1:7] and stays away from evil" (1:8; see also the narrator in 1:1). Not even the Accuser questions this assessment. He rather questions the motivation. Is Job pious out of self-interest? So Job's suffering is the result of a test of the motivation for his godliness, not because of any sin on his part.

Yet one of the ironies of the book is that Job himself shares the presuppositions of the three friends. He too believes that only the wicked should suffer. The difference, however, is that he also knows that he does not deserve to suffer, so he does not see merit in Zophar's (and the others') advice to repent. He believes God is unjust (chap. 9), and so he seeks an audience with God to set him straight (31:35–37).

6. All quotations of Job in this chapter are taken from the NLT.

7

Job will get his audience with God, but before he does, yet another character steps forward: Elihu. Elihu has waited patiently for men older (and presumably wiser) than he is to solve the problem presented by Job's sin. Elihu represents a more "spiritual" wisdom rather than one based on experience and observation (32:6–10). The irony of Elihu's speech is that though he castigates the failed arguments of the three friends, he basically parrots the same argument based on retribution theology:

> He brings the mighty to ruin without asking anyone,
>   and he sets up others in their place.
> He knows what they do,
>   and in the night he overturns and destroys them.
> He strikes them down because they are wicked,
>   doing it openly for all to see. (Job 34:24–26)

Since Elihu's argument is a repetition of the previous argument, no one even bothers to answer him. So much for youthful, "spiritual" wisdom.

Human wisdom has failed. Job's friends, Elihu, and Job himself have not arrived at the right response to Job's predicament. Human perspective gives way to the divine perspective in 38:1–42:6.

Job desired an audience with God. He wanted to set him straight. He gets the audience, but the session does not go as he anticipated in 31:35–37 ("I would tell him exactly what I have done. I would come before him like a prince"). God appears in a whirlwind, a sign that he is none too happy with Job. God does not give Job a chance to speak, but calls him to attention and then presents a barrage of questions. God here is like a professor irritated with a student who thinks he knows more than his teacher. God, in essence, presents Job with a pop exam, which he miserably fails.

The nature of the questions serves the purpose of putting Job in his place. He is unable to answer questions that only God could answer about the origins of creation ("Where were you when I laid the foundations of the earth? Tell me, if you know so much. Who determined its dimensions?" [38:4–5a]). God thus asserts his wisdom and elsewhere his power (for instance, as he describes the awesome Leviathan as his pet [41:1–11]). Job has no recourse but to repent in the presence of God (40:4–5; 42:1–6). As a result, God restores his blessings to him (42:12–17).

What do we learn about suffering in the book of Job? What does it teach about the relationship between behavior and consequences (retribution)? It is often rightly remarked that the book of Job does not provide an answer to the question of suffering. Indeed, it is right to say that the book's main subject is wisdom and not suffering. Job, after all, does answer the question "Who is wise?" All the human characters' wisdom is shown as inadequate to help Job to understand his situation. Only God is wise.

Even so, the book, while not giving an answer to the question of human suffering, does effectively debunk the view that suffering is inextricably tied to sin. Job is an example of a totally innocent sufferer. As we know from the preface, Job's suffering is not the result of his sin. Thus, the three friends, Job, and Elihu were all wrong to believe so.

Retribution in Ecclesiastes

The book of Ecclesiastes raises serious questions about divine retribution. Before examining that particular issue, however, it is necessary to discuss the book as a whole in order to properly situate our consideration of specific passages.

Most contemporary commentators today follow Michael Fox in distinguishing two voices within the book.[7] In the largest part of the book, Qohelet (the Teacher) speaks in the first person. His voice emerges in 1:12 with a typical ancient Near Eastern autobiographical introduction:[8] "I am Qohelet. I have been king over Israel in Jerusalem."[9] His speech continues through 12:7. The other voice is that of a person (who remains nameless) who talks about Qohelet in the third person: e.g., "Qohelet was a wise man . . ." (12:9). While it is conceivable that the same person lies behind these two voices and changes narrative voice for rhetorical purposes, I find this extremely unlikely and odd, since I cannot determine what the rhetorical purpose would be. The most natural way of reading Ecclesiastes is to differentiate the voices and to understand that the second unnamed wise man (Fox calls him the "frame narrator") is exposing his son (12:12) to the teaching of Qohelet and commenting

7. Michael V. Fox, "Frame-Narrative and Composition in the Book of Qohelet," *HUCA* 48 (1977): 83–106, and most recently, *Ecclesiastes* (Philadelphia: JPS, 2004). See also Tremper Longman III, *Ecclesiastes* (Grand Rapids, Eerdmans, 1998); Craig G. Bartholomew, *Ecclesiastes*, BCOTWP (Grand Rapids: Baker, 2009).

8. For the ancient Near Eastern background of Qohelet's speech, see Tremper Longman III, *Fictional Akkadian Autobiography* (Winona Lake, IN: Eisenbrauns, 1993), 120–22.

9. All quotations of Ecclesiastes in this chapter are the author's own translation.

on it in the epilogue. We can identify this second voice in the prologue (1:1–11) and the epilogue (12:8–14).[10] The most important implication of recognizing these two voices is to understand that the "theology of Qohelet" is not the "theology of the book of Ecclesiastes." The latter is to be associated with the thought of the second wise man. The book of Job is analogous, since it would be an interpretive mistake to understand the theology of the book of Job as that of the three friends, Elihu, or even Job himself. That said, it would also be a mistake to discount the importance of Qohelet's thought, if for no other reason than the book devotes so much space to the development of his ideas. Furthermore, it appears that the frame narrator does affirm the truth and importance of Qohelet's views, even while he seems to be criticizing it. I will comment on this below, but for now we need to turn to the book's teaching on retribution.

As we do so, we see that retribution is a topic that is taken up by Qohelet, not the frame narrator. Qohelet's main argument is that "life is difficult and then you die." In a word, life is *meaningless*, a word (*hevel*) that he repeats over forty times in his speech. He does so particularly in the early chapters of his speech when he is exploring different avenues of potential meaning in life: pleasure (2:1–11), wisdom and folly (2:12–17), work (2:18–23; 4:4–6), political power (4:13–16), and wealth (5:9–6:9).

Why are they all meaningless? Qohelet offers three reasons. The first is death (3:16–22; 12:1–7). For example, wisdom is better than folly because it helps one navigate life, but it does not allow the wise man to escape death. Both fools and wise people die, so what is the advantage of the latter over the former (2:12–17)?

The second factor that renders life meaningless is the inability to discern the "proper time." After all, wisdom functions by doing the right thing or saying the right thing at the right time (Prov. 15:22; 27:14). Just knowing the proverbs is not enough; one needs to know when they are relevant to a situation. For example, the only way to know whether to answer a fool or not is to discern what kind of fool one is speaking with (Prov. 26:4–5). Proverbs in the hands of a fool are useless (Prov. 26:7) or even dangerous (Prov. 26:9). Of course, Qohelet knows that God has created everything for its "proper time," but unfortunately he has not allowed humans in on the

---

10. The third-person narrator makes his presence known as the narrator of Qohelet's teaching in 7:27 with the simple "Qohelet said."

secret (Eccl. 3:1–14). This frustrates Qohelet and leads him again to conclude that life is meaningless.

For our purposes, Qohelet's third reason why life is meaningless will draw our close attention. Life is not just short and hard to figure out; it is also unfair. Qohelet raises the question of proper retribution. I will look at four passages in this regard.

In Ecclesiastes 2:18–23, Qohelet explores hard work as an avenue to meaning in life. Based on a number of proverbs (Prov. 6:6–11; 10:26; 12:11, 24, to name just a handful), one would think that hard work would lead to success and happiness since it is the route of wisdom, while laziness would lead to the opposite since it marks the behavior of the fool. Consider, for instance, Proverbs 10:4: "A slack hand makes poverty; a determined hand makes rich." Qohelet takes a penetrating look at this teaching and concludes that in the light of death, hard work is meaningless. Sure, one might even grow wealthy from working, but then the person dies, and "an individual who did not work for it" (Eccl. 2:21) gets it. Thus "all [one's] days are filled with pain and frustration" (2:23). Proper retribution does not work out, according to Qohelet.

In 3:16–22, Qohelet again observes that there is no proper reward and punishment in this life:

> The place of judgment—injustice was there!
> The place of righteousness—injustice was there! (3:16)

In the light of a present in which there is no justice or fairness, Qohelet contemplates the possibility of a later reckoning. What about justice in the afterlife?

> I said to myself concerning the human race, "God tests them so that they may see they are like animals." For the fate of human beings and the fate of animals are the same fate. One dies like the other. There is one breath for all. Human beings have no advantage over the animals, for everything is meaningless. All go to the same place. All come from the dust, and all return to the dust. Who knows whether the breath of humans goes up above and the breath of animals goes down to the depths of the earth? So I observed that there is nothing better than for people to rejoice in their work, for that is their reward. For who can bring them to see what will happen after them? (3:18–22)

Qohelet does not believe that he can be sure that everything will be straight in the afterlife, because he is not sure that there is such a thing as life after death.[11]

In 7:15–18, Qohelet moves beyond mere observation of the unfairness of life to offering advice about how to live in the face of such inequities:

> Both I observed in my meaningless life: There is a righteous person perishing in his righteousness, and there is a wicked person living long in his evil. Do not be too righteous and do not be overly wise. Why ruin yourself? Do not be too wicked and do not be a fool. Why die when it is not your time? It is good to hold on to this and also to not release your hand from that. The one who fears God will follow both of them.

These are remarkable words, especially compared with the exhortations of Proverbs to seek wisdom (note the entirety of Proverbs 2). Since retribution does not work, do not exert yourself strenuously in the pursuit of wisdom or righteousness.

Perhaps the most extensive treatment of the lack of retribution by Qohelet is found in chapter 9, where it is also intertwined with Qohelet's other nemesis, death, as well as the inability to recognize the proper time. Ecclesiastes 9:11–12 is just one example from this dark chapter:

> Then I turned and observed something else under the sun. That is, the race is not to the swift, the battle not to the mighty, nor is food for the wise, nor wealth to the clever, nor favor to the intelligent, but time and change happen to all of them. Indeed, no one knows his time. Like fish that are ensnared in an evil net and like birds caught in a snare, so people are ensnared in an evil time, when it suddenly falls on them.

In a word, people do not get what they deserve, but rather they are subject to the vicissitudes of chance.

One final example. Ecclesiastes 8:10–14 illustrates that Qohelet really struggled with this teaching. To him, it accentuated the difference between what he *knew* and what he *saw*:

> Thus, *I saw* the wicked buried and departed. They used to go out of the holy place, and they were praised in the city where they acted in such a

---

11. He is actually more pessimistic in 12:1–7 and chapter 9.

way. This too is meaningless. Because the sentence for an evil deed is not quickly carried out, therefore the human heart is filled with evildoing. For sinners do evil a hundred times and their days are lengthened—although *I know* that it will be well for those who fear God because they fear him, and it will not be well for the wicked and their days will not lengthen like a shadow, because they do not fear God. There is *another example* of meaninglessness that is done on the earth: There are righteous people who are treated as if they did wicked deeds, and there are wicked people who are treated as if they did righteous deeds. I say that this too is meaningless.

Here Qohelet begins with an observation of the lack of fairness in life. Wicked people were honored during their life and given a glorious burial. How unfair! But then his mind goes to what he knows (his theology), and he repeats standard ideas of retribution. But he cannot stop here. He then gives an anecdote (another example) based on observation that contradicts his theology. For Qohelet, life conflicts with theology. Theology does not adequately explain life.

Do Job and Ecclesiastes Contradict Proverbs?

Our presentation of the material above may lead to a misconception if not read carefully. Proverbs emphasizes the rewards that come to those who follow the way of wisdom, while Job and Ecclesiastes question the connection between behavior and consequences. Does that mean that Job and Ecclesiastes contradict Proverbs, not to speak of the other strands of the OT that imply that good things happen to good people and bad things happen to bad people?

Close study of these books suggests a negative answer. In the first place, Proverbs does not guarantee reward to the righteous or punishment for the wicked. A proverb is simply not in the business of issuing promises or guarantees.[12] Rather, a proverb states the best route to a desired end, all other things being equal. Most of the time it is true that lazy behavior will lead to poverty and hard work will result in a better living standard, but not always. An indolent person could inherit a fortune, or a hard worker might be wiped out by a natural calamity or a crooked administrator. Proverbs 13:23 acknowledges the latter when it says:

12. Bruce K. Waltke, "Does Proverbs Promise Too Much?" *AUSS* 34 (1996): 319–36.

> A poor person's farm may produce much food,
>> but injustice sweeps it all away.

Another indication that Proverbs itself does not believe there is a mechanical and absolutely guaranteed connection between wise behavior and good benefits is in its acknowledgment that the fool can have wealth—even if only temporarily:

> Wealth from get-rich-schemes quickly disappears;
>> wealth from hard work grows over time. (13:11)

But even when the wealth of fools might last, it does not really help the person:

> Riches won't help on the day of judgment. (11:4a)

Thus, a number of better-than proverbs imply that a person may have to decide between wisdom and success in life:

> Better to be poor and godly
>> than rich and dishonest. (16:8; see also 15:17; 16:16; 17:1; 22:1; 28:6)

In conclusion, Ecclesiastes and Job do not correct Proverbs, but rather they correct an overreading of Proverbs.[13]

The life of Joseph is a wonderful illustration of the complicated relationship between wisdom and consequences. Joseph in many ways is the epitome of the man who walks on the path of wisdom. Proverbs 5–7 teaches that the wise man avoids the promiscuous woman and will be rewarded with success in life for doing so. It is the fool who sleeps with the "strange and foreign woman," and he will suffer. In Genesis 39 Joseph rejects the advances of his master Potiphar's wife. Is he rewarded for avoiding the "strange and foreign woman"? No, he is thrown in jail! He suffers for his wisdom.

That at least is the short-term perspective. At the end of his life, however, Joseph can say to his brothers: "You intended to harm me, but God intended it for good to accomplish what is now being done, the saving of

13. R. C. Van Leeuwen, "Wealth and Poverty: System and Contradiction in Proverbs," *Hebrew Studies* 33 (1992): 25–36.

many lives" (Gen. 50:20 NIV). And indeed he did. His being thrown into jail meant that he came into contact with the head cupbearer and head baker of Pharaoh. They brought his skills as a dream interpreter to Pharaoh's attention. In this way Joseph came to a position to which he could help his family, the covenant family, during a horrible famine.

What looks to us like punishment could actually be a blessing. Joseph, like Job, did nothing really to deserve the abuse that he received during his youth. Even if he was an insensitive braggart (Gen. 37:1–11), he did not deserve his brothers' betrayal. His fidelity to God and Potiphar did not deserve a prison sentence. His aid to the chief cupbearer in prison did not deserve neglect once the latter was released from prison. His life, however, was on a trajectory that brought him to a position of power in Egypt. In the end, retribution worked out for Joseph. He ended his life wealthy and blessed with family.

In the End, Retribution Works Out

Yet not everyone ends life so well. Many people carry their troubles—financial, relational, emotional, health—to the grave. Remember Qohelet's statement that people "eat in darkness all the days with great resentment, illness, and frustration" (Eccl. 5:17) right after remarking "as they come so they go" (v. 16).

As mentioned above, though, the theology of Qohelet is not the theology of the book of Ecclesiastes. After exposing his son to the "under the sun" theology of Qohelet, he tells him: "The end of the matter. All has been heard. Fear God and keep his commandments, for this is the whole duty of humanity. For God will bring every deed into judgment, including every hidden thing, whether good or evil" (12:13–14).

The frame narrator does not elaborate on his advice. He does not make explicit when this judgment, at which time good and evil will get their proper deserts, will take place. As we read Ecclesiastes in the light of the NT, though, our attention is drawn to Romans 8:18–27. Here Paul says that "the creation was subjected to frustration" (v. 20 NIV) by God. This word *frustration* (*mataiotes*) is the Greek word used to translate the Hebrew word *meaningless* (*hevel*) in the Greek OT. Paul reflects on the fall, but of course, it is the effects of the fall that Qohelet so painfully experiences in his quest for meaning. But Paul says more than that God subjected creation to frustration. He also looks forward to its redemption, when "the creation itself will be liberated from its bondage to decay and brought into the glorious freedom of the children of God" (v. 21 NIV).

The good news is that Jesus has freed us from the curse of the fall. He has released us from the grip of death, and he did so by dying himself. The sting of death is taken away by his resurrection. Death is no longer the end of the story. We may agree with Qohelet that "life is hard and then you die," but then there is resurrection, which makes life now meaningful as well. In the end, the message of the NT, foreshadowed by the OT, is that retribution does work out. Only the measure is not how good or how bad we have been, but rather whether we have united ourselves with Jesus Christ our Savior.

CONCLUSION

Al suffered during his relatively brief life. His health was fragile during much of the time that I knew him. He died young, but confident in God's goodness. Even in his last days, he was more concerned with how other people were doing than with his own situation. How could he face his end with such dignity and strength?

There was more than one reason. God blessed Al with a wonderful, godly wife and gifted and pious children. He loved them deeply and was so proud of each one. But Al's profound courage in the face of death was ultimately founded on his understanding that true happiness and blessing were not found in this present world. God grant us all his courage.

2

Psalm 15: An Exposition in Honor of Alan Groves

Bruce K. Waltke

PROFESSOR ALAN GROVES exemplified in his life the kind of person who may dwell as a resident alien in God's temple. This exposition of Psalm 15, which aims to answer the question, "Who has the right to enjoy the eternal protection of *I AM*'s temple?" aims to preserve his memory and to encourage future generations to follow his example.

Translation[1]

> [1A]A psalm by David.
> [1Ba]*I AM*,[2] who may sojourn in your tent?[3]
> [1Bb] Who may dwell on your holy mountain?

---

1. All quotations of Scripture in this chapter are the author's own translation.
2. *I AM* translates the sentence name in his own mouth: "I am who I am." See Bruce K. Waltke, with Charles Yu, *An Old Testament Theology: An Exegetical, Thematic and Canonical Approach* (Grand Rapids: Zondervan, 2007), 11.
3. Fragments of Hebrew codices in the Cairo Geniza and more than twenty manuscripts in the Kennicott-de Rossi collection read the plural "in your tents" against the majority of Hebrew manuscripts and the ancient versions. Perhaps the plural is an auricular error and was understood as a plural of extension to indicate that the tent is inherently large or complex. See Bruce K. Waltke

[2Aa]Whoever lives[4] as a person of integrity:

   [2Ab]who does[5] what is right;

   [2B]and speaks truth from[6] his heart.

[3Aa]He does not slander with his tongue,[7]

   [3Ab]does not harm his neighbor;

   [3B]and does not vilify his close neighbor.[8]

[4Aa]Whoever is vile[9] in his eyes[10] is one to be rejected,[11]

   [4Ab]but he honors those who fear *I AM*;

[4B]He promises on oath to his own hurt,[12]

and he does not change,

[5Aa]He does not give his silver to the poor with interest,

   [5Ab]or take a bribe against the innocent.

[5Ba]Whoever does these things

[5Bb]will never be toppled.

LITERARY FORM AND STRUCTURE

Psalm 15 is a *torah* (catechetical teaching) psalm to teach piety and ethics, using a liturgical temple entrance formula of question and answer (cf. Ps. 24:3–5; Isa. 33:14–16; Mic. 6:1–8). The connection between liturgy and

---

and Michael O'Connor, *Introduction to Biblical Hebrew Syntax* (Winona Lake, IN: Eisenbrauns, 1990), 120, P. 7.4.1c (hereafter *IBHS*); there is no significant difference in meaning.

4. Lit. "walks" (see exposition below).

5. Interpreting *waw* as epexegetical to clarify or specify the sense of the preceding clause, and signified as such by the colon after "integrity."

6. Lit. "in" or "with."

7. Instead of the tricolon of the MT, BHS scans verse 2A as a bicolon and instead of scanning verse 3 as a tricolon combines verse 3Aa with verse 2B: "speaks truth in his heart"/"does not slander with his tongue," forming the typical parallels of "heart" and "tongue." The MT, however, has the advantage of linking the three participles of verse 2 and the three occurrences of *lo'* with three gnomic perfectives in verse 3 and of making the performing of the virtues of verse 2 parallel to abstaining from the vices of verse 3 (see exposition below).

8. Lit. "to reproach he does not lift up [the name] of his close friend" (so most versions). If so, *kherpah* is an adverbial accusative of place with a verb of motion (*IBHS*, P. 10.2.2c, nos. 8–10). TaNaK, however, glosses verse 3B by "or borne reproach for *his acts toward* his neighbor" (see exposition below).

9. *Niphal* participle functions as a gerundive (*IBHS*, 387, P. 23.3d).

10. *Paseq* syntactically links *b'enayw* with *nimas*.

11. Here the gerundive *Niphal* participle signifies what is proper (*IBHS*, 387, P. 23.3d).

12. A one-place internal *Hiphil* (lit. "to hurt himself," *IBHS*, 39–40, P. 27.2ff.). The LXX (Syr) reversed the consonants from *hr'* to *r'hw* ("to his neighbor"). The unique *plene* spelling speaks against this, facilitating reading for difficult Hebrew syntax.

piety and ethics suggests that liturgy depends on pure ethics and religion, and that liturgy reinforces Israel's covenant values. But "purity" is a matter of the heart, as the psalm makes clear. Though commentators commonly assume that the psalm was used by a temple warden to evaluate the aspiring worshiper, in truth the psalm looks to one's conscience to be the temple warden. It calls for self-examination, not judgment by others (cf. 1 Cor. 11:28, 30), for who but the worshiper knows what is in his own heart (see vv. 2, 4)? In this psalm spirituality, morality, and liturgy unite as a holy trinity.

Its structure, like other features of the psalm, is complex.[13] On the one hand, the psalm's introduction raises the question about who is worthy to sojourn in *I AM*'s protective sanctuary (v. 1); its body answers the question (vv. 2–5A); and its conclusion promises the worthy eternal security (v. 5C). This structure is similar to Psalm 24:3–6 and Isaiah 33:14B–16. The body consists of a decalogue of stipulations: 1–3 [v. 2]; 4–6 [v. 3], 7–8 [v. 4A, B]; and 9–10 [v. 5Aa, b]). The seventh, usually a favored slot in a series, pertains to the crucial requirement to fear *I AM*. On the other hand, this structure of introduction, body, and conclusion is presented rhetorically in a chiasm housing other chiasms:

A. Question: who may dwell in *I AM*'s sanctuary?—v. 1Ba, b

   B. Summary and particulars of required action and speech—v. 2
     1. Summary of prescribed virtues (participles):
       a. Summary: walks (*holekh*) with integrity—v. 2Aa
       b. Action: does (*polel*) righteousness—v. 2Ab
       c. Speech: speaks (*dover*) truth—v. 2B
     2. Particular proscribed vices (negative particle *lo'* plus
       perfectives)—v. 3
       a'. Speech: No going about as slander (*lo'-ragal*,
        "foot")—v. 3Aa
       b'. Action: No evil to neighbor (*lo'-'asah*)—v. 3Ab
       a'. Speech: No reproach against neighbor (*lo- nasa'*)—v. 3B
     X. Fears *I AM*—v. 4
       1. Socially: reject despicable but honor God-fearers—v. 4A
       2. Personally: Negative: no changing of vows (i.e., fears
       I AM)—v. 4B

---

13. Many scholars see three parts: a question in verse 1, its answer in verses 2–5A, and a promise of blessing (inviolability) in verse 5B.

    B'. Particulars and summary of righteous action and speech—v. 5
      1. Particular proscribed vices (*lo'* plus perfectives)—v. 5A
        a. Action: No interest from poor (*lo'-natan*)—v. 5Aa
        b. Speech and Action: No bribes against innocent (*lo'*
          laqakh)—v. 5Ab
      2. Summary: Does (participle, *'oseh*) these things—v. 5Ba
A'. Benediction: Assurance of eternal security—v. 5Bb[14]

The analysis above reveals the psalm's obvious theme: what does God, a consuming fire against the wicked, require of his worshipers? Not surprisingly, in true Israel's theology, so unlike pagan religion, the answer pertains to spirituality and ethics, not ritual. The psalm's chiastic structure pivots on the requirement to fear *I AM*, which entails faith in him. Biblical ethics and faith are two sides of the same coin that has eternal currency.

Let us consider this chiastic structure more closely.

A/A' (vv. 2, 5Bb): The question who may sojourn in *I AM*'s sanctuary is raised in A, and the reason one wants to dwell there is stated in A': it provides eternal security.[15] Guests of God were protected against pursuers (Pss. 23:5–6; 27:4–5ff.; 61:4–5), and granted deliverance and peace.

B/B' (vv. 3, 5A–Ba): An accepted worshiper's social obligations are stated in B, moving from a summary statement to particulars and reversing that sequence in B'. Moreover, in B the requirements become more and more focused, moving from the generalization "walks" (i.e., "lives," v. 2Aa) with integrity, to summary statements of action ("does right," v. 2Ab) and "speaks truth" (v. 2B). Conjunctive *waw* links the three clauses. The three positive, generalizing virtues of verse 2 are followed by three particular prohibited vices in verse 3, which has yet another chiastic pattern of a/a' (speech: not slander, not malign) around the pivot b' (action: do not do evil to neighbor). Also, the tricolon of virtues in verse 2 are held together grammatically by the use of three *Qal* participles, having the assonance of the *Qal* participle's infix pattern of /ō/ /ē/. Likewise, the tricolon of vices in verse 3 are linked grammatically by *lo'* plus a *Qal* perfective, having the assonance of its infix pattern /a/ and

---

14. Cf. Pierre Auffret, "Essai sur la structure literéraire du Psaume SV," *VT* 31 (1981): 385–99; Lloyd M. Barré, "Recovering the Literary Structure of Psalm XV," *VT* 34 (1984): 207–10.

15. That climactic consequence is signaled by the shift from participles and perfectives to the future imperfective ("will never be toppled"). "Never" glosses the collocation *lo' l*'o-la-m*.

/a/.[16] Turning now to B' (v. 5A), on the other side of the pivot, it states specific prohibited vices with regard to action (v. 5Aa) and speech and action (v. 5Ab), using the same grammar in sense and sound of verse 3. In yet another chiasm, verse 5B summarizes the requirements in a positive statement, using the participle infix pattern, matching the form and assonance of the *Qal* participle in verse 2.

X (v. 4): Whereas the teachings pertain to social obligations, the two teachings of the pivot pertain to God. The pivot can be analyzed as a quatrain, which consists of antithetical clauses (v. 4A), which are linked by disjunctive *waw* (v. 4Aa, b), and a semantically conditional clause ("[when] he promises on oath") and its apodosis ("[then] he does not change"). The king hinges the two semantic halves of his decalogue on the "fear [of] *I AM*" (v. 4), which has the social dimension of honoring God-fearers and rejecting the despicable, and of keeping one's vow even to one's own hurt (cf. Eccl. 5:1).

Throughout the OT, the key to social ethics is true piety, whose non-negotiable virtue is faith. Though ethics and piety are commonly treated separately by theologians, in reality ethics on the horizontal axis is inseparable from piety (faith) on the vertical axis, and vice versa. Since the focus of the psalm is on ethics, the pivot gives pride of place to the accepted worshiper's posture toward the impious and pious (i.e., the infidel vs. the faithful) before insisting that he himself fears *I AM* as shown by the litmus test that he keeps his oaths.

EXPOSITION

Superscript

The author of our psalm is none other than inspired David, Israel's greatest, covenant-keeping king. In his deathbed charge, David instructed Solomon to keep *I AM*'s *torah* in order to secure his throne forever (1 Kings 2:1–4). As soon as David transferred the ark to Zion, that mountain became holy by *I AM*'s presence. The reference to the tent uniquely applies to David's tent for housing the ark. David drew up the plans for the temple and

16. Note the alliteration of the gutturals (18x): ' [4x], *h-kh* [4x], ' (5x), and *r* (5x); note too the assonance of *'al-shono* and *'al-qᵉrovo* at the end of verse 3Aa, 3B, of *re'ehu* and *ra'ah*, and of *'asah* ("does," v. 3Ab) and *nasa'* ("lifts up," v. 3B).

composed the music and libretto for its liturgy. His question of a person's worthiness to worship there was apt as soon as that mountain was sanctified by the divine presence. Perhaps David originally intended the psalm for an individual, such as a priest or king, to secure inviolability by an affirming conscience, but more probably he intended it for all who ventured on that sacred mountain.

As the psalm functions in the Psalter, it teaches all the people of God to keep covenant, especially brotherly love, with all their heart in order to secure eternal life. David implicitly points to his greater Son, for only the Son of God perfectly satisfies these covenant requirements. Nothing less than his perfect obedience and sacrifice for his people can secure eternal inviolability in God's presence. The triune God grants that perfection and salvation to all who fear (i.e., believe in) him.

Question: Who May Dwell in *I AM*'s Sanctuary?—v. 1

The wise king introduces his catechetical teaching by asking, probably his students (i.e., his people), what *I AM*'s conditions are for the individual and nation to enjoy his security in his sanctuary. In the OT, an individual does not enter into the sacred sphere lightly or as a matter of right. Barriers inherent in the Israelite religion take ethics into account. The king likens the worshiper at the sanctuary to a resident alien. *Gur* ("sojourn") signifies to leave one's homeland for political, economic, religious, or other circumstances and to dwell as a newcomer and resident alien without the original rights of the host community for a (definite or indefinite, Ps. 61:4) time in order to find protection, a resting place, and home in another community (cf. Gen. 12:10; 19:9; 20:1; Judg. 19:16; Ruth 1:2; Jer. 42–50 [12x]). The *ger* ("resident alien") possesses no land and so is usually poor and depends on the goodwill of the host. The relationship between the landless Levite and the *ger* bears comparison (Deut. 14:29; 26:11–13; Judg. 17:4; 19:1). In Israel's daily life, apart from ownership of land, no distinction between a *ger* and an Israelite existed: the *ger* stands under *I AM*'s divine protection (Deut. 10:18; Ps. 146:9; Mal. 3:5) and is to be loved as one loves himself (Lev. 19:34; Deut. 10:19), and care must be taken not to oppress him or her (Ex. 22:20–23). The *ger* also participates in the tithe (Deut. 14:28–29), Sabbath year (Lev. 25:6), and cities of refuge (Num. 35:15) and is subject to the same law (Lev. 20:2; 24:16, 22; Deut.

1:16).[17] The word is used here poetically and figuratively of the worshiper's relationship to *I AM* in God's tent. As a sojourner, the *ger* has no natural right but depends on God's favor to give him the *protection, provision, and rest* that his tent affords. The decalogue of requirements specifies that the *ger* must have a heartfelt commitment to *I AM*, a requirement that demands a new heart (i.e., regeneration, Jer. 31:31–33). Today David's language of dwelling in God's tent is a type of the Christian's belonging to God's household (Eph. 2:19).

'Ohel ("tent") refers to a collapsible tent made of cloth or skins stretched over a wooden frame, fastened down to pegs with cords, in contrast to a more permanent *bayit* ("house") or any other kind of dwelling.[18] It may be a simple nomad's tent or a tent fit for a king. *I AM*'s tent, the tabernacle, during Israel's sojourn in the wilderness was an elaborate royal tent. Here "in your tent" (*be'oholekha*) refers to the sacred tent David pitched on Mount Zion to house the ark of the covenant, pending its installation in a permanent structure (2 Sam. 6:17; 7:2, 6; 1 Kings 1:39; 2:28–30; 1 Chron. 15:1; 16:1; 2 Chron. 1:4; Ps. 132:1–9). References to the sacred tent in the Psalter are in psalms attributed to David (Pss. 27:5–6; 61:4).[19] These texts suggest that though a tent is the essence of the nomadic way of life (Jer. 35:7–10; Hos. 12:9), the tent David pitched was more complex and beautiful than a typical nomad's tent.

In verset B, "who" is emphatically repeated; its predicate escalates God's residence from a transient tent to the security and permanence of a mountain. *Shakhan* ("dwell") means "to stay, spend time, dwell." The verb indicates nothing concerning the nature or duration of the stay. The rest of the psalm specifies those details. The semantically equivalent substantival participle, *shakhen*, denotes "one who resides in some geographically proximate relationship to another and thus may designate a next-door . . . neighbor (the neighbor close[st] 'to his house[hold]')."[20] The rest of the psalm shows that

17. In this paragraph, I lean heavily on Robert Martin-Achard, *TLOT*, 1:308, s.v. *gur*, "to sojourn."

18. From the OT little can be gleaned concerning the form or construction of tents; they may be matted or pointed. A nomad lived in a bell tent, supported in the middle by a wooden pole and composed of several dark goatskin curtains.

19. Critics who deny that David wrote Psalm 15 avoid the obvious inference that the mention of a tent sanctuary points to David's authorship and dubiously argue that the Psalter's reference to the tent preserves the memory of that tent. In Solomon's day the Tent of Meeting was at Gibeon (2 Chron. 1:3; cf. 1 Kings 8:4), and in Chronicles "tent" is used of the second temple as a memory of the Tent of Meeting (cf. 1 Chron. 9:23; 17:5).

20. R. H. O'Connell, *NIDOTTE*, 4:112, s.v. *shakhen*.

God's closest neighbors dwell on God's holy hill as a welcome guest (2 Sam. 12:20; Pss. 23:6; 27:4–6; 61:4; 84:10).

"On your holy hill" (b^ehar qodshekha) refers to Zion. God says of this mountain:

> This is my resting-place for ever and ever;
>> Here I will sit enthroned, for I have desired it.
> I will bless her with abundant provisions;
>> Her poor I will satisfy with food.
> I will clothe her priests with salvation,
>> And her faithful people will ever sing for joy. (Ps. 132:13–16)

Summary and Particular Requirements—vv. 2–3

The royal decalogue demands duty to neighbor, moving from broadly axiomatic, abstract virtues to more specific virtues and prohibited vices, moving back and forth between proper speech and action. More specifically, David's decalogue first, using independent relative participles—which tend to characterize a person—demands that the individual be a person of integrity in behavior and speech (v. 2). Then it requires specific acts, using perfectives for complete situations, which tend to be specific, with regard to speech (not slander or bring reproach on a neighbor and not do evil to him [v. 3]). The seventh requirement demands a right response to neighbor based on fear of *I AM*, and the eighth cites oath-keeping as the test of one's fear of *I AM*. Finally, the ninth and tenth require that money not be used to disadvantage the poor. Surprisingly, from a pagan perspective, David, the elaborator of Israel's liturgy, makes no mention of cultic matters such as sacrifices, ritual purity, and so forth (cf. Isa. 1:11ff.; Hos. 6:6; Amos 5:21ff.). This is so because ritual without spiritual and moral virtue is abomination to God (1 Sam. 15:22–23). The Lord's famous Sermon on the Mount shares the same spiritual impetus as the Decalogues of Moses and of David. It is surprising, however, that David's decalogue makes no mention of heinous crimes such as murder, adultery, and theft, as in the Mosaic Decalogue. The prescribed virtues of David's decalogue are more spiritually subtle (e.g., walking with integrity), and its proscriptions are commonly violated by people: taking advantage of others, gossiping about them, and breaking vows. More fundamentally, the issue is one of the heart, demanding of the worshiper self-examination.

Summary of Virtues—v. 2

Summary: lives as a person of integrity—v. 2Aa. In verse 2Aa, *holekh* ("lives," lit. "walks") is a verbal complement of *derekh* ("way"), a common metaphor denoting living according to one's world and life views. The metaphor signifies one's course of life (i.e., the character and context of life); one's conduct of life (i.e., specific choices and behavior); and the consequence of that lifestyle (i.e., the inevitable destiny of one's lifestyle).[21] *Tamîm* ("as a person of integrity"), from the root *tmm* (*tam* [adj.], *tom* [noun], *tamîm* [adjectival substantive]), denotes completeness and integrity with reference to a process that has already been accomplished in a person and "that through imminent necessity will produce either good or bad result."[22] With "walk," *tmm* denotes consistent behavior, "to do something with the completeness of one's heart." When rappelling over a cliff, a person wants a *tamîm* holding the rope. *Tmm* is a comprehensive term for a total commitment to the way of *I AM*. The next two clauses clarify what is meant by "walk as a person of integrity" with regard to action and speech.

Action: does what is right—v. 2Ab. The summary, "lives with integrity," is now broken down by two more broad abstractions pertaining to action and speech. *Po'el* ("who does") means "to execute"—that is to say, the worker puts into action the necessary means to secure the success of his enterprise, namely *tsedeq*, glossed "what is right." John Olley defines *tsedeq* ("righteousness") as "to bring about right and harmony for all, for individuals, related in the community and the physical and spiritual realms. It finds its basis in God's rule of the world."[23] In other words, *tsedeq* signifies to serve one's neighbor, not oneself (see Ps. 4:1 [2]), as defined by God's *torah*.

Speech: speaks the truth. "And" joins righteous action (v. 2Ab) with truthful speaking (v. 2B). In biblical ethics, righteous speech and actions are inseparable; one cannot do righteousness and speak vilely, and vice versa. *Dover* ("who speaks") indicates primarily "the activity of speaking," whereas its synonym, *'mr* ("say"), directs attention to the contents of the speech

21. Bruce K. Waltke, *The Book of Proverbs: Chapters 1–15*, NICOT (Grand Rapids: Eerdmans, 2004), 194.

22. K. Koch, *TLOT*, 3:1, 425, s.v. *tmm*.

23. John W. Olley, " 'Righteous' and Wealth? The Description of the *Tsaddiq* in Wisdom Literature," *Collogquium* 22 (1990): 38–45.

(see Ps. 4:4 [5]).[24] *'Emeth* ("truth") denotes words upon which one can rely. Although righteous behavior and righteous speech are inseparable, speech may be hypocritical, not righteous. Consequently, an accepted worshiper speaks truth "from his heart" (lit. "in his heart"), aiming to conform his speech to reality and to speak it sincerely, not with hypocritical flattery (see Ps. 4:4 [5], 7 [8]; cf. 12:2). He intends to speak truth, not to mislead by lies or flattery.

Particular Prohibited Vices—v. 3

The three broad virtues of verse 2 are now paired in verse 3 with three vices, which give the abstractions more specificity: *lo'-ragal* ("to not slander [with his tongue]"), a derivative of *regel* ("foot"), specifies *halakh* ("walk"); *lo'-'asah* ("to not do [evil against a neighbor]") specifies *pa'al* ("to execute [what is right]"); *kherpah lo'-nasa'* ("to not vilify [one close by]") matches *davar* ("to speak truth in his heart"). The trilogy of proscriptions in verse 3 is still quite abstract and so will receive finer specification in verse 5.

Speech: no slander—v. 3Aa. "Slander" glosses Hebrew *ragal*, a denominative of *regel*, "foot." *BDB* connects the denominative to its etymological root by the gloss: "foot it," "go about" (maliciously, as "slanderer"). "With his tongue" (*'al shono*, lit. "upon his tongue"), the body part that performs the speech act, balances the "heart" in verse 2B, where the speech act is conceived.

Action: no evil to neighbor—v. 3Ab. The second prohibition disallows "to do evil/harm" to the worshiper's innocent neighbor. The semantic range of *'asah* ("do") is very large, like its English equivalent "to make," "do." Its manifold uses depend on its subjects and objects, ranging from production ("to make") to action ("to do"), which is the sense here and so in parallel with *p'l* (v. 2). Lexicographers gloss the feminine *ra'ah* ("evil") and its gender masculine doublet *ra'*, with no difference in meaning, by "evil (ill-disposed and sin)," "wickedness," "injustice," "wrong," "calamity," "distress," "disaster," "deprivation," "misfortune," recognizing that the differences between these synonyms are often attenuated. H. J. Stoebe suggests that the basic meaning of *ra'ah* is what harms life, not what benefits

---

24. Gillis Gerleman, *TLOT*, 1:327, s.v. *davar*.

it.[25] More fundamentally, its root, *r"*, conveys the factual judgment that something is bad, whether it be a concrete physical state (e.g., "ugly" cows, Gen. 41:3; "poor/bad" figs, Jer. 24:2), an abstraction, "calamity/disaster," or moral behavior that injures others (Ps. 15:3). The value judgment that something is bad depends on the taste of the one making the evaluation, so "in one's eyes" is often added to the word (see 15:4). The phrase "to his neighbor" (*re'ehu*) is a broad term for "those persons with whom one is brought into contact and with whom one must live on account of the circumstances of life."[26] Jesus defined, not redefined, *neighbor* as anyone encountered (Luke 10:29–37).

Speech: no maligning of neighbor—v. 3B. Also, the worshiper must not defame an innocent community member. "He does not vilify" glosses *kherpah lo'-nasa'* (lit. "he does not lift up reproach"). *Kherpah* ("reproach") refers to the indelible disgrace that society heaps on an individual who seeks to break up its foundation and its social coherence; society punishes him by maligning him in order to denigrate his significance, worth, and potential influence. "Lift up" (*nasa'*) is probably elliptical for "you shall not lift up the name of" (i.e., lift up his hand and speak [that which causes society to heap insults against someone], cf. Ex. 20:7). In the phrase "against his close neighbor" (*'al-qᵉrovo*), the preposition *'al* ("against" [LXX *epi*]) has its hostile sense and *qarov* denotes a neighbor who is "close" both literally in space and metaphorically in sympathy and spirit (cf. Lev. 21:2–3; Ruth 2:20; cf. Ps. 148:14; Prov. 27:10). Reproaches and insults are rightly heaped upon sinners (cf. Jer. 29:18; 42:18; 44:8ff.), but not upon an innocent neighbor who dwells trustingly in the neighborhood and who has not done wrong (Prov. 3:29–30). *Kherpah lo'-nasa' al-qᵉrovo* can also mean "or borne reproach for *his acts on account of* his neighbor" (see note 8), investing *nasa'* with its usual meaning and *'al* with the sense of "on account of." But although the ambiguity may be intentional (see above), in a decalogue of proscribed virtues and prescribed vices that pertain to others, the clause more likely means to inflict scorn, not suffer it. This inference is further supported by the parallelism between verses 2 and 3 (see above), suggesting that verse 3B is parallel to *dover 'emeth* that entails affecting others, not self.

25. H. J. Stoebe, *TLOT*, 2:491, s.v. *tob*.
26. *HALOT*, 3:1254, s.v. *rea'*.

Fears *I AM*—v. 4

Teachings about having a right relationship with God stand at the pivot of teachings regarding maintaining a right relationship with neighbors. Foundational to acceptable ethics is the fear of *I AM*, which entails faith in him. The true worshiper shows his fear of *I AM* both socially by rejecting the vile, who do not fear *I AM*, and honoring those that fear him (v. 4Aa, b) and personally by keeping his oath whatever the cost.

Socially: rejects despicable (non-God-fearers) but honors God-fearers— v. 4A. Although the true worshiper never slanders a neighbor or alienates from society an innocent neighbor by heaping scorn on him, he draws a line with regard to piety: he rejects the impious and aims to give the pious social weight. As for *nivzeh* ("one who is vile/despicable"), its root *bzh* means "to regard as worthless and vile." As in Proverbs 1:7, the vile stands in opposition to God-fearers, suggesting that by "vile" David means those who are irreverent. "In his eyes" (*be'enayw*) may be literal because in the ancient Near East one's attitude is shown on the face, "by the look in someone's eyes."[27] The MT accents favor the interpretation of connecting "in his eyes" with "is one who should be rejected" (i.e., he views the reprobate as one to be ostracized, not honored; cf. Prov. 26:8; Isa. 32:5). One cannot understand anyone or anything without explanation, and that explanation depends on a prior understanding of reality. William Blake, I am told, makes the point tellingly: "We do not see with the eye, but through the eye." The accepted worshiper brings to a situation his "fear of *I AM*," and interprets people and/or situations with that preconceived understanding of reality. In the God-fearer's evaluation, it is proper (see note 11) to regard the vile, the non-God-fearer, as "one to be rejected" (*nim'as*). The root *m's* means "to want nothing to do with someone or something."[28]

In this single requirement of properly relating to people with regard to their piety, the *waw* ("but") is disjunctive, pitting "those who fear God" against "the vile," "the despicable." One can neither honor God-fearers and the despicable nor reject both. One who fears *I AM* loves *I AM* with all his being and so trusts him and obeys his catechetical teaching. He does so because he holds *I AM* in awe, knowing that God holds in his hands life for

27. Cf. Heinz-Josef Fabry, *TDOT*, 5:24, s.v. *khanan*.
28. Hans Wildberger, *TLOT*, 2:653, s.v. *m's*.

the pious and covenant-keepers, and death for the impious and disobedient to his teachings.[29] Whereas the accepted worshiper rejects the contemptible, he always "honors" (*ykabbed*) those who fear *I AM*. The root *kbd* means "to be heavy"; in *Piel* it means to esteem a person as having value and to declare him as such to give him social weight or prominence.[30] In other words, the acceptable worshiper aims to divest the vile from social significance and to invest the ethical God-fearer with social weight.

Personally: keeps oath at any cost—v. 4B. The true worshiper also demonstrates his fear of *I AM* by his keeping oaths made before *I AM*, whatever the cost. "He promises on oath" (*nishba'*) means "to bind oneself to a future obligation," not to confirm an existing circumstance with an oath. To swear an oath to do something assumes God's awareness of the oath. Sometimes *shb', Niphal*, involves a solemn obligation accompanied by a conditional curse (e.g., "thus may *I AM* do to me and even more if I do not . . .") or strengthened by a reference to God (cf. 2 Sam. 3:35; 1 Kings 1:13, 17, 29ff.; Ps. 132:2–5). The root of the phrase "to his own hurt" (*l'hara'*) is *ra'* (see v. 3). Even though his oath damages his well-being, "he does not change" (*yamir*) [it] by a different oath or by negating his original oath. The object "oath" is elided. Even a lightly spoken promise must be honored (Lev. 5:4). A promise made dishonestly or with false intentions, or one that simply cannot be fulfilled, is called "fraudulent" or "deceitful" and will be harshly condemned by *I AM* (Lev. 6:2, 4 [Heb. 5:22, 24]; 19:12; Jer. 5:2; 7:9). For this reason the wise caution their students against taking oaths. The preacher in Ecclesiastes draws his sayings on the danger of not keeping vows with the exhortation: "Therefore fear God" (Eccl. 5:1–7). And so to keep an oath at any cost implies that the oath-keeper fears *I AM*, for he believes God will hold him accountable to keep it. Saul, in contrast to David, failed this litmus test of piety (cf. 1 Sam. 19:6, 15 with 24:21ff.; 26:8–11).

Particulars and Summary of Social Action and Speech—v. 5A–Ba

Whereas the teachings in verses 2 and 3 moved from admonishing positive virtues to prohibited vices, now in the chiastic complement of verse 5A to verse 3, they move from prohibited vices to a positive summarizing statement

---

29. See Waltke, *Proverbs*, 100–101.
30. *IBHS*, 402–4, P. 24.2f, g.

in verse 5Ba. The accepted worshiper, who inferentially has economic power, refuses to use it to take advantage of the misery of the poor: he rejects taking interest from them and using bribes to steal from them.

Particular prohibited vices of action and speech—v. 5A. As the bicolon of verse 2, so also its chiastic parallel bicolon in verse 5A moves from action to speech, but uses the negative *lo'* plus the perfective form, as a matching chiasm to verse 3.

No interest from poor—v. 5Aa. "His silver" (*kaspo*) refers to silver as mined and smelted, not as a precious metal in its native state. The reference to silver instead of gold may indicate an early time when silver was priced higher than gold.[31] *Natan*, which "basically indicates the process through which an object or matter is set in motion," more specifically has either the sense of "to cause something to come to some" ("to give") or the sense of "to cause," "to effect," "to occasion" ("to do"), as in Proverbs 10:10.[32] Since the one giving the silver does not exact interest, one may assume that the true worshiper gives his silver to the destitute either outright or, more probably, with the expectation that the borrower will repay the loan when he is no longer destitute. "The poor" is added to "with interest" (*b^eneshekh*) because in the ten biblical occurrences of *neshekh*, half (three in the Pentateuch, Ex. 22:25 [24]; Lev. 25:36–37; and two in Ezekiel based on the Pentateuch, Ezek. 18:8, 13) explicitly refer to a charge for borrowed money from the poor. In Psalm 15:5 and Ezekiel 22:12, that precise reference is not as clear, but the latter is in the context of keeping the Mosaic covenant. According to Deuteronomy 23:20 [21], where *neshekh* occurs twice, an Israelite could charge interest from foreigners—the Gentiles charged interest from their own poor—but not from fellow Israelites. The parallel, "poor," in Proverbs 28:8 and the context (see vv. 3, 6, 11) strongly favor restricting its meaning to charging interest from the needy. In biblical times, the charge on borrowed money was about 30 percent of the amount borrowed. In any case, most scholars agree that all ten passages refer to loans made as "acts of charity for the relief of destitution as opposed to loans of a commercial nature for expanding business."[33] To make profit on another person's misery is unconscionable.

31. C. A. Robinson, "God the Refiner of Silver," *CBQ* 11 (1949): 188–90.
32. C. J. Labuschagne, *TLOT*, 2:776, s.v. *ntn*.
33. Robin Wakely, *NIDOTTE*, 3:186, s.v. *nŝk*.

No bribes taken against innocent—v. 5Ab. "Bribe" (*shokhad*) refers to a gift, usually monetary, given to or taken by a judge or a witness to convict an innocent person (Ex. 23:8; Deut. 10:17; 16:19; 27:25). So bribes pertain to both action and speech, and this subject appropriately draws this decalogue of "dos and don'ts" to its conclusion. According to J. J. Finkelstein, although there is sufficient evidence that bribery of judges was regarded at least as a moral offense in other ancient Near Eastern culture, "there is no known cuneiform law outlawing bribery specifically." He draws his essay on bribery to this conclusion: "it was not only a common practice, but was recognized as a legal transaction."[34] "Accepts" glosses *lqhk* ("to take"), which can mean "to take [i.e., to draw out of the pocket]" with reference to the one who proffers the bribe (cf. Prov. 7:20; 20:16; 22:27) or "to accept" with reference to the one who takes it (cf. Prov. 1:3; 2:1). The latter interpretation accords better with Proverbs 15:27 and fits the parallel of taking interest in Psalm 15:5Aa, but the ambiguity is probably intentional. "The innocent" (*naqi*) means "free from guilt." Both the briber and bribed aim to pervert justice "against" ('*al*) the guiltless.

SUMMARY

The relative participle, "one who does" ('*os'eh*, see v. 5Ba), complements as an inclusio the initial summarizing relative participle (*holekh*, "one who walks [i.e., lives]"). The deictic relative pronoun, "these things" ('*elleh*), refers back to the decalogue of proscribed virtues and prohibited vices. As a consequence of meeting these requirements, the true worshiper, who has already begun in the eternal way that God watches over (Ps. 1:6), dwells forever on *I AM*'s holy hill. "Never" glosses *lo'* ("not") and *le'olam*[35] ("forever," "for eternity"). '*Olam*, according to Ernst Jenni, means "the most distant time," "of unlimited and unforeseeable duration."[36] *Mot*, the root of the verb "will . . . be toppled" (*yimmot*), means concretely "to rock or shake and to fall off a base," and in Proverbs 10:30 "to never be toppled" stands in antithesis to "not dwell" (*lo' shkn*, see Ps. 15:1). The metaphor of "never toppled" connotes durability, stability, unalterability, finality, and permanence. This is so because the accepted worshiper dwells on the Eternal's

34. J. J. Finkelstein, "The Middle Assyrian *Shulmanu*-Texts," *JAOS* 72 (1952): 77–80.
35. Temporal and terminative l (*IBHS*, 206, P. 11.2.10c).
36. Ernst Jenni, *THAT*, 2:230, s.v. '*olam*.

holy mountain, a type of heaven. The world may collapse, but God never will (cf. Ps. 46:5; Isa. 24:19; 54:10). In short, David draws his decalogue to conclusion with a benediction of eternal life upon the worshiper who by faith keeps these requirements.

God's salvation from human failure to keep these virtues and to abstain from these vices comes about through the obedience of faith in reliance on God's grace for forgiveness of sins for spiritual enablement.

3

"The LORD Is Christ's Shepherd": Psalm 23 as Messianic Prophecy

DOUGLAS J. GREEN

THOSE WHO KNEW Al Groves well remember how much he loved the psalms. The Psalter was the cornerstone of his devotional life, a book he "lived in" and "lived out of" throughout his life. And those of us fortunate enough to have spent time praying with Al will recall how central the theme of "seeing Jesus" was to his piety. "Seeing Jesus" meant keeping our eyes fixed on Jesus or expecting to see him at work in our lives, and in Al's final days it took the form of a comforting and even joyful anticipation of meeting the Savior he loved face-to-face.

This essay is an exercise in Christian interpretation of the Psalter, and in particular an attempt to "see Jesus" in Psalm 23 in a fresh way. In combining two of Al's great passions—Christ and the psalms—I wish to honor the memory of my respected mentor, trusted colleague, wise friend, and godly brother in Christ, in a way that he would have appreciated.

INTRODUCTION: THE PSALTER AS A BOOK OF PROPHECY

Is Psalm 23 a messianic psalm? In other words, does this much-loved poem belong to a small group of "prophetic" psalms that have "no direct message of significance for the OT period" but "only predict the coming Messiah"?[1] First, it should be noted that many scholars do not even recognize the existence of this category of psalms. They argue that *at the level of their original composition*, even psalms traditionally defined as messianic-prophetic, for example, Psalms 2, 16, 22, 45, and 110, should be read as royal psalms, which make excellent sense in the historical context of Israelite theology in general and Davidic royal ideology in particular.[2] Furthermore, even those who argue for the existence of these original "direct prophecies" of the Messiah usually limit their number to fewer than fifteen,[3] with Psalm 23 rarely, if ever, categorized as a messianic psalm in this narrow predictive sense.

Nevertheless, since the time of the church fathers, Christians *have* engaged in a form of Christological interpretation of Psalm 23, reading its opening words, with Augustine, to mean that "my shepherd is the Lord Jesus Christ" and interpreting the rest of the psalm accordingly.[4] This line of interpretation, which has (rightly) brought comfort to Christians through the centuries, can be regarded as "messianic" in only the most general sense. From a grammatical-historical perspective, the psalm describes Yahweh's relationship with Israel (or Israel's king, David). The Christological interpretation develops in various ways out of this original meaning. Trinitarian theology, with its incorporation of Jesus into the identity of Israel's God, Yahweh, makes it very natural—for Christians!—to understand the first clause to mean "Jesus is my shepherd." Moreover, this classic Christological approach also finds textual support from a number of NT passages that refer to Jesus as the shepherd of his people, with John 10:11 and Luke 15:4–7 being two prominent examples.[5]

My sense is that the undergirding rationale for this classic Christological interpretation of Psalm 23 is not so much that Jesus fulfills a direct

1. Tremper Longman III, *How to Read the Psalms* (Downers Grove, IL: InterVarsity Press, 1988), 67.

2. For example, Longman contends that "no psalm is exclusively messianic in the narrow sense" (ibid., 68). By this he means that no psalm, as originally composed, is purely prophetic, or messianic, in character.

3. For example, Walter C. Kaiser Jr. treats only eleven psalms (2, 16, 22, 40, 45, 68, 69, 72, 109, 110, and 118) as messianic (*The Messiah in the Old Testament*, Studies in Old Testament Biblical Theology [Grand Rapids: Zondervan, 1995], 92–93).

4. Saint Augustine, *Expositions of the Psalms, 1–32*, in *The Works of Saint Augustine III/15*, ed. John E. Rotelle (Hyde Park, NY: New City, 2000), 244.

5. See James Montgomery Boice, *Psalms*, vol. 1, *Psalms 1–41* (Grand Rapids: Baker, 1994), 208; Patrick Henry Reardon, *Christ in the Psalms* (Ben Lomond, CA: Conciliar, 2000), 43–44.

prophecy concerning the identity of Yahweh in his eschatological role as Israel's shepherd, but rather that there is an analogy between Yahweh's relationship with an individual Israelite, David, and Christ's relationship with individual Christians. This analogy then allows Christians to "apply" the "truths" about the relationship described in Psalm 23 to their relationship with Christ. A good illustration of this kind of "analogical" application of the psalm's grammatical-historical meaning comes from the conservative evangelical expositor James Montgomery Boice. Initially, he takes verse 1 to refer to "Jehovah" as Israel's shepherd, but he then moves in a decidedly Christian direction by insisting that it does not stretch this OT statement "to see Jesus as our shepherd and to apply the lines of the psalm carefully and in detail to ourselves."[6]

This way of reading Psalm 23 bears witness to a certain tension in Christian (or at least modern evangelical) interpretation of the Psalter. On one hand, the commitment to grammatical-historical interpretation means that the primary question we ask is, more or less, what did the psalm mean to its original author? With this hermeneutical tether in place, it is arguable that no psalms prophesy some distant messianic future because *every* psalm addresses the "here and now" of ancient Israel. Yet Christians have always read the Psalter "toward Christ," even in the case of psalms that do not seem to have overtly messianic content. That inclination is a hint that the grammatical-historical method offers, at best, a limited starting point for the interpretation of the psalms.

The grammatical-historical approach interprets the psalms in the context of their original composition. Yet we do not receive the Psalter's 150 psalms as stand-alone texts in their original compositional context; they come to us in an expanding interpretive and canonical context.[7] First, the individual psalms are part of a canonical collection, the Psalter, the final form of which is the result of a long editorial, or redactional, process that only reached its conclusion at some point in the postexilic period. In recent years, scholarly attention has focused on this redactional process and the role it plays in determining the meaning of individual psalms. Is the shape of the Psalter—the location and ordering of the various psalms, and especially

6. Boice, *Psalms 1–41*, 208.

7. Bruce K. Waltke, "A Canonical Process Approach to the Psalms," in *Tradition and Testament: Essays in Honor of Charles Lee Feinberg*, ed. John S. Feinberg and Paul D. Feinberg (Chicago: Moody, 1981), 3–18.

the location of particular psalms at the beginning and end of the Psalter, and at the "seams" between its five books—merely an accident of history, or is there an editorial intention behind this shape? And if this shaping of the Psalter is intentional (at least to some degree), then what theological agenda guided these redactors as they did their work? And more specifically, did these redactors operate with an eschatological agenda? In other words, was the Psalter edited in such a way as to encourage readers to interpret its constituent psalms no longer simply as prayers and hymns rooted in the experience of ancient Israelites but as prophecies of events at the climax of Israel's history? This is not the place to enter this complex debate, but a growing number of scholars now agree that "the final form of the Psalter has been shaped . . . as an eschatological-predictive text,"[8] or at least that this final form is *susceptible* to being read in a prophetic direction.[9] If this approach to interpreting the Psalter is adopted, then individual psalms that did not have an eschatological orientation *at the level of their original composition* may be open to an eschatological or prophetic reinterpretation in their new literary context, that is, *at the level of the Psalter's final form.*

Even if there is uncertainty concerning the intentions of the Psalter's redactors, it is clear that in the Second-Temple period many Jews did read the psalms in a prophetic and eschatological direction. In addition to some intriguing evidence indicating that the translators of the Septuagint read the Psalter in this way,[10] it is apparent that at Qumran the Davidic psalms (at least) were being read as prophecy[11] and that the Psalter had become a book of "eschatological psalmody."[12] In other words, Qumran understood historical David to be speaking, through the gift of prophecy, the words of the Messiah who was yet to come. David, once "Israel's singer of songs" (2 Sam. 23:1),[13] had become a prophet, and his book, the Psalter, was interpreted accordingly.

8. David C. Mitchell, *The Message of the Psalter: An Eschatological Programme in the Book of Psalms*, JSOTSup 252 (Sheffield, UK: Sheffield Academic Press, 1997), 198.

9. M. A. Vincent, "The Shape of the Psalter: An Eschatological Dimension?" in *New Heaven and New Earth: Prophecy and the Millennium: Essays in Honour of Anthony Gelston*, ed. P. J. Harland and C. T. R. Hayward, VTSup 77 (Leiden: Brill, 1999), 82.

10. See Sue Gillingham, "From Liturgy to Prophecy: The Use of Psalmody in Second Temple Judaism," *CBQ* 64 (2002): 479.

11. 11QPs^a 27:2–11 refers to the psalms in the following way: "All these he [David] spoke through prophecy which was given to him by the Most High God." See Gillingham, "From Liturgy," 483–84.

12. Ben Zion Wacholder, "David's Eschatological Psalter 11Q Psalms^a," *HUCA* 59 (1988): 41.

13. All quotations of Scripture in this chapter are from the NIV, unless otherwise indicated.

Even more clearly, and more importantly for Christian readers of the Psalter, the NT authors read the psalms in the same way: not merely as ancient Israel's inspired hymnody, but as prophecy, as *predictions* of events that would occur at the climax of Israel's history. Of course, the apostles differed from Qumran in that they placed Jesus and his people—rather than the Qumran community—at the center of these climactic events.

In Luke 24:44, Jesus states that "everything must be fulfilled that is written about me in the Law of Moses, the Prophets and . . . Psalms." The obvious point is that Jesus understands the Psalter to be speaking prophetically about himself. Less obvious is the fact that in the Greek there is no definite article before "Psalms." According to Craig Evans, this means that "we do not have here an instance of the tripartite canon (i.e., the Law, the Prophets, and the Writings), but only the first two divisions—the Law and the Prophets, the latter of which was understood to include the Psalms."[14] Elsewhere in the NT, the Hebrew Scriptures, including the Psalter, are referred to as "the Law [or Moses] and the Prophets" (e.g., Matt. 5:17; 7:12; Luke 16:16, 29, 31; Acts 13:15; 28:23; Rom. 3:21). This strongly suggests that in the first century AD, the Psalter was being read in connection with—or as an extension of—the prophetic books.

Furthermore, a careful study of the use of the Psalter in the NT would show that the apostles understood the psalms as prophecies concerning a future Messiah and his people.[15] Again, this is not the place to engage in such a study, so reference to a single text will have to suffice. In Acts 2:29–30, Peter explains his quotation of Psalm 16 by saying: "David died and was buried . . . But *he was a prophet* and knew that God had promised him on oath that he would place one of his descendants on his throne." For Peter and the other apostles, David was as much a prophet as Isaiah, Jeremiah, and Ezekiel, and the psalms that bear his name were read as predictions of eschatological events, now fulfilled in the story of Jesus and his followers.[16]

In light of this full-canon approach to psalms interpretation, it is appropriate to read the *whole* of the Psalter in a prophetic and eschatological direction. More specifically, *all* of the "Psalms of David" should be read

14. Craig A. Evans, "Praise and Prophecy in the Psalter and the New Testament," in *The Book of Psalms: Composition and Reception*, ed. Peter W. Flint and Patrick D. Miller Jr., VTSup 99; Formation and Interpretation of Old Testament Literature 4 (Leiden: Brill, 2005), 551.

15. J. Samuel Subramanian, *The Synoptic Gospels and the Psalms as Prophecy*, LNTS 351 (London: T&T Clark, 2007), 2.

16. Ibid., 15.

as messianic psalms that describe different dimensions of the life—and especially the suffering—of Israel's eschatological King. Therefore, instead of treating the small group of psalms that the NT "applies" to Jesus as a special group of direct prophecies of the Messiah,[17] I regard these psalms as the tip of a prophetic and messianic iceberg. It is not that the NT quotes *all* of a small group of messianic psalms. Rather, it quotes from a *few* of a very large group of messianic psalms.[18] In other words, the apostolic authors adopted not simply a general Christological approach to reading the Psalter, wherein Christ could be "seen" in the psalms, but more specifically a decidedly *Christotelic* approach, reading it in connection with Israel's great narrative of redemption, which from their perspective had reached its surprising climax (Greek *telos*, "end" or "goal") in the story of Jesus, the Messiah.

READING PSALM 23 AS A MESSIANIC PROPHECY

Against this background of a developing interpretive and canonical context, I propose a second type of Christological reading of Psalm 23, a Christotelic reading, which will stand alongside—but not replace—the traditional Christian interpretation that places Jesus in the role of Yahweh, the shepherd ("the Lord, Jesus Christ, is my shepherd"). I will read Psalm 23 as a messianic psalm, that is, a prophecy concerning the Messiah, and set out a Christotelic interpretation in which Jesus fulfills the role played by the psalmist David, the sheep. To arrive at this interpretation, it will be helpful to consider briefly how the psalm's meaning may have developed through the different stages of redemptive history and the growth of the canon. In this way, a psalm that originally described *David's* relationship with Yahweh ("Yahweh/the LORD is David's shepherd") came to be understood as a messianic prophecy ("Yahweh/the LORD is—or will be—*eschatological* David's shepherd") until finally, with the Christian affirmation that Jesus of Nazareth fulfilled Israel's messianic hopes, the purely prophetic, forward-looking interpretation gives way to a Christological reading ("The LORD/God the Father is *Christ's* shepherd"[19]), with the psalm now understood as an abbreviated gospel narrative.

17. See Kaiser, *Messiah*, 92–94.

18. See Bruce K. Waltke, "Christ in the Psalms," in *The Hope Fulfilled: Essays in Honor of O. Palmer Robertson* (Phillipsburg, NJ: P&R Publishing, 2008), 41.

19. This nontraditional line of interpretation has already been anticipated by Vern S. Poythress, *Science and Hermeneutics: Implications of Scientific Method for Biblical Interpretation*, Foundations

Beginning at the grammatical-historical, or compositional, level, the psalm testifies to the Lord's faithfulness to David, by providing for his needs (v. 2) and bringing him through the threat of death (v. 4) into abundant life in the temple (vv. 5–6). To this basic structure we may add some details. First, Psalm 23 can be identified as a pilgrimage psalm.[20] It tells a story about a journey—not just any journey, but one that reaches its goal as the psalmist enters "the house of Yahweh," the temple in Jerusalem. More specifically, the psalmist's metaphorical journey passes through three spatio-temporal points: (1) it passes from a time and place of sufficiency and safety, depicted in the imagery of the pasturage in springtime (v. 2), (2) it moves into the quasi-exilic condition of life under the threat of death, portrayed as a descent into a deep ravine in the Judean wilderness during summer (v. 4), and (3) finally, after safely passing through the "valley of the shadow of death," the pilgrimage—or is it a return from exile?—ends in the temple in Jerusalem in early autumn at the Feast of Tabernacles (v. 5). This movement through space and time can be set out as follows:

v. 1a: Statement of Theme: Yahweh is my shepherd.[21]

> v. 1b: First Implication: I do not lack (= "Life")
> v. 2: Provision of Food and Water (Location 1: Pasturelands/Spring)
>> In pastures of spring grass he causes me to lie down;
>> Beside waters of rest he guides me.

> v. 3a: Second Implication: He restores my life (Resurrection/ Return from Exile)
> v. 3bc: Theological Orientation (Yahweh's Faithfulness)
>> He leads me in paths of (*his*) righteousness[22]
>> for the sake of his reputation.
> v. 4: From "Death"/Exile (Location 2: Wilderness/Late Summer)

---

of Contemporary Interpretation 6 (Grand Rapids: Zondervan, 1988), 154–56; repr. in Moisés Silva, ed., *Foundations of Contemporary Interpretation* (Grand Rapids: Zondervan, 1996), 523–24.

20. Mark S. Smith, *The Pilgrimage Pattern in Exodus*, JSOTSup 239 (Sheffield, UK: Sheffield Academic Press, 1997), 132–42; Craig C. Broyles, *Psalms*, NIBCOT 11 (Peabody, MA: Hendrickson, 1999), 123–24.

21. All renderings of Psalm 23 in this chapter are the author's own translation.

22. John Goldingay, *Psalms*, vol. 1, *Psalms 1–41*, BCOTWP (Grand Rapids: Baker, 2006), 350.

> (So) even when I walk in the valley of the shadow-of-death
> I will not fear the danger
> because you are with me.
> Your rod and your staff—they calm my fears.
>
> v. 5: To "Life Plus" (Location 3: Temple/Early Autumn—Feast of Tabernacles/Ingathering)
> You arrange a banquet-table before me—
> opposite my adversaries—
> You have anointed my head with olive-oil.
> My cup overflows.
>
> v. 6: Extension of v. 5 (Return to the Temple)
> Surely, (your) goodness and covenant faithfulness will pursue me
> all the days of my life
> and I will keep coming back into the house of Yahweh
> for a lengthening of days.[23]

Read as a movement from pasturage to wilderness to temple, Psalm 23 gives specific expression to the most basic outline of the story of redemption. In its simplest form, this recurring "redemptive pattern" can be described in terms of the development "Good → Bad → Better." This can be restated in a variation such as "Life → Death → Abundant Life," "Promised Land → Exile → Restoration," or, even more broadly, "Eden → Exile from the Garden → New Jerusalem" and "Life → Death → Resurrection and Exaltation." This pattern will provide the framework for the different ways of reading the psalm.

In its grammatical-historical context, Psalm 23, as a psalm of King David, can arguably be further defined as a royal psalm,[24] but read as prophecy, it becomes a messianic psalm. "David" is no longer historical King David, but rather "eschatological David." In continuity with the grammatical-historical

---

23. For a detailed defense of my grammatical-historical interpretation of Psalm 23, see Douglas J. Green, "The Good, the Bad and the Better: Psalm 23 and Job," in *The Whirlwind: Essays on Job, Hermeneutics and Theology in Memory of Jane Morse*, ed. Stephen L. Cook, Corrine L. Patton, and James W. Watts, JSOTSup 336 (Sheffield, UK: Sheffield Academic Press, 2001), 67–81.

24. See John H. Eaton, *Psalms*, Torch (London: SCM, 1967), 76–79; John H. Eaton, *Kingship and the Psalms*, 2nd ed., The Biblical Seminar (Sheffield, UK: JSOT Press, 1986), 36–38; Michael Goulder, "David and Yahweh in Psalms 23 and 24," *JSOT* 30 (2005): 463–73.

meaning, the psalm now predicts that Yahweh will be faithful to his promise to protect and preserve his Messiah at every point in his life's journey. Given the movement from images of restfulness to a darker, more threatening image of "the valley of the shadow of death," and finally to a picture of restoration, victory, and abundance in the Lord's presence, Psalm 23 establishes the outline of Messiah's story. His final destiny will be glorious: a return to the abundance of Eden in the Lord's temple, with (defeated) enemies arrayed before him (v. 5). Before this climax, however, Messiah must pass through the valley of the shadow of death—perhaps a brush with death, or some deathlike condition (e.g., exile). In other words, Messiah's story will conform to the pattern "Life → Death → Life Plus."

The final interpretive step is to engage in a Christotelic reading that builds on the grammatical-historical and prophetic interpretations of the psalm but ultimately conforms to what actually happened in the story of Jesus of Nazareth.

I take the opening words of the psalm ("Yahweh is my shepherd") to be a short monocolon that functions as a title or introductory statement of the theme developed in the rest of the poem. Throughout his pilgrimage, David finds Yahweh to be true to his promise to "be with" him, first by providing for his daily needs (v. 2), summarized by the statement "I do not lack" (v. 1b), and second, by rescuing him from the threat of death and bringing him into a life of blessing (vv. 4–5). This latter dimension of Yahweh's faithfulness is summarized in verse 3a by the statement "He restores my life." Moving beyond David, and reading the psalm as fulfilled prophecy, the metaphor of sheep and shepherd also provides an accurate picture of the relationship that Jesus enjoyed with his heavenly Father. While the NT does not use shepherd-and-sheep imagery to depict *this* relationship, it is fair to say that in *his* pilgrimage, in *his* life, death, and resurrection, Jesus finds Yahweh—the LORD, his heavenly Father—to be *his* faithful shepherd, the One who provided for *his* daily needs and restored *his* soul by rescuing him from death. In other words, the gospel, from beginning to end, is a story of how "the LORD was Christ's shepherd."

The psalm's metaphorical journey begins in the springtime in the pasturelands to the east of Jerusalem and Bethlehem, the liminal zone between the grain-producing land of the Judean highlands and the wasteland of the Judean wilderness. This is "ordinary time" in the life of the sheep: when the shepherd leads them to fresh spring grasses and pools of water remaining from the winter rains (v. 2). This is that stage of the pilgrimage that can be brought under the rubric of "I do not lack" because the shepherd provides the psalmist's daily needs. But this section can also be reread as a prophecy of Yahweh's sustaining of the Messiah: fulfilled in such stories as Luke's account of the temptation of Christ in the wilderness: "If you are the Son of God, tell this stone to become bread" (Luke 4:3). Jesus, of course, chooses against the way of self-trust, and chooses instead to trust in his Father to give him each day his daily bread (Luke 11:3). This episode provides a window on the life of Messiah Jesus: in the ordinariness of life—in the pasturelands of springtime, as it were—he discovered that the Lord, his heavenly Father, was the shepherd who supplied his needs, allowing him to say, "Because the LORD is my shepherd, nothing do I lack."

In my grammatical-historical reading of Psalm 23, I take the words "He restores my life" (v. 3a) not as the conclusion of verse 2 but as a short summary of what will transpire in the following narrative of verses 4 and 5: Yahweh will "restore" the psalmist's life by bringing him safely through the threat of death (v. 4) into the blessed life described in verse 5. I can give the rest of verse 3 only passing mention by offering this paraphrase: "Yahweh leads me in paths of *his* righteousness, paths where he fulfills *his* obligations to the psalmist-sheep and does so in order to maintain his reputation as a covenant-keeping God." Read Christotelically, the Lord's fidelity to Jesus, his Servant-Sheep—especially seen in raising him from the dead—is the ultimate witness to his reputation as a faithful God.

"Soul restoration" is marked by a movement from negative to positive conditions. To state the obvious, the negative is described in verse 4, "the valley of the shadow of death," the second spatio-temporal point on the psalmist's pilgrimage. Metaphorically, he has left the pasturage and traveled farther east—in an "exilic" direction—into the deep ravines that cut through the Judean wilderness and run down to the Dead Sea. While it is not explicitly stated, I set this verse in late summer. The wholly negative character of this place is emphasized in three ways: it is, forebodingly, "the valley of the shadow of death," it is a place where danger (literally, "bad") threatens (probably in the form of wild beasts and precipitous cliffs), and finally, it is a place of fear.

Verse 5 (read in concert with verse 6), on the other hand, provides the counterpoint to verse 4 and marks the destination of the psalmist's pilgrimage, which can also be analyzed as a return from exile. The journey from the pasturage through the wilderness now reaches its goal in "the house of Yahweh," the temple in Jerusalem. Judging by the banquet imagery of verse 5, the movement from spring to summer ends in early autumn at the great harvest festival—the Feast of Tabernacles/Sukkot (Ingathering)[25]—the pinnacle experience of salvation for ancient Israelites. The threat of death gives way to life, or more accurately "life *plus*," since the quality of the life of verse 5 (the banquet table and overflowing wine) far exceeds that of verse 2 (grass and water): from the bare necessities to abundance, from plain fare (for a sheep!) to banquet richness. The "bad" that threatens the psalmist in verse 4 gives way to God's pursuing "good," in verses 5 and 6. The fear of death is replaced by sabbatical rest as the psalmist's enemies are subdued. This is what it means to have one's "life (or soul) restored": it is being led from death (or in this case, the threat of death) to "life plus" (the abundant life of sabbatical rest).

Even in their grammatical-historical context, verses 4 and 5, with their images of escape from the threat of death and (possibly) return from exile, tell an incipient resurrection story. Read prophetically, these verses echo the story of the Isaianic Servant as they depict the Messiah's journey through some kind of suffering, which will subsequently change into his enjoyment of the blessed life, and more specifically to an eschatological banquet. It must be admitted, however, that the psalmist does not actually die—"the valley of the shadow of death" is not death itself—so it is difficult to see how even a prophetic interpretation of this psalm can transform it into a prediction of the actual *death* and subsequent bodily *resurrection* of the Messiah. Nevertheless, Christotelic exegesis cannot be satisfied with either a grammatical-historical or a prophetic interpretation of Psalm 23, although it is indebted to both. If Jesus Christ is indeed the *telos*, or goal, of Israel's story, and more specifically the fulfillment of the OT's messianic prophecies—including the Psalter understood as a prophetic book—then Christian interpretation of the OT must be an exercise in reading backwards, of rereading earlier texts so that their meanings cohere with what God has actually done in history in Jesus Christ.[26]

Adopting this approach means that I read Psalm 23:4–5 as a prophecy of the *death* and *resurrection* of Christ, even though these verses, in either

25. Mark D. Futato, *The Book of Psalms*, Cornerstone Biblical Commentary 7 (Carol Stream, IL: Tyndale House, 2009), 103.

26. Francis Watson, "The Old Testament as Christian Scripture: A Response to Professor Seitz," *SJT* 52 (1999): 229–30.

their earlier grammatical-historical or prophetic sense, do not directly predict these specific events.[27] Christ's death and resurrection "expand" the earlier meanings of these verses. Psalm 23, read from an original (postexilic) prophetic perspective, looks *forward* with an expectation that the coming Messiah would in some way walk into the valley where death metaphorically casts a shadow. But read from a Christotelic perspective, we discover that eschatological David actually keeps walking . . . into the *next* valley, into Death's own valley. Psalm 23:4 should be reinterpreted as a prophecy of the *actual* death of Messiah, and not a metaphorical death (like exile), or being under the threat of death. In short, when we read Psalm 23:4 in this Christological manner, we should no longer hear the word *shadow*! Likewise, verse 5 becomes a way of speaking about Jesus' resurrection and exaltation to "life plus" at the right hand of the Father and depicts the welcome that Jesus receives as he reenters heaven as the risen and exalted King. "The house of the LORD" in verse 6 no longer refers to the temple in Jerusalem. Implicit in every Christian reading of this verse is the idea that the temple was merely a sign pointing forward to the reality of God's heavenly dwelling and ultimately to the eschatological reality of heaven on earth.

Reading Psalm 23 in this way opens up a rich and complex perspective on the death of Christ. Viewed through the lens of Psalm 23 (and verse 4 in particular), the crucifixion can be seen as the moment when Jesus boldly asserts in the face of death itself, "I will not fear because my heavenly Father is with me." Of course, at this point, my Christotelic interpretation seems to have hit an immovable obstacle, precisely because God the Father was *not with* Jesus in his death, as proved by Jesus' cry of dereliction, "My God, my God, why have you forsaken me?" quoting from the immediately preceding Psalm 22! Nevertheless, we may find a side path around this barricade by asking whether God abandoned Jesus on the cross. I suggest that the answer is both yes *and* no. For Matthew and Mark, the answer is clearly yes, since they both record Jesus' words of abandonment (Matt. 27:46; Mark 15:34). Luke, however, paints a quite different picture. He omits the cry of dereliction; instead, Jesus' final words in Luke are more appropriate for a man experiencing God's comforting presence in death: "Father, into your hands I commit my spirit" (Luke 23:46). Also of interest is Luke 22:43, which

---

27. Similarly, Psalm 16, which in its original, compositional context speaks "merely" of *protection from dying*, is read expansively by Peter as a prophecy of Messiah's *rescue out of death* (i.e., resurrection) (Acts 2:25–31).

records that during Jesus' agony in the garden of Gethsemane, "an angel from heaven appeared to him and strengthened him." Again, this datum is omitted from Matthew and Mark, and I suggest that it is part of Luke's distinctive portrayal of the passion of the Messiah. For Luke, Jesus goes to his death comforted by the confidence that his Father *was* in fact with him![28] In other words, Psalm 23:4, interpreted Christotelically, can be read as the words of the Lukan Jesus: "Even though I walk through the valley of death, I will fear no evil. I entrust my life into your hands for you are with me; I trust you to restore my soul [i.e., raise me to life]."

We cannot here attempt an explanation for these two perspectives on Jesus' experience of God in his final moments. Somehow the Father was *both* absent from and present with Jesus on the cross. We should not be surprised by this paradox. It has its origins in the Psalter, where Psalm 22 ("God has abandoned me") and Psalm 23 ("God is with me") sit side by side as two equally true expressions of David's experience of God in times of deep distress.

We come at last to the final verse of the psalm—a verse that I have refrained from commenting on until now. My translation of the Hebrew ("*and I will keep coming back into* the house of Yahweh *for a lengthening of days*") departs significantly from the received tradition. Some brief observations on two elements in this verse are in order. The traditional (KJV) translation ("*I will dwell* in the house of the LORD") is not based on the MT (*weshabtî*) but on the LXX (which assumes *weshibtî*, lit. "and my dwelling [will be]"). I find it difficult to read the MT's *weshabtî* in any other way than as a *weqatal* (or *waw* consecutive plus perfect) form of *shûb* ("return, come back"). Additionally, the final words of the psalm do not speak of *eternal* life: the Hebrew can be literally translated as "for a lengthening of days" and simply refers to a long life. From a grammatical-historical perspective, the MT of verse 6 does not depict the psalmist living in the temple forever. Rather, it expresses the expectation that he will experience the blessing of a long life and the happy prospect of making pilgrimage to the temple year after year to enjoy the blessings of Sukkot, described in verse 5. Verse 6, in effect, casts the psalmist back to verse 2 to commence the pilgrimage all over again.

28. Maarten J. J. Menken, "The Psalms in Matthew's Gospel," in *The Psalms in the New Testament*, ed. Steve Moyise and Maarten J. J. Menken, The New Testament and the Scriptures of Israel (London: T&T Clark, 2004), 79, also cites John 16:32 ("Yet I am not alone, for my Father is with me") as further evidence of an early Christian tradition, in which "Jesus' closeness to God, even in his passion," coexisted with a tradition that emphasized the fact that he was abandoned by God.

"I will keep coming back into the house of Yahweh" does not reflect the traditional translation of this verse, but is a good rendering of its grammatical-historical meaning. Nonetheless, it does not "work" Christologically. Once Christ ascends into the *heavenly* house of the Lord, he stays there (Heb. 1:3b); he does not return to earth and make annual pilgrimages back to heaven! Accordingly, whether the LXX reflects the better textual tradition or not is beside the Christological point. "I will dwell" may or may not be a good translation of the original Hebrew, but it is an excellent translation of the gospel. Read in the light of the story of Jesus, the Messiah, we must follow the LXX: the eschatological David has been brought from the valley of death into the heavenly house of the Lord, to *reside* there!

I can make a similar interpretive point even more strongly with respect to the final words of the psalm. Even when read from a postexilic prophetic perspective, all that the Davidic Messiah can expect is a *long life* after his brush with death. But read from a Christotelic perspective, then the right interpretation, if not the right translation, of the Hebrew *is* "forever" because God has in fact granted Messiah Jesus a lengthening of days *that stretches out into eternity*. So in the end, while the KJV tradition ("I will dwell in the house of the LORD *for ever*") may not be quite true to Hebrew grammar, it is true to the grammar of the gospel!

CONCLUSION

Psalm 23, read as a fulfilled messianic prophecy, tells the story of Jesus Christ from the perspective of God's shepherd-like care for him: in life, through death, and on to glorious entry into the heavenly temple. Moreover, it tells the story of those who have been united to Christ by faith. Jesus' story has become our story; his pilgrimage has become our pilgrimage. In the end, this alternative Christological reading of the shepherd psalm should bring the same encouragement to Christian readers that comes to them through the traditional Christian interpretation. "The LORD" (understood as God the Father) "is Christ's shepherd" transposes easily—by virtue of our union with Christ—into "the LORD is the Christian's shepherd." In fact, we face the valley of (the shadow of) death without fear because God has already brought the lead Sheep from his great flock safely through that dark valley. Because the Great Shepherd has led Jesus from the valley of death to the Temple Mount, he will provide the same death-defeating, life-restoring protection to all who follow in Jesus' tracks.

4

Ecclesiastes according to the Gospel: Christian Thoughts on Qohelet's Theology

P E T E R   E N N S

ECCLESIASTES IS A VERY difficult book to interpret. This is not only the case with individual verses here and there, which are shrouded in mystery or complexity (although, in either Hebrew or English, the meaning of what Qohelet[1] says here and there is plain enough). Rather, the real difficulty with Ecclesiastes is what the book as a whole is saying. This is a discussion that has been active since at least the first century AD in Jewish circles, and is still very evident today.

For example, for nearly any OT book, you can ask any ten reasonably informed people about its contents, its basic story line. To use Genesis as an example, these different people might emphasize different aspects of the

---

1. *Qohelet* is the name given to the main speaker of the book of Ecclesiastes. In some translations this name is rendered *Preacher* or *Teacher*, but both of these are highly interpretive and of questionable value. Along with most other scholars, I simply prefer to leave his name as is. For a discussion of the name and its meaning, see Peter Enns, "Ecclesiastes," in *Dictionary of the Old Testament: Wisdom, Poetry, and Writings*, ed. Tremper Longman III and Peter Enns (Downers Grove, IL: InterVarsity Press, 2008), 121–32; Tremper Longman III, *Ecclesiastes*, NICOT (Grand Rapids: Eerdmans, 1998), 1–2.

book, but somewhere they would likely all mention creation, Adam and Eve, the flood, the Tower of Babel, and various episodes of the patriarchs. Likewise, for Exodus, the main themes to arise might be slavery, Moses, deliverance, the Red Sea, and Mount Sinai, with variations on those main themes. No one, I think, would say of Genesis, "It is about the destruction of the world, how Adam and Eve passed the test, that wonderful tower project, and how God rejected the patriarchs in favor of Egyptians." And no one would say that Exodus speaks of God's enslaving of the Israelites and Pharaoh's efforts to liberate them. The basic content and meaning of these books are not in serious question by informed readers. There may be differences of emphasis or disagreement on some minor points, but it is hard indeed to "counter-understand" Genesis and Exodus.

Yet with Ecclesiastes (Song of Solomon being another example), the main issue at hand is not matters of emphasis or degrees of difference. Rather, the issue has been and remains this: "What is the very basic message of the book?" To put it somewhat bluntly, is Qohelet right or wrong? You do not have to read too far in the book before Qohelet sets you back on your heels. He makes numerous observations and complaints that are a bit stark, to say the least, and he arrives at some conclusions that may make some of us want to cover our ears and eyes.

Although by no means universal, two common ways of handling "the problem of Qohelet" are: (1) to allow Qohelet to vent for eleven chapters, say "duly noted," and then cancel out his words by a particular reading of the epilogue (12:8–14); and (2) to try to make Qohelet look more "orthodox" than he really is by dulling the impact of his words. In my opinion (and again, I want to stress that these two options represent something of extremes), the answer lies somewhere in the middle, and it is the epilogue that holds the key for understanding the message of the whole. To briefly summarize my conclusion:

> Qohelet is indeed making stark, harsh, unsettling observations about the nature of reality, observations that put his words in tension with much of Israelite thought. The epilogue, however, considers Qohelet, nevertheless, to be a wise man, but still encourages readers not to linger with Qohelet but to move beyond.

What follows is, first, a summary of Qohelet's theology, focusing on the opening chapter of the book. Second, I will briefly address Qohelet's view of God, or at least one important aspect of it, particularly with respect to the so-called carpe diem ("seize the day") passages. Third, we will look at the epilogue to see how Qohelet's words are evaluated by the narrator of the book.[2] These three issues will help us form a working knowledge of the theology of Qohelet. I will then conclude by bringing this theology into brief conversation with the Christian reality of being united with the crucified and risen Christ. In my view, the theology of Qohelet, however unsettling it might be, should not be discounted by the church but be instructive to it.

A SUMMARY OF QOHELET'S THEOLOGY ACCORDING TO CHAPTER 1

One can summarize Qohelet's theology in a number of ways, but allow me to boil it down to a brief statement and then illustrate by following the argument presented in chapter 1.

> Everything, and I mean everything, is *absurd*. No matter what you do, you have *ultimately nothing to show for it*. You live and then you die. The only thing you have is the *portion* God gives you. And this is how God has set things up.

This doesn't seem to preach well, I admit, but that does not mean the summary is inaccurate. In fact, these themes recur throughout Ecclesiastes. The italicized portions refer to three keywords in Ecclesiastes that help bring some order to the message. "Absurd" is a translation of the word *hevel*, which is more often translated "meaningless" or, as in the KJV, "vanity." "Absurd," however, better reflects Qohelet's exasperation at the human condition.[3] Another common and loaded term in Ecclesiastes is *yitron*, which is typically translated "profit," as in a surplus, a return on your investment. Qohelet claims that there is no *yitron* in anything you do, that you ultimately have nothing to show for your work. Why is that? Because we *all* die (2:14; 3:20). All we really have, and it isn't much, is the day-to-day work that God has given us to do, our "portion" or "lot" (*kheleq*). This is what life is like, and it is God who is to blame for making it so.

2. To be precise, the actual words of Qohelet begin at 1:12 and end at 12:7. Qohelet's words are framed by a narrator, who introduces us to Qohelet's words in 1:1–11 and then evaluates them in 12:8–14.

3. Michael V. Fox, *A Time to Tear Down, A Time to Build Up: A Rereading of Ecclesiastes* (Grand Rapids: Eerdmans, 1999), 30–42.

Perhaps the best way of easing into Qohelet's rather dismal outlook is to look at chapter 1. The narrator introduces the book in verses 1–11, and then Qohelet himself introduces his thoughts in verses 12–18.

As I said at the outset, the overall meaning (and value) of Ecclesiastes is debated, but it seems to me that there can be little doubt as to the point that Qohelet is trying to get across. The narrator has even been kind enough to summarize Qohelet's words for us, first generally in verses 2–4 and then in more detail in verses 5–11. Verses 2–4 may be translated as follows:[4]

> Utterly absurd . . . utterly absurd, everything is absurd. What profit is there in anyone's labor under the sun?[5] A generation goes [dies] and another one comes; the world remains unchanged.

The narrator leaves little doubt about what will occupy both Qohelet and the readers' attention for the next twelve chapters. Moreover, the fact that 12:8, the first verse of the epilogue, is a virtually verbatim repetition of 1:2 makes it clear that this thought frames the words of Qohelet throughout. The narrator is handing us Qohelet's message on a silver platter.

Verses 5–7 are an extended illustration in which the narrator appeals to creation in support of his summary. Unlike the Psalter, which praises God for his creation, Qohelet sees creation as confirming the futility of existence. The sun rises and sets, every day the same thing (v. 5). The image drawn here is of the sun rising, setting, and then "panting" (šʾp) to get back in place in order to do it all again the next day. But what is in it for the sun? What profit does the sun have? Its existence is absurd, just like ours. It is as if Qohelet is saying, "You don't believe all of life is absurd? Just look out the window." The same goes for the wind (v. 6). From north to south, round and round it goes on its rounds, a never-ending cycle. Then in verse 7, we see how the rivers flow into the ocean, but for all their hard work, the oceans are never full: there is no profit.

Beginning in verse 8, Qohelet moves from analogues taken from the natural world to human activities (namely, speaking, seeing, and hearing),

---

4. All quotations of Ecclesiastes in this chapter are the author's own translation.

5. The term "under the sun" is often misunderstood to mean something like "on earth, *as opposed to* in heaven." The point would be that if only Qohelet would take his gaze off earthly things, he would see that a heavenly perspective holds the answers. But this is not at all what he means. Rather, the phrase is meant to refer to the exhaustive nature of Qohelet's search. He has left no stone unturned; nothing has been left uninvestigated, as the subsequent chapters make clear.

and the result is the same: they amount to nothing. All words just make one weary; they just don't get you anywhere. So, too, with seeing and hearing: the eye never has enough and the ear is never "full."

Verses 9 and 10 make the same point but in more direct language, without recourse to natural or physical imagery. In fact, we may say that verses 9 and 10 summarize in plain language the points made thus far: "Whatever *has* happened is what *will* happen. Whatever *has* been done is what *will* be done. There is nothing at all new under the sun" (see also 3:15). This summary notion is very strong: "There is nothing at all new anywhere on earth ['under the sun'; see verse 3 above], in neither the past, present, nor future." This "circle of life" is for Qohelet not a source of stability or comfort, but the very expression of the absurdity of life, since "the cycle" ensures that nothing that happens or nothing we do will make any difference. "Oh, sure," Qohelet continues in verse 10, "someone might look at something and say, 'look, this is new,' but it really isn't. It's just the same old thing. It has been here 'forever.' "[6]

Verse 11 concludes the introduction to the book and brings us to another summary statement of sorts, one that will become a dominant theme throughout Ecclesiastes: death. Not only is there no *thing* new under the sun—no permanent deed or human activity—but this holds for *us* as well. In fact, the very existence of previous generations is forgotten. Likewise, those who are yet to be born will eventually, after their own deaths, be forgotten by generations who will come after them. This is no throwaway line; its sentiment should echo with anyone familiar with the OT, for it is precisely a blessed memory that is the hope and comfort for God's people. To live in such a way as to live on in the memories of one's descendants is a mark of a life lived in communion with God and God's covenant faithfulness to his people (e.g., Ps. 112:6; Prov. 10:7). In 1:11, Qohelet does not leave room for the memory of the righteous: nonremembrance is the ultimate lot of *all* the living. The point is made more clearly in 2:16: "There is no memory for the wise man, like the fool, forever; in days to come both will be forgotten. Like the fool, the wise man too must die!"

With this thought we come to the end of the narrator's introduction and begin the words of Qohelet. Whatever winding path Qohelet will choose to take in subsequent chapters to arrive at his points of destination,

---

6. The Hebrew phrase is *l'olam* and does not mean "forever" in the sense of "eternity." It means something more like "from time immemorial and on and on into the future."

we must keep before us the fact that the narrator has already pointed us in the ultimate direction in which Qohelet is headed.

> The cycle of life, as illustrated even in nature itself, assures that there is no payoff for any of our activities and efforts. All that we do in any corner of our existence collapses to absurdity. Moreover, the ultimate indication of absurdity is the fact that we will all die, and even the hope of being remembered by our descendants is an empty one.

To the narrator's summary is added Qohelet's own in 1:12–18. After announcing himself in verse 12, he declares how he has "given his heart" to the wisdom task of investigating everything done under the sun. One might think a wise search of the things of the world would be a worthwhile task, but not for Qohelet. No sooner do we read this than he follows with the dismal observation at the end of verse 13, "It [the search just announced] is a grievous task that God has given to humanity by which to occupy them." After raising a spark of hope in the reader's eye, he immediately undermines that quest with what is one of the more significant verses not only in the introduction, but also in the book as a whole. To paraphrase the last portion of verse 13: "God sure has made it difficult for us." As we will see in a bit more detail below, Qohelet's complaint is not about what *happens*, but, somewhat like lament psalms, about *God* who *lets* things happen—or, for Qohelet, even more starkly, who *makes* things happen this way. He follows up on this notion in verses 14–15. He claims to have seen[7] everything done under the sun, and he declares it all absurd and a "chasing of the wind." Moreover, this state of affairs is what it is; there is nothing that anyone can do about it. As he says in verse 15: "What is made crooked cannot be straightened; what is lacking cannot be counted." In other words, this state of affairs that Qohelet has observed, this grievous task, this crooked situation, cannot be undone. The implication, particularly in view of the latter portion of verse 13, is that it is *God* who is responsible.

Clearly, Qohelet has a bone to pick, and he is not starting off his monologue in a manner that will win him many dinner invitations. That his problem is with God is something we will return to in a moment, but let us first bring chapter 1 to a close. In what seems like another immediate

---

7. *Seen* should not be understood in the literal sense, but figuratively, i.e., in his mind's eye. Elsewhere in Ecclesiastes the word also means "experienced."

reversal, Qohelet again announces his attainment of wisdom. In fact, he has more wisdom than any other who has ever ruled over Jerusalem (v. 16). He has given himself over to the task of knowing wisdom and knowledge as well as madness and folly (v. 17): he covers the entire spectrum and leaves no stone unturned. One would think Qohelet had put himself back on the right track, but once again, he brings any such optimism to an abrupt halt: "I know that this, too, is a chasing of the wind." As the book continues, one will see Qohelet weaving in and out of this realization, but already here, at the outset of his words, he makes the announcement that puts him in tension with the heart of Israel's faith: *wisdom does not really work.* In fact, as he concludes in verse 18, much wisdom brings much anger; adding knowledge adds pain. One would be hard-pressed to find such a statement in Proverbs, where wisdom is "more precious than rubies" (see Prov. 3:13–20).[8]

This opening chapter is extremely important for setting the stage for what is to come. We have, from both the narrator and Qohelet himself, a clear indication of where he will end up, when all is said and done. He will have spasms of optimism and submit to traditional notions now and then, but in one form or another, he will return to the broader realization that everything is absurd, that nothing can be done, and that God is responsible.

GOD IS THE PROBLEM

We have already seen in 1:13 and 15 how Qohelet seems to have a thinly veiled gripe with how God is running things. This is a theme that surfaces with more force in subsequent chapters, particularly in the context of the carpe diem passages. I would like to look briefly at two of them here, 3:1–15 and 5:17–19 (Eng. 18–20).

First, let's look with a bird's-eye view at 3:1–15. The first eight verses are well known to many, being the topic of a famous folk song written by Pete Seeger and popularized by The Byrds, "Turn, Turn, Turn." There is a time for everything, a time for being born, a time for dying, etc., etc. One might be tempted to think of this litany of "times" as a positive statement on Qohelet's part: "Look at the rhythms of life. Aren't they wonderful? There is a time for everything, so don't fret." Actually, this is far from Qohelet's mind. Think back on 1:5–7 and the rhythm of the created world. This is what demonstrates the *absurdity* of life. The same holds here. One need

---

8. All quotations of Scripture in this chapter, other than Ecclesiastes, are from the NIV.

only continue reading to 3:9, where Qohelet interprets verses 1–8: "What *profit* is there for the one who does something in which he toils?" In other words, things are the way they are. There are "times" for everything, and so all our toiling to make a difference amounts to nothing. Then, in verse 10, he repeats essentially the sentiment expressed earlier in 1:10, "I have seen the task God has given to humanity by which to occupy him," and he is none too happy about it.

None of what Qohelet is describing here is good. The remaining verses in this passage are key. "He [God] does everything fitting[9] in its time." *Time* is the same word found throughout 3:1–8, which Qohelet has already evaluated as something without profit. In other words, God does what he does when he does it, and he has "put 'time-consciousness' into our hearts." ("Time-consciousness" is an attempt to translate the root *'lm* we saw before often mistranslated as "eternity.") This first portion of verse 11 is often misunderstood as a word of praise to a good God who, despite the ups and downs of the "times," has nevertheless given humanity a yearning for heaven, or something like that. This is completely contrary to Qohelet's thinking. He is actually saying that God acts when he pleases, and he has given humanity *the ability to comprehend this*, to conceive of time immemorial and on and on into the future, *to frustrate them further*. The point is made clear in verse 11b: "Humanity cannot find out what God has done from beginning to the end."

What follows in verses 12–15 is the actual carpe diem passage, which, like the earlier verses, is often given a positive spin that would send Qohelet off in a huff. In view of all that he has been saying thus far, in the book as well as in this passage, Qohelet's words here can hardly be taken as encouraging. To paraphrase verses 12–15:

> I know that there is nothing better for them [people] than to be joyful and do worthwhile things in their lives. In fact, this is what sums up our human existence[10]: eat, drink, and experience some good in one's labor. This is what

9. The Hebrew root here, *yph*, can also mean "beautiful," but "fitting" is better given the context. Qohelet is not remarking on how God's actions here are beautiful, but how they fit in their proper (i.e., God-determined) time.

10. The Hebrew here is *kol-ha'adam*, literally "all the man." The phrase appears in the next carpe diem (5:18), concerning death (7:2), and then once more in the epilogue (12:13). This is an important phrase, and we will return to it below. For a more detailed interaction with how this phrase helps us understand the theology of Ecclesiastes, see "*Kol-ha'adam* and the Evaluation of

God gives us to do. I know that whatever God does lasts [*l'olam*]: you can't do anything to change it. God does these things so that humanity might fear him. What is already was; what is to be already was.[11]

For Qohelet in this passage, life has a rhythm ("times") that is in God's hands, not ours, and so what we do has no profit. To make matters worse, God endows us with a real understanding of the grand expanse of time, which frustrates us all the more. In light of this state of affairs for which *God* is responsible, Qohelet *resigns* himself (i.e., "there is nothing better than") to finding some alternative meaning in life, one of taking it as it comes and finding some enjoyment in what one does. This is what sums up the human condition. What God does cannot be changed (note the echoes of 1:15 in 3:14), and so we fear him, not in a Proverbs 1:7 "the fear of the LORD is the beginning of knowledge" kind of way, but fear as one would have for a capricious ruler. Qohelet is not happy.

A similar sentiment is found in a second carpe diem passage, 5:17–19 [Eng. 18–20], and so we can treat it much more briefly. Eating, drinking, experiencing good things as the fruit of one's labor is our *lot* in life, that is, our *portion* [*kheleq*]. In fact, he adds here, rather dismally, "the number of days of our lives." This allusion to the inevitability of death, and how it cancels out any hope of any sort of *profit*, raises its ugly head again. And everyone to whom *God* gives wealth, possessions, and the ability to enjoy them—well, that is God's "gift." Note here, too, that the ability to enjoy the fruit of one's labor is *God's doing*. In fact, as verse 19 concludes, humans don't remember much of their lives because God keeps them so busy with the "pleasure of their hearts," that is, the fruit of their labor. None of it lasts. None of it is profitable. It is merely our *portion*, that which this God deigns to give us.

Qohelet's frustration with, even anger toward, God is not limited to these two passages,[12] but they give enough of a sense of where Qohelet is coming from. In summary, the words of Qohelet hit on a lot of issues, and he is anything but consistent in his train of thought. But what unites his thinking is the fundamental commitment to the absurdity of life:

Qohelet's Wisdom in Qoh 12:13, or The 'A Is So, and What's More, B' Theology of Ecclesiastes," in *The Idea of Biblical Interpretation*, ed. James Kugel (Leiden: Brill, 2003), 125–37.

11. I have left untranslated the very last clause in verse 15. It is a bit enigmatic and does not affect the general picture given here.

12. E.g., 5:1; 6:10; 7:13.

At the end of the day we have nothing to show for our lives, we die and are forgotten, and this is how God set it up. The best we have is to try to enjoy the fruit of our daily labor, even though that, too, will come to naught. Yes, absolutely everything under the sun is absurd.

Qohelet's despondency is palpable on every page.

The Epilogue's Evaluation of Qohelet's Theology

Surely, one would think, such a theology has no place in the Hebrew canon—yet there it is. It is also no wonder why some interpreters have tried to minimize the force of Qohelet's observations either by toning down his rhetoric or by claiming that the epilogue (12:8–14) corrects Qohelet's errant teaching. In my view, Qohelet's words are too many and too clear to tame. And as a review of the epilogue will show, the frame narrator hardly corrects or condemns Qohelet's error, but affirms Qohelet in a very sincere way.

After summarizing Qohelet's words in 12:8 (see 1:2), the narrator says in verse 9 that (1) Qohelet was a wise man, (2) he taught people knowledge, (3) he heard, investigated, and put in order many proverbs. In fact, he sought (exerted effort) to find "pleasing words," meaning the right words to get his point across, and his written words were honest (v. 10). Now, this may not be what readers expect to hear at this point. Was Qohelet really a wise man, with all his dismal words and despondent rhetoric? It seems that, according to the narrator, he was. He must have anticipated the discomfort this would give to his readers, as we read in verse 11: "The words of the wise are like goads, like firmly embedded nails are the 'masters of collection' [either those who collect wise sayings or the collection itself] given by a shepherd." I do not think the reference to a shepherd here is necessarily a reference to God. The imagery is simply that of sheepherding. The goad, with its nail at the tip, is meant to keep the sheep in line. And yes, sometimes that process hurts, just like Qohelet's words.

The narrator continues with a warning to his son in verse 12: "There is no end to the making of books [better, *writings*], and much study wearies the body." Although this is a favorite verse of seminarians during final exams, it has nothing to do with applying oneself to one's studies. Rather, the narrator is shifting now from what was praise of Qohelet in verses 9–11 to a cautionary note *to his son*. He is saying that one can go on and on as Qohelet has done, multiplying example after example, going round and round on this issue (write more books like this); that is wearisome. Rather, as he says in verse 13, "The end of the matter, all has been said" (i.e., no more needs to be said). And then the narrator reveals the lesson that he wants his son to take away from his reading of Qohelet's words:

> Fear God and keep his commandments. Indeed, THIS[13] is what sums up the human situation.

Qohelet is wise, to be sure, and his words hurt. What do you expect from wise sayings? But remember, my son, in the midst of any sort of similar stresses and doubts that you yourself might experience, no matter how unnerving and "unorthodox" a question may come from your lips, no matter how much you are frustrated and even angry with God himself, remember this: fear God and keep his commandments.

This is not cheap advice, but gets at the heart of much of Israel's traditional faith. The narrator is not saying, "Just shut up and do your Bible lesson." He is saying that however wise Qohelet's observations are, that wisdom does not let one off the hook of continuing to fear and follow God *no matter what. This* is what your duty is. Verse 13 is the fourth use of the phrase *kol-ha'adam* in the book, the previous three pertaining to the matter of seeking temporary satisfaction in one's work (3:13 and 5:18) and the inevitability of death (7:2). But here, the narrator is saying that what trumps all is the duty to fear and follow God even as you work through the ups and downs of life. At the end of the day, God will judge justly, even though you don't see it now (12:14). To put it succinctly, the narrator is saying, "Yes, Qohelet is wise. Pay attention to what he says, as painful as it might be. But in the midst of all this, the higher good is to fear and follow God, who will eventually set all things right." This is the theological message of the epilogue, and it intersects quite well with the message of the gospel.

ECCLESIASTES ACCORDING TO THE GOSPEL

The narrator does not discount Qohelet's anguish, doubt, and anger, but affirms them and even lauds Qohelet as wise. The proper perspective to take is not to minimize Qohelet's suffering (as Job's friends did with him), but neither

---

13. The Hebrew is quite emphatic: *ki-zeh.*

is it to wallow there in endless speculation and despair. Neither option is left open for his readers. Rather, they are to fear and follow God, that is, remain an Israelite in covenant with God, regardless of what may come.

The significance of Ecclesiastes for Christians involves us in a question of the nexus between "what it meant" and "what it means," or, if you will, the overused word *application*. How one gets from then to now has in my experience proved to be a complex interpenetration of factors both obvious and subtle.[14] But to speak of the Christian significance of any OT book is to say that the setting of the interpreter (whether individual or community, however defined) presents itself as an influential factor in interpretation. To put it another way, the Bible does not have contemporary "significance" for anyone apart from a conceptual framework within which one makes sense of anything.[15] This certainly entails one's individual time and place in world history. But for Christians, that conceptual framework is centered first and foremost not on our particular or personal life-settings, but on the gospel, which is to say on what God has done for his people and the world in and through the person and work of Christ.

For the gospel to form our grid for understanding Ecclesiastes is not a call to "see Christ" in every verse, or even every passage of the book, nor is it to discount Qohelet because we "know better." Rather, the gospel forms our basic "hermeneutical posture": that point of view from which we read and to which the meaning of Ecclesiastes will be applied. It is to acknowledge that the very questions we raise, the very way in which we interact with an ancient Hebrew book such as Ecclesiastes, is profoundly shaped by our having been raised and united with the crucified and risen Christ. It is, in my view, precisely a failure to recognize this vital hermeneutical posture that has fostered the notion that a faithful, Christian reading of Ecclesiastes is demonstrated by deriving some immediate moral lesson from the book—an approach that will, in my opinion, drive one to ignore, overlook, brush aside, or actually mishandle portions of the book. Our outlook must rather be shaped by the knowledge that, on the one hand, Ecclesiastes has something

14. I explore some of these issues, albeit briefly, in "Apostolic Hermeneutics and an Evangelical Doctrine of Scripture: Moving beyond the Modernist Impasse," *WTJ* 65 (2003): 263–87, esp. 279–87.

15. See, for example, the comment by Dan G. McCartney: "When a person within a certain social context, who shares with the culture a certain way of thinking about reality, comes to a text, he or she understands that text in categories drawn from an already-extant understanding of everything," from "The New Testament's Use of the Old Testament," in *Inerrancy and Hermeneutic: A Tradition, A Challenge, A Debate*, ed. Harvie M. Conn (Grand Rapids: Baker, 1988), 104.

to say on its own terms, and on the other hand, how we hear it and use it will be shaped in a most fundamental way by our living in the privileged setting of the postresurrection cosmos.

All this is to say that any Christian interpreter of any OT book, including Ecclesiastes, must purposefully endeavor to allow the two horizons of then and now to be in conversation with each other. And they must be in conversation. To repeat, I do not think the cross and resurrection mean that the challenging peaks and valleys of Ecclesiastes can now be ignored. But it is still a conversation that embraces the powerful and liberating realization that we are living in the age of the inaugurated eschaton. It is this final, climactic stage in the drama of redemption that we now look back on and say, "Now that we know where Israel's story ends up, what difference does that knowledge make in how we understand previous stages in the story?" In other words, the "now" with which the "then" must be in conversation is not *exclusively* the "private now" of my personal experiences (although the personal dimension is certainly in play), but the "eschatological now" of the new age (2 Cor. 6:2) that dawned when Christ, the climax of God's covenant with Israel, was crucified and raised from the dead. Only after this eschatological posture is allowed to exert its proper force do we as Christians bring Ecclesiastes to bear on the particular circumstances of our individual and corporate lives.

A Christian reading of Ecclesiastes must allow its own prominent peaks and valleys to define our hermeneutical landscape, while at the same time bearing in mind that there is another, grander landscape beyond the immediate horizon, against which Ecclesiastes can be seen in a different light. Interestingly, an analogy with the book of Ecclesiastes itself may illustrate the point. Just as reading the epilogue brings us to say to Qohelet, "Yes, you're right, but there is something more," so, too, does our postresurrection vantage point bring us to look at Ecclesiastes as a whole and say, "Yes, you're right, but there is something more." The difference, of course, is that the "something more" of the epilogue is a reiteration of Israel's traditional categories of fear and obedience. For us, the "something more" is the complex realization that, however bound we are to this same formulation, it is now reconfigured in the crucified and risen Christ, who paradoxically embodies *and* transforms Israel's story.

Such an approach to understanding Ecclesiastes should ring true with those familiar with the role of suffering, doubt, despair, even anger toward God in the Christian life. It is in this sense that Ecclesiastes can be seized by the church as the Word of God, not the ramblings of a tired, pessimistic heretic in need of a little faith. After all, it is only people of faith who speak as Qohelet does. Rather, Qohelet forces us to see our own struggles and sufferings for what they are, never for a moment thinking that they should be sanitized or sugarcoated in any way, while also driving us to see how we, too, are to move through and ultimately beyond the suffering.

In this respect we see two ways in which the NT is very much in harmony with the reading of Ecclesiastes that I have presented above. The NT is replete with passages in which suffering and doubt are not minimized, but encountered. No one who has been a Christian for any length of time is a stranger to suffering of some sort, and the NT is not at all shy about telling us that this is to be expected. When I as a Christian read Ecclesiastes, even in his darker moments, at times I think to myself, "Yup, I hear you. I have felt that way, too." Even though Qohelet may put things in a somewhat provocative way, few Christians I know would argue that his thoughts are unknown to them—even when it comes to crippling doubt and accusing God of some wrongdoing.

The difference between Ecclesiastes and the NT, however, is that the intensity of the suffering of the Christian is, by the power of the Spirit, matched only by the joy and privilege of knowing that precisely *in our suffering* we are following in Jesus' footsteps, even to the extent that we are filling up what is "lacking" in Christ's suffering (Col. 1:24). The narrator says to his son, "Keep moving: fear God, keep the commandments." Jesus says to us:

> Suffering will come. When you suffer you are becoming more like me. Do not allow your deepest, darkest thoughts to overcome you, even though I, more than anyone else, understand what those thoughts feel like. I affirm your pain. I have known it. Follow me anyway. Keep moving. Even when *none* of it makes sense, and the easiest thing to do is to cry out, "This is all absurd; I am getting nowhere." I am not asking you to understand. I am asking you to follow—to pick up your cross and follow. I have uttered that very cry myself, when the Father was nowhere to be found. Follow me anyway, as I followed the Father.

The book of Ecclesiastes presents a particular kind of cry, one of despair, doubt, frustration, and anger in which God himself is called to account. A Christian who cries out as Qohelet did should not minimize or dismiss the sage's observations, but press on in the Spirit, knowing that what sums up all of our existence is, to paraphrase 12:13–14, "Follow Jesus anyway, no matter what."

5

Biblical Theology and Missional Hermeneutics: A Match Made *for* Heaven . . . on Earth?

Michael B. Kelly

IT IS A TREMENDOUS honor to offer some thoughts in memory and honor of my friend, mentor, and colleague James Alan Groves. As I considered my contribution to the present volume, one phrase kept coming to mind: *involving others in conversation*. Al's life was a model of selfless orientation toward others. At places such as professional meetings I often saw Al with people who didn't know one another, providing the "glue" to get a conversation started between them. Many of us were beneficiaries of countless conversations with Al, and we remember the great gift Al was to the people of God.

The point of this essay is to bring together a few conversations, and will be a first step toward a synthesis of sorts, namely, between *mission* and *biblical studies*. The two have operated at too great a distance from each other. Harry Daniel Beeby writes that there has been in recent years

a deepening awareness of the crises that exist in biblical interpretation and some acknowledgement that one way to begin to resolve them is not only to recover the Bible's missionary message for pulpit and classroom, but to be immersed equally in the missiological and missional. . . . *Notoriously, biblical studies, on the whole, proceed comfortably without even a nodding acquaintance with mission or missiology.*[1]

I would like to bring together two approaches to biblical interpretation for the current readership: in the first place, the *biblical-theological* approach in the redemptive-historical tradition, which, though well established, is still expanding and deepening in its method and results. Second, I will engage the relatively recent conversation regarding *missional hermeneutics*. Space here prevents a full academic engagement; I will only introduce the conversation by first highlighting what, to my mind, undergirds each approach and motivates some engaged in them, and then offering a synthesis attempting to bring these two approaches into an initial conversation.

Throughout the essay I will use two terms repeatedly. The first, *Christotelic*, pertains to the biblical theology conversation. The term attempts to capture a hermeneutical posture that understands Jesus Christ as the goal, the end point, the purpose of the OT. The OT, in all its literary and historical complexity and diversity, "drives toward" Jesus Christ. The second term is *missiogenic*, meaning that a *good* biblical-theological—Christotelic—reading of an OT text will be generative of mission in God's world, sweeping up the readers and their communities in the great story of redemption being "told" by the ongoing application of the gospel of Jesus Christ to every corner of creation. A good reading will shape readers to align themselves with God's mission.

BIBLICAL THEOLOGY

Our first dialogue partner is biblical theology, as understood in the tradition of Geerhardus Vos. Admittedly, the term *biblical theology* is open to a variety of understandings concerning the approach the term describes.[2] As encapsulated by Vos, biblical theology aims to be "that branch of exegetical

1. Harry Daniel Beeby, "A Missional Approach to Renewed Interpretation," in *Renewing Biblical Interpretation*, ed. Craig G. Bartholomew, Colin J. D. Greene, and Karl Möller (Grand Rapids: Zondervan, 2000), 278 (emphasis added).

2. See C. H. H. Scobie, "History of Biblical Theology," in *New Dictionary of Biblical Theology*, ed. T. Desmond Alexander, Brian S. Rosner, D. A. Carson, and Graeme Goldsworthy (Downers Grove, IL: InterVarsity Press, 2000), 11–20.

theology which deals with the process of the self-revelation of God depos-
ited in the Bible."[3] Several key concepts emerge in this brief, yet seminal
definition. Primarily, we understand that biblical theology in the Vosian
tradition is exegetical, and pays careful attention to Scripture. Second, and
of vital significance for our conversation with missional hermeneutics, Vos
understands biblical theology to be dealing with a *process*. Revelation unfolds
through time. And as it unfolds, more is seen, greater vistas are opened to
the interpreter, until that unfolding revelation finally opens to the full flower
of the climactic revelation in Jesus Christ.

Vos has helpfully introduced *history* into the exegetical and theological
task, which will be crucial to our dialogue with missional hermeneutics.
Rooting revelation in historical moments, Vos states that "Biblical Theology
imparts new life and freshness to the truth by showing it to us in its original
historic setting. The Bible is not a dogmatic handbook but a historical book
full of dramatic interest. Familiarity with the history of revelation will enable
us to utilize all this dramatic interest."[4] Similarly, Vos writes, "Because God
desires to be *known* . . . He has caused His revelation to take place in the
milieu of the historical life of a people. . . . All that God disclosed of Himself
has come in response to the practical religious needs of His people as these
emerged in the course of history."[5]

To engage missional hermeneutics, I will draw out two implications of
the Vosian approach to biblical theology. First, this rootedness of revelation
in history leads to a hermeneutical corollary. Given the fact that Scripture
is so historically rooted, a responsible hermeneutical approach to Scripture
involves an understanding that God communicated through *ancient* means—
languages, literary genres, worldviews, and so on—to *ancient* people. This
move introduces a historical distance between the contemporary reader and
the text, a distance that requires study and work to bridge. I raise this point
not to question the clarity of Scripture in presenting all that is necessary to
be known for salvation, but to raise an important issue arising from Vos's
language that "His revelation [takes] place *in the milieu of the historical life
of a people.*" I believe we must take the implications of that statement very
seriously as we consider Scripture's *communicative* impact. In Scripture God
authoritatively and effectively *communicates* to an ancient people and, as

---

3. Geerhardus Vos, *Biblical Theology* (Grand Rapids: Eerdmans, 1948), 13.

4. Ibid., 26.

5. Ibid., 17 (emphasis in original).

the Scripture comes to us, communicates to a modern people as well. The question we must consider is "communicates to what end?"

A second important implication arising out of these statements by Vos is the narrativity of revelation; the Bible *tells a story*, a story commonly considered in the four stages of creation, fall, redemption, and destiny. In his recent book *Who Gets to Narrate the World?* Robert Webber challenges his readers to relearn the biblical narrative in all its richness, with the goal of recapturing the imaginations of people in the twenty-first century with the *true* narrative of the world, "told" by God in the pages of Scripture.[6] The biblical narrative concerns God's *vision for the entire world!*

This vast scope might immediately raise the question, "If the biblical narrative is so grand, involving all of creation, what holds this narrative together?" Does anything occur as a point of cohesion of such a rich, dramatic, and sprawling narrative? Building on Vos, several writers over the past half century have, indeed, articulated just such a point of cohesion to this *historically rooted* and *historically developing* approach to Scripture: Jesus Christ, in his incarnation, life, death, resurrection, and ascension. Jesus Christ functions as the end point, or the goal, of the OT, and the center of the NT. In recent discussions, the term *Christotelic* has been used to describe this approach to the task of biblical theology as it relates to the OT. This term focuses more explicitly than does another commonly used descriptive word, *Christocentric*, on how, in the full light of the unfolding of redemption, Jesus Christ, in his life, death, and resurrection, functions as the goal, the *telos*, of the OT.[7] In doing this, we today share with the NT authors the core conviction that the OT has at its core a story, a narrative, that finds its end point in Jesus Christ. For biblical theology, the "unifying element is always the end point of the process, not the process itself. Its wisdom is always defined in terms of the administration of the mystery hidden in ages past, revealed in Christ, made known among all the world's cultures, and consummated at his return (Eph. 3:8–10; Rom. 16:25–26; Col. 1:25–27)."[8]

6. See Robert Webber, *Who Gets to Narrate the World?* (Downers Grove, IL: InterVarsity Press, 2008).

7. See the seminal article by Dan McCartney, "The New Testament's Use of the Old Testament," in *Inerrancy and Hermeneutic*, ed. Harvie Conn (Grand Rapids: Baker, 1988), 101–16. While not coining the term *Christotelic* in this article, McCartney, in pointing out that contemporary Christian interpreters must maintain Jesus Christ as the "hermeneutical *goal*" of OT interpretation, certainly anticipates the term.

8. Harvie M. Conn, *Eternal Word and Changing World: Theology, Anthropology and Mission in Trialogue* (Grand Rapids: Academie Books, 1984), 226.

We find this approach explicated in the writings of Edmund Clowney, whose book *Preaching and Biblical Theology* contains a helpful diagram.[9] It captures visually what the historical unfolding of redemptive history looks like, as it culminates in Jesus Christ. See Figure 1, slightly revised and expanded from the version offered by Clowney.

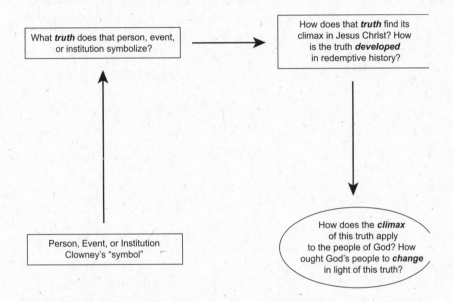

Fig. 5.1. Christotelic Biblical Theological Application.

Clowney introduces this figure in his discussion of symbolism. The vertical arrow on the left arises from a "symbol," upward to the "truth" symbolized. The symbol can be an OT person (e.g., David), an event (e.g., the exodus), or an institution (e.g., the sacrificial system). The horizontal arrow on the top, taking us from the truth symbolized to its climax in Jesus Christ, is the arena of unfolding redemptive history. How, in the unfolding narrative of redemption, is that truth developed to find its goal in Jesus Christ? The significant challenge arises when we seek to drop down from the fulfillment in Jesus Christ to the application of that "truth" to God's people. Admittedly, this is often where adherents of biblical theology in the Vosian tradition have struggled to make biblical theology "relevant."

9. See Edmund Clowney, *Preaching and Biblical Theology* (Philadelphia: Presbyterian and Reformed, 1961), 110.

And so Christian interpreters who understand that they must consider Jesus in the interpretation of an OT passage might quite comfortably proceed from the symbol to truth symbolized (the left-hand, upward arrow), possibly resulting in some principle or example arising from the text. But then, bypassing the *development* of that truth in redemptive history toward its *Christotelic climax* (the horizontal line on top of Figure 1), readers may make an immediate attempt to apply the truth to the contemporary audience. Aware of their inability to live up to this truth, the audience is exhorted to find remedy in Christ (back up the diagram, vertically on the right-hand side). So rather than forming a "box" around which the interpreter navigates, allowing the symbol to find its climax in Jesus Christ by following redemptive history along the top of Figure 1, this approach to "Christocentric" interpretation forms the shape of an *N*. If the truth is too much to keep, we flee to Jesus for comfort for our afflicted consciences (see Figure 2).

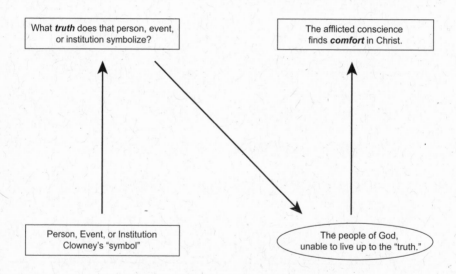

Fig. 5.2. Application with No Redemptive-Historical Development.

Christ *is* introduced into interpretation, but only after the inability of the hearer to live up to the truth is emphasized. In other words, a "Christological" interpretation along these lines is one that does not simply tell people what they must do in light of the passage (traditional moralism), but convinces the hearers of their inability actually to *do* what the text tells them to do. In light of that, the interpretation takes them back up the vertical line to Christ. This *N*-shaped approach may avoid illegitimate allegorization, but does it lose the glorious fulfillment of redemptive history in Jesus Christ? Now, certainly, there is some merit to this approach to interpretation. Humanity is sinful and unable, of our own efforts, to live fully in line with the will of a holy God. We *do* need Jesus for the forgiveness of sin! But does a Christotelic approach open another window for interpretation and application? This only anticipates another, larger question: how, exactly, is a Christotelic approach applicable?

The connection between fulfillment in Jesus Christ and applicability to contemporary audience *is* precisely the place at which a Christotelic and missiogenic reading intersect, and thus the insights from *both* biblical theology and missional hermeneutics are needed to engage the issue of application. In union with Jesus Christ, and empowered by the Holy Spirit, we join in the continuing mission of God[10] to bless the world through the signs of new creation dawning in our world today.

This approach to biblical theology, with its embrace of the historical context of revelation, its deeply narratival approach to biblical interpretation—placing an OT text in the larger narrative of the unfolding of redemption—and the climactic role it assigns to Jesus Christ will prove to . be an ideal and enriching dialogue partner for the growing conversation regarding missional hermeneutics.

Missional Hermeneutics

There is a growing dialogue regarding a *missional hermeneutic*, which, as I see it, contains at least three elements. First, a missional hermeneutic is *historically rooted* in reflecting concrete and historical concerns of God's people. A missional hermeneutic understands revelation as delivered *in* history, in order to align the people of God to his mission in the world. Revelation, in other words, is generative of mission—revelation is *missiogenic*. Second, a missional hermeneutic is *hermeneutically centered on Jesus Christ*, following the hermeneutical goal of the NT authors themselves.

---

10. By *mission of God*, I mean simply the all-encompassing and relentless work of the triune God in history to "set the world to rights" (to use N. T. Wright's felicitous phrase) by the work of Jesus Christ and ongoing application of his work by the Holy Spirit. The mission of God will involve the inbreaking of the reign of God and the dawn of new creation. Though never *complete* until the second coming of Jesus Christ, the marks of new creation and divinely accomplished restoration are nonetheless real.

Third, a missional hermeneutic, bearing in mind the whole of the story of the Scripture, is *holistically oriented* toward creation, and opens up rich theological reflection in the full range of human existence.

Unfortunately, the use of the word *missional* has become somewhat confusing given its wide use by a variety of Christian communities and movements; defining the term is vital for any dialogue. I should state up front that I am not using the term as "code" for *emergent*. In its most straightforward meaning, *missional* is simply an adjective deriving from the word *mission*. When applied to the church, for example, *missional* simply draws attention to the constitutive reality of the "sent-ness" of the church.[11] The church consists of those gathered around Jesus Christ who are *sent* into the world; mission orients the church to its reason for existence, creating an identity for the church as to what it is to *be* in the world. Applying this simple "mission-as-identity-forming" to my own understanding of what shapes a missional hermeneutic begins to draw our attention to the hermeneutical task of attending to the mission of God in our reading of Scripture. It is that simple, but at the same time seems so foreign to the way many of us instinctively read the Bible—reading it as a collection of messages to me personally, not as a cosmic message of what God has *accomplished* in Jesus Christ, and continues to *apply* by the Holy Spirit.

Missional, then, is a hermeneutical posture before the Scripture that assumes several things. It assumes that the Bible itself is a *product of* the mission of God in revealing himself to fallen humanity, providing humanity with the authoritative vision of God's will for the universe. God revealed himself in history to correct, encourage, warn, and comfort his people; he spoke concretely in historical contexts, and the Bible is the result of that speaking. He addresses, as we previously saw through Vos, the "practical religious needs of His people as these emerged in the course of history."[12]

A missional hermeneutic also assumes a posture that Scripture is a *witness to* God's work in the world. Scripture truly narrates God's intention for creation, the problem in creation, God's solution in Jesus Christ for creation, and the destiny of creation. Scripture narrates the mission of God for the *whole* of the cosmos. In other words, the Bible authoritatively lays out for us the overarching, single story of God's mis-

---

11. I am aware that *missional church* has also taken on a meaning within a particular movement. See the seminal work Darrell Guder, ed., *Missional Church* (Grand Rapids: Eerdmans, 1998).

12. Vos, *Biblical Theology*, 17.

sion for the world, with its climax in Jesus Christ and his accomplished redemption and extending to every corner of creation. *Missional* demands a broad vision.

There is a growing body of literature related to this approach to hermeneutics, and many authors, while agreeing on some elements of the approach, bring different concerns to bear in their own discussion.[13] Among the most helpful and thorough is the recent book by Christopher J. H. Wright, *The Mission of God*.[14] In this ambitious and wide-ranging book, Wright seeks to offer a comprehensive picture of God's relentless and creation-wide plan of redemption as told through the story of the Bible, finding at its center the "mission of God."

Wright lays out his own parameters for how he will define *missional hermeneutics*. To engage in this hermeneutical posture is to read the Bible in light of:

- God's purpose for his whole creation, including the redemption of humanity and the creation of the new heavens and new earth;
- God's purpose for human life in general on the planet and of all the Bible teaches about human culture, relationships, ethics, and behavior;
- God's historical election of Israel, its identity and role in relation to the nations, and the demands he made on its worship, social ethics, and total value system;
- The centrality of Jesus of Nazareth, his messianic identity and mission in relation to Israel and the nations, his cross and resurrection;
- God's calling of the church, the community of believing Jews and Gentiles who constitute the extended people of the Abrahamic covenant, to be the agent of God's blessing to the nations in the name and for the glory of the Lord Jesus Christ.[15]

13. Several excellent articles on the topic of missional hermeneutics, showing some of this diversity, are available at www.biblicaltheology.ca/bluearticles.htm.

14. Christopher J. H. Wright, *The Mission of God: Unlocking the Bible's Grand Narrative* (Downers Grove, IL: IVP Academic, 2006).

15. Ibid., 67–68. Many of Wright's concerns in this book reflect the biblical-theological and missional concerns that I am addressing in this essay. I am attempting to contribute to the conversation in this essay by introducing the notion of speech act into biblical theology and missional hermeneutics (see the section below on "Scripture as a Communicative and Mission-Generating Speech Act"), and self-consciously highlighting the role of inaugurated eschatology.

I quote these five points here to indicate how vast the scope of Wright's program is, and how comprehensive a picture one must bear in mind to engage in a *missional* hermeneutic as he (and I) understand it. A missional hermeneutic will not be content to address only what we may have traditionally understood by *missions*—namely, evangelism. A missional hermeneutic will, indeed, make room for other crucially important areas—for example, creation care, social justice, and cultural engagement.

While in full agreement with Wright and the points he raises to bear in mind while engaging in a missional hermeneutic, I would like to expand the elements by adding another, one that is very significant as we think about our conversation between biblical theology and missional hermeneutics: eschatology, specifically understood in the familiar description of the kingdom *already* having come in Jesus Christ (Matt. 12:28; Mark 1:14–15), but *not yet* present in fullness (Rom. 8:23–25). In other words, the last days have been *inaugurated* at the first advent of Jesus Christ, and *await* the final consummation at his second coming.

For the contemporary Christian to engage in a missional hermeneutic is to read the Bible self-consciously as those "upon whom the ends of the ages have come" (1 Cor. 10:11 NKJV). This will ground both the *scope* of a missional hermeneutic and our *expectations* of such a hermeneutic. The *scope*, because we approach the interpretive task fully expecting to draw out from the Scripture an understanding of the real, earthly, new-creation-having-dawned reality begun in the resurrection of Jesus Christ. John Bolt, in his editorial introduction to chapter 18 of Herman Bavinck's *Reformed Dogmatics: Holy Spirit, Church and New Creation*, picks up on one important strand of Bavinck's thought from that chapter:

> Biblical hope, rooted in incarnation and resurrection, is creational, this-worldly, visible, physical, bodily hope. . . . The salvation of the kingdom of God, including communion with God as well as the communion of the saints, is both a present blessing and a future, consummated, rich glory. The kingdom of God has come and is coming.[16]

Bolt, summarizing Bavinck, wonderfully picks up on the "between the ages" character of our current existence. A missional hermeneutic, I believe, should

---

16. Herman Bavinck, *Reformed Dogmatics*, vol. 4, *Holy Spirit, Church and New Creation*, ed. John Bolt, trans. John Vriend (Grand Rapids: Baker Academic, 2008), 715.

produce just this sort of hope. Echoing back to our discussion of Christopher Wright, a missional hermeneutic will involve approaching Scripture—the whole story, including God's intention for creation and humanity—with eyes to see how we might be drawn into this very real and visible, bodily hope in our world. Biblical hope is *creational*.

But the already-and-not-yet nature of our current existence also tempers our *expectations*. We do not expect perfection and, indeed, still do our interpretive work, engaging us toward the intention of God for creation, fully within the reality of the "not yet"—even while enjoying the blessing of the "already." Paul Marshall puts it well:

> We do not live now in a time of perfection and wholeness, for the kingdom of God has not yet come in completeness. But neither do we live in a time exclusively of pain and failure, for the kingdom of God is already here. We live in the time before the final winnowing, the time when the wheat and the tares will continue to grow together. We cannot and should not expect any immediate final victory over evil. But we can expect what Francis Schaeffer has called "substantial healing"—real change and real fruits of peace and love.[17]

A missional hermeneutic engages self-consciously in this time of tension, and allows the interpreter full appreciation of the pain so often experienced in this world. A missional hermeneutic is not idealistic or triumphalistic, but brings real healing to places of real pain. The title of this essay suggested "heaven on earth." Really? Doesn't our world at many times seem more like *hell* on earth? Even the occasion of this festschrift screams of loss. Yes, we await the *final* victory over death and pain. But in the meantime, by the Spirit, we can experience now "real fruits of peace and love" and, again only by the power of the Spirit, minister those real fruits in the broad context of creation and God's suffering people.

Finally, I would like to view missional hermeneutics not simply as a descriptive undertaking but, as I mentioned in the introduction to this essay, as becoming a hermeneutical model that seeks to interpret Scripture so as to be generative of mission. Mission should not be considered an afterthought, but rather a vital component in the essence of the interpretive model. The

---

17. Paul Marshall, with Lela Gilbert, *Heaven Is Not My Home* (Nashville: Thomas Nelson, 1998), 229–30.

text certainly narrates the mission of God—that is clear both in light of biblical theology and in light of what we have seen about the nature of the Bible itself as a "missional" document. But Scripture, obediently read, should also generate a response that will call the reader to align himself or herself with the mission of God in the world—what I call a *missiogenic* reading. For this to happen, we will need to find an interpretive model to employ for this synthesis of biblical theology and missional hermeneutics. I suggest that speech-act theory may provide such a helpful model, and to this synthesis we now briefly turn our attention.

SCRIPTURE AS A COMMUNICATIVE AND MISSION-GENERATING SPEECH ACT

We are now at the place where, in light of the previous two sections, I can briefly lay out a model that might provide a way forward and synthesize these two crucially important conversations. We have already seen significant overlap between a Vosian approach to biblical theology and the concerns of a missional hermeneutic. If I am correct in advocating for these two significant strands in interpretation—that interpretation be both Christotelic and missiogenic—just how do they relate? What does a Christotelic approach *uniquely* demonstrate to us about the mission of God and how we are to live in this world? The question boils down to this: can a Christotelic approach be generative of mission, and if so, how?

I would like to suggest here that some insights from *speech-act theory* can be of tremendous assistance to begin to answer this question. Speech-act theory, growing out of the work of J. L. Austin and developed by others, is a linguistic theory concerned with what is accomplished through verbal utterances. In particular contexts, utterances *do* things. Words spoken in particular contexts alter reality. Classic examples are a bride and groom saying "I do" during a marriage ceremony, followed by the subsequent words of a minister, "I now pronounce you husband and wife." What has happened? The couple has entered into a covenant with each other by saying these words, and the minister has accomplished a legal binding of the two individuals. The words, given the particular context, have accomplished something.

It will be helpful to draw a further distinction from speech-act theory for the purpose of bringing together Christotelic and missiogenic readings. In the first place, words are intended to affect a hearer. What impact does an utterance have? What do I accomplish in my utterance? For example, is a hearer or reader warned, comforted, motivated, or admonished? Of course, the context in which the verbal utterance is spoken or written will have a significant impact on the force of the utterance. Second, and important to our missiogenic reading of Scripture, what does a speaker want his hearers or readers to do as a result of his words? How does he want them to act differently? What response is expected as a result of the utterance, if the utterance is properly understood? The key insight of speech-act theory is that speakers do things with words, both in the impact the words have on hearers and in the subsequent actions that follow.[18] Words truly alter reality and accomplish things.

For example, if my wife, sitting in our drafty living room, says "I'm cold" while nodding at the front window, she intends to alter my reality and accomplish something. She is communicating a request to me. She is asking me to do something even though the words, on the surface, do not contain a request. Further, the effect she intends to have on me is that I will get up and go close the window. She does not actually *say*, "Please close the window," but given the context, I know what she is asking and what she wants me to do. Far from being academic abstraction, or hairsplitting linguistic distinctions, these categories may indeed prove useful as we bring together a biblical-theological and missional hermeneutic.

Understanding Scripture as a divine speech act embedded in real historical human contexts, intended to change both the *thinking* of its readers and the *actions* of its readers, may indeed provide a helpful way to think about how Scripture functions as generative of mission. We must admit that not every text in the Scripture speaks *directly* of the mission of God (Psalm 67, for example). But might we say that the overarching, divinely intended effect of the story to which biblical theology attends is that its readers align themselves with God's mission in the world, his intention for all creation as that intention finds its climax in the life, death, and resurrection of Jesus Christ? In other words, might the whole Bible, narrating as it does the mission of God in the world, be one sweeping, all-reality-encompassing, sustained speech act?[19]

18. See J. L. Austin, *How to Do Things with Words*, 2nd ed. (Cambridge, MA: Harvard University Press, 1975).

19. Speech-act theory initially operated at the level of the sentence, but has subsequently taken up the question of whole discourses. Kevin Vanhoozer has addressed this for biblical literature. See Kevin Vanhoozer, "The Semantics of Biblical Literature," in *Hermeneutics, Authority and Canon*,

Christian missional obedience, then, goes beyond obedience to individual passages here or there (as vital as that obedience is when a passage is properly interpreted). The Bible, while offering real words of hope to a pilgrim community, also sends that pilgrim community into God's world to be agents of blessing to every corner of the world. Christian missional obedience extends to actively aligning *our* story with the true story of the world as narrated by God through Scripture, as the Scripture comes to us and encourages, motivates, admonishes, comforts, warns, and promises. In other words, can we say that Scripture functions to *shape* its obedient readers toward God's comprehensive mission in the world, to act in accord with this mission, a mission seen climactically embodied in the life, death, and resurrection of Jesus Christ?[20]

Here the insights of biblical theology, and the Christotelic approach advocated earlier in this essay, become quite significant. To put it simply: the mission of God seen through Jesus Christ was a mission of suffering and grief, in the hope and promise of restoration. Our Christotelic approach guards us from triumphalism, giving both a grief and a confidence to our being swept up into the mission of God. We understand the mission of God not simply in creational (or new creational) categories, but also in the categories of incarnation, humility, and sacrifice. The story of Jesus Christ, in both his death and resurrection, in pain and joy, shapes our living into God's mission. In other words, biblical theology gives the shaping function of Scripture a decidedly Christotelic cast. As we are united to Christ in both his death and resurrection (Rom. 6:3–5), our expected missiogenic reading of Scripture will be a call to suffering and to hope. Interpreting Scripture as speech act in Christotelic perspective, on our side of the cross and resurrection, will shape the interpretive community in light of the cross toward suffering, sacrifice, and pain. At the same time, interpretation will be generative of mission in a new creational, holistic, multiethnic, Spirit-empowered shape, as the text journeys forward in redemptive history also to shape readers united to Christ,

---

ed. D. A. Carson and John D. Woodbridge (Grand Rapids: Baker, 1995), 53–104. What I suggest above is an overarching view of the whole Bible as a sustained discourse narrating the mission of God in the world.

20. Jeannine K. Brown, in her excellent book *Scripture as Communication* (Grand Rapids: Baker Academic, 2007), draws on the significance of speech-act theory for developing a model for hermeneutics as well. Particularly in chapter 12, she raises the issue of the shaping reality of Scripture on its readers. In full agreement with Brown, I suggest in this essay that the shaping reality is particularly toward the comprehensive vision of the mission of God.

who is the end of the story, to the mission of God in all its comprehensive and Christ-centered scope.

Finally, in keeping with biblical theology and missional hermeneutics, we consider two final factors important to the nature of the speech act that I am suggesting we consider the Bible, as God's Word, to be. First, it is *communicative*. By this I mean that revelation, as given in its original historical context, communicates as an ancient document written to ancient people. As stated earlier in this essay, this is *not* to say, in any way, that what is necessary for salvation is not plainly known by reading the Scripture *without* a knowledge of its ancient context. At the same time, I suggest that growing in knowledge of the ancient contexts in which Scripture was given may lead to a greater appreciation and understanding of what the Scripture, as revealed in history, was intended by God to accomplish. Attending to the wonderful diversity in the Bible—for example, its different literary genres—is crucial to understand what the Scripture is intended to accomplish. A historical narrative, an epic poem, a parable, or apocalyptic literature—each of the great variety of genres in the Scripture—accomplishes a different thing as a speech act germane to its particular form.

Second, as seen repeatedly throughout this essay, Scripture is a *mission-generating* speech act, both in its ancient context and, by virtue of its inspiration, in our contemporary context. I have suggested in this essay that the biblical texts were, in part, originally given to align the readers to the mission of God, in keeping with the redemptive-historical context in which they were given. Bearing in mind the redemptive-historical context is vitally important, as we ask questions along the lines of how we see a particular text witnessing to the mission of God to restore the world, and what effect this text might have had on the ancient audience to align themselves with God's glorious mission. Further, as we read on this side of the cross and resurrection, we ask how, having seen Jesus Christ as the goal of revelation, we might be called by this particular text to align ourselves with God's mission in the world.

CONCLUSION

This essay intended to bring two worlds together, two worlds that I believe will richly benefit from ongoing dialogue. I can think of no better context in which to offer this essay, in a volume honoring Alan Groves, a man who always looked toward the "other" (and in that sense was "missional") and who had a deep love for biblical theology. As the title of the essay suggests, and as was developed in the second portion, the approach I am suggesting will indeed seek to bring the marks of new creation—"heaven," if you will—to bear on earth. Biblical theology and missional hermeneutics prove themselves very useful dialogue partners. Biblical theology reminds us of the inherent suffering involved in the mission of God, because of the death of Jesus Christ, while at the same time, in union with the risen Christ, we are empowered boldly to take up the mission of God in the world and be a new-creation people. Missional hermeneutics aids biblical theology from falling into a merely descriptive undertaking, reminding those engaging in biblical theology of the necessity of other perspectives and other voices in seeing *how* Jesus functions as the center of the Scripture.

I recognize that space limitations allowed me only to lay out the theory; future essays and writings will flesh out with concrete examples what a biblical-theological interpretation of a text that engages in the mission of God will look like. I have simply tried to suggest here that in our interpretive task as biblical theologians, it may be profitable to raise the question of how a text shapes the reader, not just the ancient reader, toward the comprehensive mission of God to bless the world in the name of Jesus Christ by the power of the Spirit. Might this be a way forward, toward the question of "applied" biblical theology?

6

The Fifth Gospel

Adrian T. Smith

HISTORICAL GEOGRAPHY field trip, January 2000. The walls of Jerusalem. The fortress Masada. The Sea of Galilee. The caves of Qumran. Hundreds of photographs. Indelible memories, kaleidoscopic and poignant.

Most poignant, my memories of Professor Al Groves. Al led our seminary field trip, accompanied by his wife, Libbie, and their four children—Alasdair, Rebeckah, Éowyn, and Alden. Characteristically, Al was the patriarch of our seminary tribe. For three weeks, we all became members of his extended family.

His physical hindrances notwithstanding, Al labored to create community "in Christ." Each day, we ascended tells and descended wadis. Each evening, at our communal meal, Al found strength to lead us in song. His favorite song focused on Christ our supreme treasure. This Christocentric focus was, I believe, the secret of Al's extraordinary influence on all who were privileged to know him.

Al loved and knew intimately the texture of Holy Scripture. He taught us that the multiple strands of the rich biblical tapestry all join together in Christ. Al's penetrating OT scholarship was guided by the conviction that the Law, Prophets, and Writings all speak of Christ (Luke 24:44).

Al delighted in the story, the imagery, and the "motifs" of the OT as gifts from God for grasping Christ. Consequently, Al encouraged students to experience firsthand the *topography* of the biblical story. Al understood the insight of those church fathers who regarded the *places* of Jesus' earthly ministry as a "fifth Gospel."

This essay expands the patristic insight concerning the fifth Gospel. My expansion moves toward a narrative theology. The Bible unfolds, from Genesis to Revelation, as a cosmic epic. Its life-giving story may be retold in manifold ways. One fruitful retelling views the gospel as the Story of Land: a paradise lost—and restored in Christ.

ORIENTATION

Israel? Palestine? The Holy Land? Our disagreements over nomenclature make an eloquent point: geographical space is an ideological construct; turf and terrain are more than real estate; physical space symbolizes political and religious values.

The religious symbolism of land in the Bible is rich and variegated—a polyvalence that resembles the topographical diversity of the terrain itself. The OT has the idiom "All Israel, from Dan to Beersheba." Both places were visited on the field trip led by Professor Groves. When we visited Beersheba in the Negev (dry land), it resembled a desert. When we visited Dan near Mount Hermon, it seemed like a tropical paradise in comparison. Wilderness and paradise—the religious experience of God's people oscillates between both.

Here we glimpse the value of the land theme for grasping, communicating, and embodying the gospel. Walter Brueggemann pioneered the art of telling the story of redemption via the imagery of its geographical setting.[1] Brueggemann makes three proposals:

1. Land is a central, integrating theme of the Bible.
2. In both testaments, the semantics of land oscillate dialectically between turf and symbol; land stands for terrain, but land also stands for an idea.
3. The land theme is a point of contact for the gospel, with powerful appeal to the physically and the spiritually landless.

1. Walter Brueggemann, *The Land: Place as Gift, Promise, and Challenge in Biblical Faith*, 2nd ed. (Minneapolis: Fortress, 2002).

Here are some dimensions of contemporary landlessness or homelessness; these provide points of contact for the gospel to reach people who experience life as a state of exile.

Numerous geopolitical, socioeconomic, and technological factors contribute to this exilic condition. For many people, homelessness and exile are literal realities: the beggars on our city streets, the innumerable refugees, fleeing war and famine. But there are also multitudes of voluntary exiles, living a life of endless geographical mobility in pursuit of careers. Capitalism itself entails the reduction of land to a commodity for profit. (Sub)urbanization tends to destroy venerable and well-loved neighborhoods. Many seek refuge in cyberspace, only to find it a poor substitute for land-based, physical community.

Then there are philosophical factors behind the loss of a sense of place we can call home. The Cartesian/Newtonian homogenization of mathematical space reduces all space to the axes x, y, and z. The evolutionary cosmology, according to the biologist-philosopher Jacques Monod, leaves humans as aliens in a universe radically indifferent to their deepest aspirations.[2] Furthermore, pluralism has evicted many from their metaphysical homes in traditional religions.[3]

As we turn to the Bible to address both physical and spiritual homelessness, we will trace the land theme from the OT, through the intertestamental period, and into the NT. Beginning in the OT, we will explore ways that the Promised Land persistently pointed to something bigger than itself. The seeds of these symbolic associations germinate during the intertestamental era, and are harvested in the NT.

THE LAND THEME IN THE OT

At the start of our journey, we need to underscore the *paradise* theme. The garden of Eden is the gateway to understanding the land of Canaan. If we read Genesis as the prologue to the story of the Bible, then we would expect the prologue to sound the opening notes of the symphony of Scripture.

This literary conviction is reinforced by subsequent echoes of paradise. Intriguingly, the cherubim motif occurs both in the garden of Eden and

2. Jacques Monod, *Chance and Necessity: An Essay on the Natural Philosophy of Modern Biology*, trans. Austryn Wainhouse (New York: Knopf, 1971), 180.
3. Peter L. Berger, Brigitte Berger, and Hansfried Kellner, *The Homeless Mind: Modernization and Consciousness* (New York: Random House, 1973), 183–84.

in the decorations of the tabernacle and the temple (Gen. 3:24; Ex. 26:31; 1 Kings 6:23–29). What might this suggest? Through the temple, the lost Eden is returning! The temple, centralized in Israel, defined the Holy Land. By reusing the cherubim motif and other Edenic motifs, the temple signaled that the Holy Land was a partial restoration of paradise.

This symbolism is reinforced by the echoes of Eden in the prophetic literature. The Prophets use recurrent motifs to portray the restoration of Canaan that will follow the Babylonian exile. These motifs include peace, fertility, trees, and water. Interestingly, these four motifs are richly attested in the ancient Near Eastern iconography of paradise. Isaiah 51:3 describes post-restoration Canaan in these terms: "He has made her wilderness like Eden, and her desert like the garden of Yahweh."[4] Significantly, in Old Aramaic, the cognate of *Eden* means "fruitfulness." This significance emerges in the descriptions of Canaan as a fertile paradise. It is a "land flowing with milk and honey" (e.g., Ex. 3:8; Deut. 26:9). The covenantal blessings depict paradise-like degrees of fertility (e.g., Lev. 26:3–10). These descriptions echo the paradise concepts of the Canaanite nature religions. In all these persistent echoes, the OT sounds a clear note: *the land of Canaan was a microcosm of paradise being restored.*

Next, let us notice the themes of *exile and alienation* in the primeval history. The plot turns with Adam and Eve being expelled from paradise. Likewise, Cain gets banished from God's presence. But then comes Noah, named in the hope that he would bring *rest* (Noah's name is a wordplay on the Hebrew word for "rest"). "And Noah's father called his son Noah [*noakh*], saying, 'He will bring us *rest* [verbal root *nuakh*] from our labor caused by the ground [*'adhamah*] that Yahweh has cursed'" (Gen. 5:29). Noah's father desires a reversal of the post-Edenic, alienated condition of humankind.

If we jumped ahead in our story, we would see that the concept of rest is integral to the book of Joshua, which uses the same Hebrew root (*nuakh*) to describe the inheritance of the land of Canaan (Josh. 1:15). This verbal echo of Genesis once again images Canaan as a microcosm of paradise being restored.

We resume the story with the *Abrahamic covenant*. The promises to Abraham are God's answer to the alienated, exilic condition of humanity. This linkage is implied by Genesis 11:27, in which the *toledot* formula hinges Abraham's history onto the primeval history: "These are the generations

---

4. Quotations from the OT, LXX, and NT in this chapter are the author's own translation.

[*toledot*] of Terah: Terah begat Abram." The book of Genesis repeatedly uses the formulaic "these are the generations of" as a red thread to tie together different epochs of salvation history. Consequently, the alienated, post-Edenic human condition, depicted in Genesis 3–11, provides the essential context for understanding the Abrahamic promises.

This linkage is reinforced by the initial promise to Abraham, which clearly functions to reverse the curses, exile, and alienation experienced in the primordial history:

> And Yahweh said to Abram, "Go from your land . . . to the land which I will show you, that I may make you a great nation, and bless you, and make your name great that you may be a blessing, and that I may bless the ones blessing you—and as for the one who despises you, I will curse him. Then all the clans of the earth ['*adhamah*] may gain a blessing in you." (Gen. 12:1–3)

This promise is the motor that drives the narrative of the entire Pentateuch (and beyond). The word *bless* occurs five times, reversing the litany of curses delivered in chapter 3 of Genesis. Furthermore, the blessing is for all the clans of the '*adhamah*—the ground that was cursed in Genesis 3:17. In sum, the land promised to Abraham was, from the outset, *part of a "package deal" for the reversal of the curse*. The Promised Land was inseparable from the global goals of the redemptive drama.

This linkage explains some curious literary phenomena. These phenomena suggest that the OT itself viewed the land as an *ideal* and as an *eschatological symbol*.

The land has fuzzy borders. Sometimes its boundaries are narrow and precise; sometimes its boundaries are vague and expansive.[5] Furthermore, the depiction of the conquest has a "now and not yet" character. In the book of Joshua, the conquest is portrayed as both complete *and* incomplete.[6] On the one hand, verses such as Joshua 11:23 portray a complete conquest: "So Joshua took the entire land . . . and he gave it as an inheritance to Israel." On the other hand, Joshua 15:63 is representative of verses that tell a different story: "Judah could not dislodge the Jebusites, who were living in Jerusalem; to this day the Jebusites live there with the people of Judah." Such phenomena

5. Cf. Deut. 11:24 and Num. 34:1–12.
6. Cf. Josh. 11:23; 12:7; 18:10; 21:43–45 and Josh. 13:1; 15:63; 23:4–5.

encouraged the ancient reader to view the land as something that eludes capture, as something that remains tantalizingly out of reach, as something capable of indefinite expansion. All this makes sense if the Holy Land represented a God-given vision of paradise restored. Ultimately, the fuzzy borders, and the "now and not yet" quality of the inheritance, suggest that the *land was viewed by the OT as an ideal and as an eschatological symbol.*

Furthermore, the land was a *symbol of the covenant* itself. This is another facet of the paradise theme, because *shalom* with God is the essence of paradise. The covenant relationship was epitomized in the formula "I will be your God / You will be my people" (e.g., Ex. 6:7; Lev. 26:12; Rev. 21:3). Every "component" of this formula was open to representation via the polyvalent symbol of land.

The covenantal dynamic of *mutual fidelity* was highlighted by the land symbol. The book of Joshua repeatedly reminded Israel that the land gift confirmed Yahweh's oath to the patriarchs (Josh. 1:6; 21:43). When the Israelites needed assurance that Yahweh was trustworthy, the ground under their feet uttered a sacramental pledge. Specific features of Canaan's topography reinforced this assurance: "As the mountains surround Jerusalem, so Yahweh surrounds his people" (Ps. 125:2).

The land also functioned as an index of Israel's covenant fidelity. Many of the covenantal blessings/curses in Leviticus and Deuteronomy are, so to speak, "grounded" in land-based realities (Lev. 26; Deut. 28). The topography of Canaan was woven into the rhetoric of the OT. On visiting the town of Shechem (modern Nablus), one sees two hills: Gerizim, the hill for reciting covenantal blessings, and Ebal, the hill for reciting covenantal curses (Deut. 27:12–13). Gerizim is green with vegetation; Ebal is barren and dry.

In addition, the location and climate of Canaan were, providentially, a testing ground for Israel's faith. Not only was Canaan dependent on unpredictable rainfall, but its strategic location made it ever vulnerable to invasion by the Egyptian and Mesopotamian superpowers. The land, therefore, testified eloquently to the challenging nature of Israel's covenant fidelity.

Furthermore, the land represented *both parties* of the covenant. The vocabulary of Psalm 16:5–6 indicates that the gift of land pointed beyond itself to the giver: "Yahweh is my chosen portion [*kheleq*] and my cup; / You are the one who holds my lot [*goral*]. / The lines [*khabalim*] have fallen to me in pleasant places; / indeed, I have a beautiful heritage [*nakhlah*]." These

Hebrew terms designate the land in the Joshua inheritance accounts.[7] The psalmist, in a move of stunning poetic boldness, applies these terms to Yahweh. The land symbolized God himself!

The land also symbolized the people of God. We see this in Deuteronomy 29:21–27, where God's anger is directed not at the people themselves, but against the land that represents them. More specifically, the land testified to God's ideal for unity among his people. In the Deuteronomic theology, the fact that God is one demanded a unity among his people, and that unity was symbolized by the land as the shared inheritance of all Israel. This sharing is underscored in the litany of allotment [*goral*] in the book of Joshua, which drives home the point via repetition of the formulaic refrain, "The allotment of [Tribe X]" (e.g., Josh. 15:1; 16:1; 17:1; 18:11; 19:1, 10, 17, 24, 32, 40).

To conclude this OT section, we highlight the *Jubilee* as a synthesis of our themes. The land represented the ideal unity of the people of God, and the land was a microcosm of paradise becoming restored. These two semantic connotations of the land come into focus in the Jubilee. This institution had the following requirements: resting the land; freeing slaves; canceling debts; returning land to the dispossessed (Lev. 25). Through these requirements, the land bore witness to the ongoing story of redemption, since the Jubilee explicitly embodied the values of the exodus. The statutes that demanded the liberation of Hebrew slaves grounded this imperative in the indicative of the exodus event: "He and his children are to be released [in the year of Jubilee] . . . for they are my servants, whom I brought out of Egypt" (Lev. 25:40–42). In sum, *the land reminded Israel of Yahweh's inclusive and liberating goals.*

We have scratched the surface of the meaning of land in the OT. We have seen that the land of Canaan was a microcosm of paradise becoming restored. The Promised Land was part of a "package deal" for reversing the exiled condition of humanity. Canaan could also symbolize God himself, his people, and the covenant relationship. Canaan, via the Jubilee, reminded Israel of the social ethics generated by the story of redemption. Let us now briefly examine the land theme in the second-temple[8] period.

---

7. For example, *kheleq* (Josh. 19:9); *goral* (Josh. 16:1); *khabalim* (Josh. 17:5); *nakhlah* (Josh. 13:23). Cf. Ps. 142:6 (MT): "You [Yahweh] are my portion (*kheleq*) in the land of the living."

8. The *second-temple period* is conventionally referred to as the *intertestamental period*, and the same general time frame is indicated by both terms. The former term pertains to the period between the building of the second temple under the Persian king Cyrus in 516 BC and its destruction by the Romans in AD 70. This term is now preferred by biblical scholars, since it gives greater

THE LAND THEME IN THE SECOND-TEMPLE PERIOD

This period saw some interesting thematic developments within Judaism's view of the Promised Land. These developments shared the following traits: first, they utilized OT trajectories of meaning; second, they utilized the symbolic polyvalence inherent in the theme of land; third, they were historically conditioned.

This third trait deserves elaboration. As James Kugel has phrased it, the return from Babylonian exile partook of "the messiness of history."[9] The restoration was a disappointment when compared with the glorious hopes of the Prophets, who had viewed the return from exile as akin to a return to the garden of Eden. The reality was a lot messier.

One dimension of this messiness was the ongoing Diaspora: most of the twelve tribes were still in exile. Then there was the stubborn fact of Gentile dominion over the Holy Land: the monotonous succession of Persians, Greeks, and Romans (depicted as a sequence of grotesque beasts in Daniel 7). Another dimension was the palpable spiritual decline within Judaism: many pious Jews bemoaned the impiety that accompanied assimilation into cosmopolitan empires. Ezra summed up one aspect of the disappointing restoration when he described the community in Jerusalem as if they were still in exile, needing a new exodus: "But now . . . Yahweh our God has been gracious in . . . giving us . . . a little relief in our bondage. Though we are slaves, our God has not deserted us in our bondage" (Ezra 9:8–9).

Let us now focus on some of the more interesting developments of the land theme during the second-temple period. In all these modifications, the referent of Israel's inheritance is redefined, moving away from the physical land and toward a more "spiritual" construal.

The Greek apocryphal book Wisdom of Ben Sira has a lengthy eulogy of wisdom (*sophia*) in chapter 24. This eulogy identifies wisdom with the law of Moses, and calls the law Israel's *inheritance*, using the technical term for the Promised Land: "All this [wisdom] is the covenant-book of God Most High, the law [*nomos*] which Moses enacted for us, the inheritance [*kleronomia*] of the synagogues of Jacob" (Sir. 24:23).

---

weight to the many developments in Jewish thought over that time, rather than simply regarding it as a holding period between two testaments.

9. James L. Kugel and Rowan A. Greer, *Early Biblical Interpretation* (Philadelphia: Westminster, 1986), 40–51.

Moving along a more eschatological trajectory, we also see the semantic shift whereby Israel's inheritance is construed as "life." In contrast to sinners, whose "inheritance [*kleronomia*] is Hades and darkness and destruction," stand "the saints of the Lord," who "will inherit [*kleronomeo*] life [*zoe*] in happiness" (Pss. Sol. 14:9–10).

In the apocalyptic literature, this eschatological redefinition of Israel's inheritance as *eternal* life becomes explicit: "The fourth [angel], who is set over all actions of repentance unto the hope of those who would *inherit eternal life*, is Phanuel by name" (1 Enoch 40:9).[10] Earlier in the same vision, the "portion" of the elect is depicted as the heavenly abode, the ultimate divine presence: "In those days, whirlwinds carried me off from the earth, and set me down into the ultimate ends of the *heavens* . . . And I saw a *dwelling place underneath the wings of the Lord* of the Spirits . . . There . . . I wanted to dwell . . . Already my *portion* is there; for thus it has been reserved for me" (1 Enoch 39:3–8).[11]

In this brief tour of second-temple literature, we have seen how the messiness of history led many Jews to redefine the land promise. Instead of turf, they conceptualized Israel's heritage along more spiritual lines. Instead of Middle Eastern terrain, Israel's inheritance was the gift of *wisdom* in Torah, or *everlasting life*, or the divine presence in *heaven*.

Another response to the messiness of history was the sense of ongoing *exile*—despite having reoccupied the Holy Land. For the holistic mind of the ancient Jew, exile was as much a spiritual and cultural condition as a geographical one. We can readily document this feeling of ongoing exile.[12]

For instance, Josephus informs us that around AD 45, a Jew named Theudas persuaded a large mob to accompany him to the Jordan River, where he announced that he was a prophet, at whose word the waters of the Jordan would divide (*Jewish Antiquities* 20.5.1). This yearning for a new exodus/conquest attests to the widespread conviction among Jews inhabiting the Holy Land that their condition was one of exile.

From within the borders of the Promised Land, the Dead Sea Scrolls lament the condition of Judaism as an ongoing exile:

10. E. Isaac, "1 (Ethiopic Apocalypse of) Enoch," in *The Old Testament Pseudepigrapha*, ed. James H. Charlesworth (New York: Doubleday, 1983), 1:32 (emphasis added).

11. Ibid., 1:30–31 (emphases added).

12. Carey C. Newman, ed., *Jesus and the Restoration of Israel* (Downers Grove, IL: InterVarsity Press, 1999), 77–110.

"You have raised us through the years of our generations, [disciplining us] with terrible disease, famine, thirst, even plague and the sword—[every reproa]ch of Your covenant. For You have chosen us as Your own . . . That is why You have poured out Your fury upon us, [Your ze]al, the full wrath of Your anger. That is why You have caused [the scourge] [of Your plagues] to cleave to us, that of which Moses and Your servants the prophets wrote: You [wou]ld send evil ag[ain]st us in the Last Days [. . .]" (*Words of the Luminaries*, 4Q504 3:7–14).[13]

As we move into the NT, we will hear clear echoes of these second-temple themes of new exodus, and the spiritual and eschatological construals of the land promise.

THE LAND THEME IN THE NT

The student who turns from the pages of the OT to the pages of the NT is tempted to ask, Whatever happened to the land promise? The Hebrew word for *land* ('*erets*) is the fourth most frequent noun in the OT (around twenty-five hundred occurrences); the Greek equivalent (*ge*) is relatively infrequent in the NT.

Do these statistics reflect disinterest or development on the part of the NT writers? Probably both. The success of the Gentile mission outside the Holy Land must have exerted pressure to de-emphasize the Promised Land. The NT does not drop the land promise, however, but develops it in continuity with OT and second-temple trajectories. Furthermore, the NT redefinition of *land* has a decidedly Christocentric quality.

Our exploration will take the following pathways: exile and Jubilee in Luke; sacred space in John's Gospel; land typology in Hebrews; inheritance in Paul. Theological diversity will emerge along the way, in keeping with Geerhardus Vos's insight: "From the organic character of revelation we can explain its *increasing multiformity*, the latter being everywhere a symptom of the development of organic life."[14]

We begin with the themes of *exile* and *Jubilee* in *Luke*. Multiple threads of the Lukan tapestry converge in depicting *the cross as the exile that terminates the exilic human condition*. For instance, Jesus characterized him-

---

13. Michael Wise, Martin Abegg Jr., and Edward Cook, *The Dead Sea Scrolls: A New Translation* (New York: HarperSanFrancisco, 1996), 411.

14. Geerhardus Vos, *Biblical Theology* (Edinburgh: Banner of Truth, 1975), 7 (emphasis added).

self as a radically homeless person: "Foxes have dens, and birds . . . nests, but the Son of Man does not have anywhere to lay his head" (Luke 9:58). Furthermore, Luke portrays Jesus' mission as an exodus and a journey—a recapitulation of Israel's story. The Greek text of Luke 9:31 literally refers to Jesus' impending death as his "*exodos*, which he was about to fulfill in Jerusalem." Luke's central section makes repeated reference to a "journey" (e.g., Luke 9:57; 13:22). On this journey, Jesus gives instruction to his followers, just as Moses instructed Israel in the wilderness.

Arriving at the cross, we are encouraged to view the crucifixion against the backdrop of two additional OT plotlines, namely, the Psalter's story of the righteous sufferer and Isaiah's story of the Suffering Servant (Luke 23:46–47 / Ps. 31:5; Luke 22:37 / Isa. 53:12). By activating these OT plotlines, Luke ties the cross into the story of Israel's humiliation and exaltation, or exile and restoration. The exilic connotations of Isaiah 53 are crystal clear: the servant was "cut off from the *land* of the living" (v. 8); his reward is described using the land-term *kheleq* ("portion," v. 12). Finally, the cross in Luke is strongly connected to the restoration of paradise. Jesus' words to the dying thief were: "*Today* you will be with me in paradise [*paradeisos*]" (Luke 23:43).

Interpreting Jesus' mission as an exile that ushers in paradise resonates with another land-related Lukan theme, namely, the *Jubilee*. Luke portrays Jesus' ministry as a contextualized, eschatological Jubilee.

Luke 4:16–21, located at the inception of Jesus' public ministry, has a clear programmatic function. Jesus reads from the scroll of Isaiah: "The Spirit of the Lord is on me, for he has anointed me to preach good news to the poor. He has sent me to proclaim freedom [*aphesis*] for the prisoners, . . . to send forth the oppressed in freedom [*aphesis*], to proclaim the year of the Lord's favor." Then Jesus declares, "*Today* this scripture is fulfilled in your hearing." The Greek word *aphesis*, used twice in Luke's account, signifies "Jubilee" in the LXX (Lev. 25:50, 54). As Luke's Gospel unfolds, we see Jesus' restoration of the socially marginalized: widows, lepers, Samaritans, tax collectors, prostitutes. Jesus' ministry embodied the restorative and liberating values of the Jubilee.

Next, we consider the topic of *sacred space* in *John's Gospel*. Here Jesus actualizes the reality symbolized by Judaism's holy institutions. This theme finds expression in the prologue: "The Word became flesh and *tabernacled* among us" (John 1:14, which uses the verbal form of the noun *skene*, used of the tabernacle in the LXX). As Jesus begins his ministry, he implies that his presence transcends Judaism's most holy location: in clearing out the temple, he alludes to the fact that his body is the true temple (John 2:21). Similarly, when Jesus conversed with the Samaritan woman, he relativized all holy places, including Jerusalem, by declaring the arrival of the age of the Holy Spirit—an age in which the presence of God is no longer focused in the temple (John 4:21–23).

The implications of this theme have been inimitably stated by W. D. Davies. Since the temple and Jerusalem have been transcended, then the entire Holy Land is transcended (because Jerusalem and the temple were regarded by Judaism as the "quintessence" of sacred space). The gospel has "shattered the territorial chrysalis" of Judaism. The gospel is about "a Jew, Jesus of Nazareth, who proclaimed the Jubilee only to die accursed on a cross and so to pollute the land, and by that act and its consequences to shatter the geographic dimension of the religion of his fathers." Subsequently, sacred space is "Christified"; wherever Jesus, by his Spirit, is present, we should take off our shoes, for we are on holy ground.[15]

The *land typology* in *Hebrews* is familiar to most readers of the NT. In the light of the new covenant inaugurated by Jesus, Hebrews (11:8–10, 13–16) clearly reinterprets the land promise as referring exclusively to the heavenly [*epouranios*] city/country (and attributes this viewpoint to Abraham himself!). This heavenly city/country is described in remarkably concrete terms: "a city with foundations, whose architect and builder is God" (v. 10). This concreteness preserves the material dimension of the land of Canaan, and discourages us from viewing heaven in purely spiritual, ethereal, Platonic terms (notwithstanding the numerous scholarly efforts to rank the author of Hebrews with the school of Plato).

We conclude our survey of land theology with the topic of *inheritance* in *Paul*. *Inheritance* is the key term through which Paul filters the land promise into the new covenant. In the LXX, the Hebrew terms for *inheritance* were translated by cognates of the stem *klero-* (*kleronomia, kleronomeo*, etc.). We need to be wary of mechanical semantic transfers from the Hebrew to the LXX to the NT. Nevertheless, transfer is greatest with technical religious terms, and land inheritance was a fundamental component of Israel's religion.

Here are some of the ways in which Paul refers to *inheritance*. In Romans 4:13, Paul makes a semantic move characteristic of second-temple Judaism, equating inheritance with the *cosmos*: "It was not through the law that the promise was made to Abraham or to his posterity, that he would be heir

15. W. D. Davies, *The Gospel and the Land* (Berkeley: University of California Press, 1974), 131, 368, 375.

of the world [*kosmos*]." Elsewhere, Paul equates the inheritance with the *kingdom* of God: "Those who do such things will not inherit [*kleronomeo*] the kingdom of God" (Gal. 5:21; cf. 1 Cor. 6:9–10); "flesh and blood cannot inherit [*kleronomeo*] the kingdom of God" (1 Cor. 15:50).

Next, Paul appears to equate the Abrahamic promise/blessing and the *Holy Spirit*! We discern this from a careful translation of Galatians 3:13–14: "Christ redeemed us . . . in order that [*hina*] the blessing of Abraham might come to the Gentiles in Christ Jesus—i.e., that [*hina*] we might receive the promise—the Spirit—through faith." These verses identify "the promise" and "the Spirit," and make this promise parallel to "the blessing of Abraham." In other words, Paul identifies the Spirit as "the blessing of Abraham." The full impact of this identification emerges when we read Jacob's blessing of Isaac in Genesis 28:1–4: "May God Almighty . . . give you and your descendants *the blessing of Abraham* so that you may inherit *the land*." In other words, Paul, by echoing this patriarchal promise, sees the Holy Spirit as the ultimate referent of the land. Intriguingly, he goes on to speak of the "*fruit* of the Spirit" (Gal. 5:22–23), since this abundant fruitfulness is a harvest of virtues akin to the abundant fertility of the land of promise.[16]

Finally, the eulogy at the beginning of Ephesians implies that the inheritance is ultimately found "*in Christ*." Cognates of the *inheritance* term (*klero-*) occur in Ephesians 1:11 and 14 in a context saturated with the phrase "in Christ" and its synonyms. The Christian is "appointed" (*kleroo*) in Christ (v. 11), and, in Christ, believers are "sealed with the promised Holy Spirit," who is "the guarantee of our inheritance [*kleronomia*]" (vv. 13–14).

This spatial emphasis—"in" (*en*) Christ—is another way in which the NT conserves yet transforms the locational particularity of the OT land promise. Consequently, having hinted that Christ is the ultimate sacred space, Paul depicts the church "in Christ" as the temple, the epicenter of sacred space (Eph. 2:21).

Conclusion

The history of redemption involves continuity and discontinuity. As the biblical story unfolds, the ultimate meaning of the Promised Land becomes progressively clearer.

The climax of the covenant entails discontinuity regarding the significance of geographical Israel. The land of Canaan has been transcended and

---

16. I owe this last insight, on the fruit of the Spirit, to my colleague Douglas Green.

is no longer focal in salvation history. The land of Canaan was a microcosm of paradise restored, and therefore a type of new covenant realities such as these: union with Christ, the Holy Spirit, the church, the kingdom of God, and the new heaven and the new earth.

On the other hand, there are deep continuities along the redemptive plotline. The OT provides the NT with "the grammar of redemption." We can describe the theological texture and trajectory of the OT, and use the results as a heuristic to explore the NT. Using this heuristic, here are six suggestions for viewing the *church* through the lens of the functions of the *Promised Land*:

1. The Holy Land was the venue for numerous *theophanies*—moments when God became palpably present. By analogy, we may view the church as the primary arena for new covenant theophanies. In other words, the church is a gathering where, through Scripture and sacrament, God may be encountered as palpably present.

2. The land was a *token* of divine faithfulness—a tangible expression of God's trustworthiness. Likewise, the visible church is a token of God's fidelity. Contemplation of God's providential preservation of the church down through the ages can be a great tonic to our faith.

3. The land was a symbol of the ideal *unity* of God's people. Viewing the church as the eschatological land encourages *ecumenicity*; the diverse denominational "tribes" of today's ecclesiastical landscape all have an equal share in the inheritance that is Christ.

4. The land functioned as a *barometer* of Israel's covenant fidelity, since so many of the blessings/curses found expression via the land. By analogy, perhaps the *shalom* of the institutional church is an index of the covenant fidelity of its members. For instance, three fundamental goals for the Promised Land were its *unity*, *purity*, and *extension*. These goals are shared by the visible church, and failure to realize them can provide a reality check on our degree of covenant faithfulness.

5. The land functioned as a *new Eden*. Intriguingly, the rituals of patristic baptism symbolized the conviction that the church is the begin-

ning of paradise restored: "The baptismal waters and the fragrance of the ointments were likened to the rivers of Paradise and the perfumes of the fragrant trees of Eden, whilst the octagonal shape of the baptistery symbolized the return of the eighth day, the golden first age of mankind in innocence."[17]

6. Finally, the land theme reinforces the *material* and *social* dimensions of salvation. Luke, the theologian of *Jubilee*, clearly grasped this when, in Acts 4:34, he said of the primitive church that "there was not any impoverished among them." In the Greek text, this sentence is a neat verbal echo of Deuteronomy 15:4 (LXX)—a verse whose context spoke of Jubilee-style debt cancellation. In the NT, "fellowship/communion" (*koinonia*) is strongly *economic* in character.

As we end this essay, a word on Middle East politics seems proper. Readers convinced by the hermeneutic of this essay must challenge the dispensationalist (Zionist) assumptions about the modern state of Israel that dominate mainstream American evangelicalism.[18] I firmly support the right of Jews to inhabit the Holy Land today. But I do not base this right on the Abrahamic covenant; rather, I affirm this right on humanitarian grounds. On the other hand, the gospel challenges American Christians to express communion with the more than one hundred twenty thousand Palestinian/Arabic Christians who call on the name of the Lord Jesus inside the West Bank and in the refugee camps of the Gaza Strip.[19] The Holy Land has been defiled by generations of bloodshed. And yet that same land was designed by God as a symbol of paradise restored, as an emblem of union with Christ, in whom the dividing wall of ethnic hostility has been overthrown (Eph. 2:14–16).

These thoughts lead me back to Al Groves. Gripped by God's kindness toward him, Al was utterly indiscriminating in extending that kindness to everyone. A visit to the Groves household was, and is, an experience of paradise restored.

17. George H. Williams, *Wilderness and Paradise in Christian Thought* (New York: Harper, 1962), 29–30.

18. For an irenic critique of dispensationalism, see Vern S. Poythress, *Understanding Dispensationalists*, 2nd ed. (Phillipsburg, NJ: P&R Publishing, 1994).

19. Statistics taken from Gary M. Burge, *Who Are God's People in the Middle East?* (Grand Rapids: Zondervan, 1993), 149.

7

"He Bore Our Sins": Apostolic Reflections on Isaiah 53

KAREN H. JOBES

THERE SEEMS TO BE no better way to honor the memory of a colleague, scholar, and brother in Christ than to call attention to the work he has left as part of his life's legacy. In 2004, J. Alan Groves contributed an article to a festschrift entitled "Atonement in Isaiah 53: 'For He Bore the Sins of Many' " to honor one of his esteemed colleagues.[1] This present essay extends his work on the atonement in Isaiah 53 by briefly considering his conclusions about the Hebrew text in light of its ancient Greek translation and by surveying the use of Isaiah 53 by the NT writers.

"Isaiah 53," a conventionally shortened reference to the passage that actually extends from Isaiah 52:13 to 53:12, is one of the passages best known to Christians from the book of Isaiah, if not *the* best known, perhaps because it speaks of the Suffering Servant. The Hebrew phrases in Isaiah 53:11 and 53:12 include two different verbs in the Hebrew, which Groves translated

---

1. J. Alan Groves, "Atonement in Isaiah 53: 'For He Bore the Sins of Many,' " in *The Glory of the Atonement: Biblical, Historical, and Practical Perspectives. Essays in Honor of Roger Nicole*, ed. Charles E. Hill and Frank A. James (Downers Grove, IL: InterVarsity Press, 2004), 61–89.

"to bear guilt" and "to carry sin," respectively, and he related these phrases to the overall concept of atonement in the book of Isaiah. Since the end of the nineteenth century it has been argued that Isaiah 53 cannot be about atonement because it contains none of the language found in passages about sacrificial atonement performed by Israel's cult elsewhere in the OT.[2] Against this view, Groves concluded that " 'bearing guilt' is uniquely presented in Isaiah 53 and that it is indeed vicarious" and therefore accomplishes an atonement.[3] Groves pointed out that the distinction between cultic and noncultic language has led in the wrong direction when discussing Isaiah 53 for three reasons: (1) the concept of "making atonement" in the Hebrew Bible is not limited to cultic contexts only; (2) Isaiah's vision of Yahweh's global presence makes atonement centered on the cult of the Jerusalem temple moot because the vision implies that a more universally efficacious atonement is needed; and (3) in Isaiah's vision, Yahweh has rejected the cult and its sacrifices.[4]

After studying atonement language throughout the Hebrew Bible, Groves based his conclusions on the observation that the context for atonement is not limited in the OT to the setting of priestly sacrifice as a cultic ritual but "is best understood as made by an act that purifies something in such a manner that the outbreak of Yahweh's holy wrath is either arrested or prevented, which is appropriate in a particular situation."[5] He further countered the argument that Isaiah 53 could not be about atonement by pointing out that Isaiah predicts a universally efficacious purification corresponding to Yahweh's global presence. Isaiah envisions "Yahweh's glory, the signature expression of his presence in the holy of holies," to be *everywhere* when the seraphim of heaven declare that "the whole earth is full of [God's] glory" (Isa. 6:3).[6] Because Yahweh's glory is everywhere, his holy wrath might break out anywhere, and hence holiness is needed everywhere, not just in the temple precincts.[7]

---

2. The word *cult* is used here in the sense of "a particular system of religious worship esp. with reference to its rites and ceremonies," in this case the sacrificial system of the Jerusalem temple (*The Random House Dictionary of the English Language*, College ed., s.v. "cult" [New York: Random House, 1968]).

3. Groves, "Atonement," 64.

4. Ibid., 65.

5. Ibid., 66.

6. Ibid, 67. All quotations of Scripture in this chapter are from the TNIV, unless otherwise indicated.

7. Groves, "Atonement," 67.

Third, Groves argued that according to Isaiah's vision, Yahweh has rejected the efficacy of ancient Israel's sacrificial system, declaring at the beginning of the prophecy, " 'The multitude of your sacrifices—what are they to me?' says the LORD. 'I have more than enough of burnt offerings, of rams and the fat of fattened animals; I have no pleasure in the blood of bulls and lambs and goats' " (Isa. 1:11). In fact, Isaiah's vision promises a purification from sin that the cult with its ritual sacrifice could not achieve; therefore, "the cult plays little or no positive role in Isaiah" and atonement language shifts to a different context, that of the atoning work of the Suffering Servant.[8] Groves identified "the real problem [as] whether or not Isaiah 53 uses the language of atonement (an action that arrests or prevents Yahweh's wrath), and if so, how the suffering and death *of a human being to make atonement* can be explained."[9]

Groves pointed out that the uniqueness of an atonement achieved by the Suffering Servant is reflected even in unusual syntax within the Isaiah 53 passage. After a thorough and detailed examination of the syntax and context of the phrases "bearing guilt" and "carrying sin" in the Hebrew Bible, Groves observed that "the syntax of the two bearing-guilt clauses in Isaiah 53:11–12 are unique" within the OT corpus and that therefore they may "have a meaning peculiar to their syntax."[10]

The Old Greek (OG) translation of Isaiah 53 seems to amplify the theme of atonement, corroborating that long before the coming of Jesus, those Jewish translators also saw atonement language in the passage. Because of differences in the structures of the Hebrew and Greek languages, it would not be expected that the OG translation necessarily preserve the unique Hebrew syntax that Groves observed, and it doesn't. But two other features of the OG of Isaiah 53 corroborate that the passage was indeed read as referring to atonement. Where the Hebrew text of Isaiah 53:4 reads, "Surely he took up our pain and bore our suffering," the OG reads, "This one *bears our sins* and suffers pain for us."[11] Furthermore, in Isaiah 53:11–12 the OG translates the Hebrew verbs and their corresponding direct objects in the phrases "he will bear their iniquities" (53:11) and "he bore the sin of many" (53:12) with

8. Ibid.

9. Ibid., 69 (emphasis added).

10. Ibid., 77.

11. *A New English Translation of the Septuagint and the Other Greek Translations Traditionally Included under That Title*, ed. Albert Pietersma and Benjamin G. Wright (New York and Oxford: Oxford University Press, 2007) (emphasis added).

the same Greek verb *anaphero* ("bear") and noun *hamartia* ("sin") in both phrases, even though the Hebrew words are not the same in both phrases. The collocation of this particular Greek verb and noun is found in only three other places in the OG canonical books that refer to atonement (Lev. 9:10; 16:25; 2 Chron. 29:21). It appears that the ancient Greek translators of Isaiah saw more atonement language in Isaiah 53 than many modern interpreters today will allow.

This amplification of the idea of atonement in the OG translation of Isaiah 53 is one example of how the Greek translation of the Hebrew Scriptures is, in God's providence, congenial to the purposes of the NT writers as they proclaim the gospel in Greek. Adolf Deissmann once commented that Hellenistic Judaism had with the ancient Greek translation of the Hebrew Scriptures ploughed the furrows for the gospel seed in the Western world.[12] F. F. Bruce added that it was the Christian preacher quoting the Septuagint who sowed that seed of the gospel.[13] Bruce noted several places "in which the Septuagint translators used a form of words which (without their being able to foresee it, naturally) lent itself to the purposes of the New Testament writers better than the Hebrew text would have done."[14]

In addition to the unique syntax of the Hebrew phrases of Isaiah 53, Groves pointed out other unique features of the Isaiah 53 passage "that suggest a unique action in the Servant's 'bearing guilt'" that, because of its unique nature, is naturally unprecedented elsewhere in the OT.[15] Isaiah 53, with all its unique qualities, describes "the *extraordinary* nature of the purification of which Isaiah spoke," which is "its most distinctive contribution to redemptive history."[16] Groves explained:

> The Torah knew no atonement that produced the universal and permanent purification envisioned in Isaiah. Such extraordinary purification required an atonement of equally extraordinary and radical nature. . . . Only an atonement based on the Servant's sacrifice could accomplish the purification that Isaiah envisioned.[17]

12. Adolf Deissmann, *New Light on the New Testament: From Records of the Graeco-Roman Period*, trans. Lionel R. M. Strachan (Edinburgh: T&T Clark, 1907), 95.

13. F. F. Bruce, *The Canon of Scripture* (Downers Grove, IL: InterVarsity Press, 1988), 50.

14. Ibid., 53.

15. Groves, "Atonement," 80.

16. Ibid., 88 (emphasis in original).

17. Ibid., 88–89.

Apostolic Reflections on Isaiah 53 in the NT

The book of Isaiah is directly quoted, most often in its ancient Greek translation, in six NT passages written by the apostles Matthew, Luke, John, Paul, and Peter. Given the differences among these men and the audiences to whom each wrote, it seems clear that Isaiah 53 was widely known and deeply rooted in the earliest proclamation of the Christian gospel. Luke suggests that the origin of this tradition was indeed with Jesus himself.[18]

Luke 22:37, Quoting Isaiah 53:12

On the last evening of Jesus' life, Luke reports that Simon Peter, in a moment of sincere bravado, told Jesus, "Lord, I am ready to go with you to prison and to death" (Luke 22:33). Jesus immediately predicted that instead, before that very night was over, Peter would three times deny that he even knew Jesus. Jesus went on to quote Isaiah 53:12, saying, "It is written: 'And he was numbered with the transgressors' " (Luke 22:37). He concludes, "And I tell you that this must be fulfilled in me. Yes, what is written about me is reaching its fulfillment."

Poignantly, the clause in Isaiah 53:12 immediately before the one explicitly quoted by Jesus is "he poured out his life unto death." Jesus quotes one part of Isaiah's prophecy in Isaiah 53 to allude to another. NT writers often use phrases from the OT to bring to the reader's mind an entire passage. By quoting a line from Isaiah 53:12, Jesus invoked the entirety of Isaiah 53, to which he is referring when he says, "And I tell you that this must be fulfilled in me. Yes, what is written about me is reaching its fulfillment" (Luke 22:37). The point apparently was not lost on the disciples that night. Their minds must have gone to the violence that the Servant is predicted to suffer, for their immediate response is, "See, Lord, here are two swords"—implying their readiness to defend Jesus (Luke 22:39). What had been written all those many centuries before about "the *extraordinary* nature of the purification of which Isaiah spoke"[19] reached its fulfillment in the life, and the inevitable execution, of Jesus.

18. M. D. Hooker, "Did the Use of Isaiah 53 to Interpret His Mission Begin with Jesus?" in *Jesus and the Suffering Servant: Isaiah 53 and Christian Origins*, ed. W. H. Bellinger and William R. Farmer (Harrisburg, PA: Trinity, 1998), 88–103.

19. Groves, "Atonement," 88 (emphasis in original).

Matthew 8:17, Quoting Isaiah 53:4

In Matthew's Gospel, the Prophets are frequently quoted to show that the events of Jesus' life fulfilled ancient prophecy. Matthew 8:14–17 relates the story about Jesus coming into Peter's house in Capernaum, where Peter's mother-in-law lay in bed with a fever. Jesus touched her hand, and she recovered well enough and quickly enough to wait on him. Later, many demon-possessed and ill people were brought to Jesus, and Matthew reports that Jesus drove out spirits with a word and healed all the sick.

As Matthew observed and later reflected on these remarkable acts of healing that Jesus did in Capernaum and elsewhere, he recognized a fulfillment of prophecy. After telling the story of the healing of Peter's mother-in-law, Matthew quotes from the Hebrew version of Isaiah 53:4, "This was to fulfill what was spoken through the prophet Isaiah: 'He took up our infirmities and bore our diseases.' " Matthew's connection of Jesus to this prophecy shows first, and perhaps most significantly, that he understood Jesus to be the One of whom Isaiah spoke in the Suffering Servant passage. Second, Matthew construes this part of the prophecy to mean that the Servant has the power and the will to take up and take away human maladies, including both the physical and the spiritual. Matthew does not seem to pick up on the aspect of atonement in his use of Isaiah 53. As Robert Gundry pointed out, however, "Insofar as Mt. represents Jesus' healings as illustrations of his redemptive work, visible pledges of his taking away sin, and the compassion exercised and the healing virtue expended as beginnings of his passion, the evangelist has caught the thought of Is."[20]

John 12:38, Quoting Isaiah 53:1

The Gospel of John includes a narrative of events from Jesus' life structured around seven miraculous signs that John presents as evidence that the long-promised Messiah is none other than God himself in human flesh (1:19–11:57). Within this narrative of Jesus' life, the "first of the signs through which he revealed his glory" was to change water into wine at the wedding in Cana (John 2:11). The revelation of Jesus' glory culminated in that most spectacular sign of raising Lazarus from the dead (John 11:1–44) that was accompanied by Jesus' declaration, "I am the resurrection and the

---

20. Robert H. Gundry, *The Use of the Old Testament in St. Matthew's Gospel, with Special Reference to the Messianic Hope* (Leiden: Brill, 1967), 230.

life. Anyone who believes in me will live, even though they die; and whoever lives by believing in me will never die" (vv. 25–26). At the conclusion of the seven signs, John 12:37–50 forms a summary of Jesus' public ministry. In this summary John marvels that even after all of Jesus' miraculous signs and powerful teaching, those who had witnessed these things "still would not believe in him" (12:37).

The rejection of Jesus as the long-awaited Messiah by the very people who were being prepared through the centuries for his coming—through the Prophets, the Law, the temple, the sacrificial system—is surely the greatest irony of human history. And it no doubt was one of the nagging questions in the minds of the apostles as they began to preach Jesus as the resurrected Messiah. John announces this perplexing fact in the prologue to his Gospel, that "he came to that which was his own, but his own did not receive him" (John 1:11). It is within this context of the rejection of Jesus and his message that John quotes Isaiah 53:1. The NT writers consistently point to the experience and message of the prophet Isaiah as they reflect on the stunning rejection of the Messiah (cf. Matt. 13:13–15; Mark 4:12; Luke 8:10; Rom. 10:16). John's summary of the public ministry of Jesus seems to say that it was largely ineffective because "even after Jesus had performed so many signs in their presence, they still would not believe in him" (John 12:37).

One of the great ironies in John's Gospel occurs when Jesus explains and demonstrates that he is "the resurrection and the life" by calling Lazarus out of the tomb (11:25, 43–44) and when that very sign provoked a meeting of the Sanhedrin in which they "plotted to take his life" (John 11:53). It is a great blindness indeed that any should presume to take the life of the One who is Life! That they succeeded in executing Jesus was a fact that the apostles themselves struggled to understand.

John and other NT writers point to the forewarning that God gave to Isaiah at his commissioning as a prophet, an ominous forewarning that his message of repentance and mercy would go largely unheeded (Isa. 6:1–13). And yet Isaiah was to go and preach, for though rejected by the people his preaching would nevertheless fulfill God's purpose. As John ponders the widespread unbelief in Jesus, he quotes OG Isaiah 53:1, "Lord, who has believed our report? And to whom has the arm of the Lord been revealed?" (John 12:38). The phrase "the arm of the Lord" was familiar to readers of the Jewish Scriptures. It refers to God's mighty acts in the exodus story—for instance, in Deuteronomy 7:19, "You saw with your own eyes the great trials, *the signs* and wonders, the mighty hand and *outstretched arm*, with which the LORD your God brought you out" (see also Ex. 6:6; 15:16; Deut. 4:34; 5:15; 9:29; 11:2; 26:8). In spite of the great signs that God displayed to the exodus generation, their hearts grew hard toward God. And centuries later at the consummation of the covenant God made with Israel, the arm of the Lord had again been revealed in the signs of Jesus, but their significance was again not comprehended by the people most prepared to understand them.

John recognizes a fulfillment of Isaiah's prophecy in the people's unwillingness to allow the signs of Jesus to lead them to faith in him. John's words in 12:38 are an exact quotation of the OG version of Isaiah 53:1, which exactly follows the syntax of the Hebrew text, adding only the vocative "Lord" at the beginning. John then reaches to another part of Isaiah's prophecy (Isa. 6:10) to explain this amazing blindness of those who failed to recognize Jesus as the Suffering Servant: "He has blinded their eyes and hardened their hearts, so they can neither see with their eyes, nor understand with their hearts, nor turn—and I would heal them" (John 12:40). Here John's quotation of Isaiah 6:10 follows neither the Hebrew nor its Greek translation exactly, but the statement of God's willingness to heal in John's quotation stands closer to the Greek OT text.[21]

The tragic *effect* of Isaiah's prophetic ministry would be to make the ears of the people dull and to close their eyes, even though its *purpose* was to reconcile God's wayward people to himself. Similarly, the *purpose* of Jesus' signs was to reveal his glory as the Word made flesh and to bring people to faith in him as the Messiah, who was none other than God himself (John 2:11; 20:30–31). And as John points out, many did in fact come to faith in Jesus through his public ministry (John 12:42). But the simultaneous effect of Jesus' signs was to harden others who saw the miracles but had priorities and motives that caused them to miss the significance of the signs Jesus performed and consequently to reject him as a threat to their self-interests.

John includes a pronoun when he alludes to Isaiah 6:10 that is found neither in the Hebrew of Isaiah 6:10 nor in its OG translation: "*He* has blinded their eyes and hardened their hearts" (John 12:40). Although the pronoun ("he") is most often taken to refer to God, in John's context it more

---

21. For a detailed comparison of Isaiah 6:10 in its Hebrew version, Greek translation, and quotation in John 12, see Raymond E. Brown, *The Gospel according to John (i–xii): Introduction, Translation, and Notes*, 2 vols., 2nd ed., AB 29A (1966; repr., Garden City, NY: Doubleday, 1987), 485–86.

specifically refers probably to Jesus, whose signs at once both drew some to faith and hardened others.[22] Hearts were hardened and ears dulled by the prophecies that Isaiah pronounced; the signs that Jesus performed had the same effect. But for those who did see and hear Jesus and turn, God ("I") did heal them.

John goes on immediately to say that Isaiah "saw Jesus' glory *and spoke about him*" (John 12:41). In other words, John claims that in Isaiah 6, where the prophet sees the *glory* of the Lord seated on a throne high and exalted, Isaiah was seeing the *glory of Jesus* (if not the preincarnate Jesus himself) and that the rejected message of the Suffering Servant (Isa. 53:1) was a prophetic prediction that the Messiah, despite signs that revealed his *glory* (John 2:11), would be rejected.

Throughout John's Gospel, Jesus' teaching highlights the sovereignty of God in drawing people to himself (e.g., John 6:37, 44, 65). And yet those who reject him are not absolved of responsibility, as if this blinding and hardening were happening without their culpable involvement. Throughout John's Gospel the presence of Jesus forces a difficult decision on those who encounter him. Many responded from self-interest, choosing to reject Jesus rather than suffer the losses that would come by following him as the Messiah. When Caiaphas the high priest heard about the raising of Lazarus, he acknowledged that if Jesus were not stopped, "everyone will believe in him, and then the Romans will come and take away both our temple and our nation" (John 11:48). While responsible discharge of duty is admirable and preservation of the nation was a noble cause, both were achieved at the cost of rejecting the One for whom that nation had waited for centuries. John was not the only NT writer to reflect on that incredible fact and to find an answer in Isaiah 53. The question also concerned the apostle Paul.

Romans 10:16, Quoting Isaiah 53:1

Romans chapters 9–11 are those in which the apostle Paul explains how it is that so few of his fellow Israelites recognized God's consummation of the covenant in Christ's sacrifice (Rom. 9:1–5). This amazing fact caused for Paul deep anguish from which emerged the truth about God's covenant people that "not all who are descended from Israel *are* Israel" (Rom. 9:6).

22. Note that most English Bible versions include the pronoun inside the quotation, obscuring this point (e.g., TNIV, NASB, NRSV, ESV).

Paul had to wrestle with a theological question that must have shaken him to his very core: had God's word failed (Rom. 9:6)? After all the promises, covenants, and prophets, after all that God had said and promised, would it all come to naught because Abraham's descendants in Paul's generation had blindly allowed the Messiah to be killed?

Paul's statement "It is not as though God's word had failed" implies that the question had indeed gone through his mind (Rom. 9:6). In the face of the rejection of Christ by so many, one of two conclusions would have been close at hand: that God's word had indeed failed or that Jesus was not truly the Promised One. Paul, knowing that neither conclusion honored the truth, reflects on the prophecy of Isaiah 53 to arrive at yet a third conclusion while pondering why the Gentiles responded to his proclamation of the gospel while his own people did not. Paul writes, quoting Isaiah 53:1, "But not all the Israelites accepted the good news [of Jesus Christ]. For Isaiah says, 'Lord, who has believed our message?'" (Rom. 10:16). In explaining the failure of all Israel to accept the good news of the gospel, Paul asks first, "Did they not hear?" (Rom. 10:18), and quickly answers, yes, of course they did! He cites Deuteronomy 32:21 and Isaiah 65:1 to point to the ancient prediction that the Gentiles, "a nation" that was not seeking God, would find him. And concerning Israel, Paul cites Isaiah, who proclaimed that God was holding out his hands to "a disobedient and obstinate people" (Rom. 10:21, quoting Isa. 65:2). When confronted with the grace of God, many simply chose stubbornly to disobey.

Acts 8:32–33, Quoting Isaiah 53:7–8

"He was led like a sheep to the slaughter, and as a lamb before its shearer is silent, so he did not open his mouth. In his humiliation he was deprived of justice. Who can speak of his descendants? For his life was taken from the earth" (Acts 8:32–33, quoting Isa. 53:7–8). After reading this passage from the book of Isaiah, the Ethiopian eunuch asked Philip, "Tell me, please, who is the prophet talking about, himself or someone else?" (Acts 8:34). And then "Philip began with that very passage of Scripture and told him the good news about Jesus" (v. 35). As we saw above, Luke records in his Gospel that Jesus himself quoted from Isaiah to explain to the disciples in the garden of Gethsemane what was about to transpire (Luke 22:37). In his sequel to his Gospel, Luke here again quotes the OG of Isaiah as he relates the story of how Philip met the Ethiopian eunuch as he was reading the prophecy of Isaiah.

Being prompted by the Spirit, Philip approached the eunuch and engaged him in conversation that led the eunuch to ask, "Who is the prophet talking about . . . ?" Philip was one of the earliest leaders in the Jerusalem church (Acts 6:1–7), and his answer indicates that the identification of Jesus as the Suffering Servant in Isaiah 53 was present very early in the development of Christian thought. Though Luke does not record Philip's exposition of Isaiah 53 with respect to the life, death, and resurrection of Jesus Christ, it must have been quite compelling, for the eunuch jumped down from his chariot to be baptized by Philip into faith in Christ. Another of the Lord's apostles, Peter, quotes this same verse to give us the fullest exposition of Isaiah 53 in the NT.

1 Peter 2:20–25, Quoting Isaiah 53:4–6, 9

From the OG translation of Isaiah, the apostle Peter gives us the most fully developed reflection on Isaiah 53 among the NT writings.[23] He does so, however, not as an exposition of Isaiah 53, but as a reflection on how Jesus suffered in the last days of his life. Writing his letter to Christians who were suffering in various ways because of their faith in Christ, the apostle Peter sets forth the suffering of Jesus as the model of the Christian life. Peter creatively weaves a description of Jesus' suffering with phrases and allusions from LXX Isaiah 53 that interpret aspects of his trial and suffering. As Hooker notes, Peter does not simply use Isaiah 53 as a proof text, but moves beyond a "simple appeal to 'what is written' to the explanation of its *significance*."[24] The extensive and creative use of Isaiah 53 in 1 Peter 2:20–25 is highlighted by quotations of it in boldface and allusions to it in italics:

2:20b—if because of doing good you suffer and endure it, this is grace before God.

2:21—for to this you were called, because Christ also suffered on your behalf, leaving you an example in order that you might follow in his footsteps.

2:22—[He,] who did not commit sin, neither was deceit found in his mouth [Isa. 53:9];

23. See Karen H. Jobes, *1 Peter*, BECNT (Grand Rapids: Baker Academic, 2005).
24. Hooker, "Use of Isaiah 53," 93 (emphasis in original).

2:23—[He,] who when reviled *did not retaliate*, when he suffered *he did not make threats* [Isa. 53:7c, d], but instead *trusted* [Isa. 53:6c, 12] *the one who judges justly* [Isa. 53:8a];

2:24—[He,] who **himself bore our sins** [Isa. 53:4a, 12] in his body upon the tree, so that being separated from sins we might live to righteousness;

[He,] by whose wounds you are healed [Isa. 53:6a].

2:25—For **you were like wandering sheep** [Isa. 53:6a], but now you have returned to the Shepherd and Overseer of your souls.

As Paul Achtemeier notes, Peter uses the *language* of Isaiah 53, but the *order* of 1 Peter 2:22–25 follows the sequence of events in the passion of Jesus, with verses 22 and 23 alluding to the trial and verse 24 to the crucifixion.[25] Leonhard Goppelt has also pointed out that this passage reflects three fundamental aspects of the passion narrative as described in Mark's Gospel:[26]

1. Jesus is the target of verbal abuse, referring to slander by the Sanhedrin (Mark 14:65), ridicule by the Roman guards (15:12–20), and derision by the crucified thief (15:29–32).
2. Jesus accepts injustice without retaliating; in fact, he accepts it in silence (14:61; 15:5).
3. Jesus entrusts judgment to God, thereby leaving the preservation of justice to God the Father alone (14:62).

That the description of Jesus' suffering in 1 Peter should follow the passion narrative as found in Mark supports the theory that Mark's Gospel preserves Peter's memories of the Lord.

Peter's use of Isaiah 53 demonstrates that the death and resurrection of Jesus Christ was not only a historical event but also a hermeneutical event that opened new understandings of the OT. Apparently Peter did not set out to do an exposition of Isaiah 53; rather, he began with the fact of Jesus' suffering and death and searched the OT to make sense of the tragedy and to understand its significance (cf. Luke 24:25–27, 44–48). First Peter 2:21–25 is a remembrance of Jesus' suffering as explained and

25. Paul J. Achtemeier, "Suffering Servant and Suffering Christ in 1 Peter," in *The Future of Christology: Essays in Honor of Leander E. Keck*, ed. Abraham J. Malherbe and Wayne A. Meeks (Minneapolis: Fortress, 1993), 180.

26. Leonhard Goppelt, *A Commentary on I Peter*, trans. John E. Alsup (Grand Rapids: Eerdmans, 1993), 211.

interpreted by Isaiah's prophecy that allowed Peter to make sense of the sufferings of the Christ. But conversely, Jesus' suffering also allowed the apostle to make new sense of Isaiah 53. Peter's new understanding of the ancient prophecy allowed him to explain that it was the Spirit of Christ who inspired Isaiah and other prophets (1 Peter 1:10–12), bringing continuity between the Jewish Scriptures and the writings of the Christian apostles.

In citing Isaiah 53, Peter puts the atonement at the center of this teaching. In 1 Peter 2:24 he writes that Jesus himself bore our sins (cf. Isa. 53:4a, 12) in his body on the tree. The crucifixion is the heart of atonement in Peter's reflection on the significance of Jesus Christ as understood through Isaiah's prophecy. Contrary to liberal Protestantism, which rejects the supernatural and places Jesus' moral and ethical teachings at the center of the Christian message, Peter elaborates on what it meant to bear our sins. The Suffering Servant atones not by providing ethical and religious instruction but by bearing our sin—and just to make certain what "bearing our sin" involved, Peter adds a reference to Jesus' crucifixion, *in his body as he hangs upon the cross.* As Groves pointed out, the universal and permanent purification envisioned in Isaiah was of such an extraordinary and radical nature that its fulfillment would require an unprecedented, and indeed unique, event.[27] The apostle Peter considered that fulfilling event to have been the crucifixion of Jesus Christ.

Peter's use of Isaiah 53 also explains why the prophecy both in the Hebrew and in its Greek translation seems to shift in pronouns and syntax between the singular and plural. The Suffering Servant passage in Isaiah can be read to refer to an individual or collectively to the nation of God's people. The apostle Peter's reflections on Isaiah 53 in 1 Peter 2:24 explain that the purification envisioned by Isaiah means being separated from sins and living to righteousness. Choosing not to sin in a society that doesn't know the meaning of the word, however, will inevitably lead to suffering at times and to some extent. Just as it was God's will that his Servant should suffer (Isa. 53:10), Peter writes that it is God's will for Christians to follow in his footsteps and choose to suffer rather than to sin (1 Peter 3:17). Isaiah envisioned both the singular suffering of the Servant and its consequences for those who follow him.

27. Groves, "Atonement," 88–89.

SUMMARY

Isaiah 53 is quoted in six passages of the NT written by five different apostles—Matthew, Luke, John, Paul, and Peter. The contexts of those quotations show that Jesus identified himself with the Suffering Servant of Isaiah (Luke 22:37) and that the identification became an important part of the church's earliest teachings as evidenced by Philip (Acts 8:32–33). Moreover, Matthew, John, Peter, and Paul carried that teaching to very different and widespread segments of the first-century church—Christian converts from Judaism and from paganism, converts living in Syria, Asia Minor, and Rome. This foundational, early, and widespread application of Isaiah 53 justifies why "in studies of atonement in Isaiah, the Song of the Servant in Isaiah 52:13–53:12 is the text to which almost all attention tends to be devoted."[28] Groves has shown how the phrases "to bear guilt" and "to carry sin" relate to the overall concept of atonement in Isaiah, which is so foundational to orthodox Christology.[29]

28. Ibid., 61.

29. The author wishes to acknowledge and thank her teaching assistant, Laurie L. Norris, for her assistance in preparing this article.

8

True Israel's "Mother and Brothers": Reflections on the Servants and Servanthood in Isaiah

CHRISTOPHER J. FANTUZZO

SERVANTHOOD IS A central theme of Isaiah.[1] We like the thought of servanthood: we like to be served. We may even be attracted to the concept of servant leadership; it is fresh and sounds benevolent and agreeable. But we must consider God's way, according to his Word. As we consider servanthood, then, with particular reference to the servants (*'avadhim*) in Isaiah 54–66,[2] let us reflect on the character of God, his work in redemptive history, and the company we keep. As servants before his throne, let us kneel before the Holy One of Israel (cf. Isa. 6:4ff.; 45:23) and tremble at his Word (cf. Ex. 19:16; Isa. 66:2).

1. I am grateful to the editors for kindly inviting me to contribute this article in honor of my esteemed mentor and friend, Al Groves. "If anyone serves me, he must follow me; and where I am, there will my servant be also. If anyone serves me, the Father will honor him" (John 12:26).

2. In Isaiah, *servant* (*'evedh*) occurs in the singular for the last time at 53:11; thereafter, it occurs only in the plural (cf. 54:17; 56:6; 63:17; 65:8, 9, 13 [3x], 14, 15; 66:14).

THE "STORY" BEFORE ISAIAH

The epoch recounted in the Pentateuch from creation and the era of the patriarchs up to and including Moses prefigures and impacts all future time.[3] God's singular purpose reaches out from creation, grasps the life of Israel for a special vocation through Abraham, and stretches to the horizon of God's universal vision to establish his kingdom throughout the world (Isa. 45:23; Rom. 14:11; Phil. 2:10). Israel's own role dynamically unfolds against the backdrop of creation and the fall (Gen. 1–3), yet Israel's self-transcending history has its eschatological horizon in new creation (cf. Isa. 65:17; 66:22). Israel was born for an illustrious mission: God fashioned Israel to bear his image as a covenant partner (Ex. 19:5–6) in his plan to establish a kingdom, not for this nation only, but for the entire world. Hence, God's choice of Israel is subservient to the divine purpose of establishing worldwide sovereignty in a new creation. Apart from this instrumental purpose, *Israel has no reason for being.*[4]

The role of God's people in this unfolding program began *before* the birth of the Israelite nation out of Egyptian bondage. Within the Pentateuch, the exodus event is the climactic divine indicative: Yahweh delivered his people by his outstretched arm and the mediation of his servant, Moses. Nevertheless, Israel's beginning in redemptive history resides in a promise to Abraham, whom God called out of Mesopotamia for a special covenantal relationship involving the birth of offspring (*zera'*, "seed") for the blessing of all nations (Gen. 12:1–3; 15:18; 17:4ff.), thereby reaffirming the Creator's original intentions for image-bearing humanity (Gen. 1:26; cf. 3:15). God had chosen a servant, Abraham (and by extension Israel), "that he may charge his children and his household after him to keep the way of the LORD [*derekh YHWH*] by doing righteousness and justice [*tsdaqah umishpat*], so that the LORD may bring to Abraham what he has promised him" (Gen. 18:19 RSV).[5]

3. Hence, the conception and use of the term *torah* for this section of the canon may be extended beyond the Pentateuch, as it was in Judaism. According to Ephraim Urbach, " 'Torah' was not a word but an 'institution', embodying the covenant between the people and its God, and reflecting a complex of precepts and statutes, customs and traditions linked to the history of the people and the acts of its rulers, kings, and prophets" (Ephraim E. Urbach, *The Sages: The World and Wisdom of the Rabbis of the Talmud* [Cambridge, MA: Harvard University Press, 1975], 289).

4. Jon Levenson expresses the instrumentality of Israel's election well: "The chosen people does not withdraw from the human family, but exercises a special office within it, an office defined by the character and will of their universal God." Jon D. Levenson, "The Universal Horizon of Biblical Particularism," in *Ethnicity and the Bible*, ed. M. G. Brett (Leiden: Brill, 1996), 155.

5. The Pentateuch narrates the partial fulfillment of God's promises to the patriarch Abraham (and after him, Isaac and Jacob): land, descendants, a special covenant relationship, and

The Judge of all the earth (Gen. 18:25) desires to dwell in circles character-ized by justice and righteousness. He will keep his end of the commitment, and he aims, by way of Abraham's seed, to see his fundamental standard[6] reproduced throughout the world (cf. Ps. 85:10–13).

Consequently, Israel's bond of love and loyalty to Yahweh—including the Sinai (Horeb) covenant—is not ultimately grounded in the exodus, but in God's promises to and covenant with his servant Abraham (cf. Gen. 26:4–5; Deut. 4:30; 5:31; 6:20–25; 9:5, 27). So as far as Israel is concerned, this covenant is unconditional; yet it established by divine oath the unfail-ing direction for Abraham's offspring: *a life of servanthood in covenant with God.* Only after Abraham, and in subordination to God's plan through him, does the biblical conception of vocation become refocused for Israel in the covenant mediated by Moses at Horeb, realized anew at Moab for life in the land. Israel's covenant-historical identity, then, is linked directly to the calling of Abraham; and its calling as a servant people under the sanctions of the Mosaic covenant presumes a universal redemptive mission.

Moses' *torah*, however, generates a tension, inwrought in redemptive history, between legislating for a present historical theocracy and the devel-oping vision of the kingdom of God (cf. Deut. 10:16; 30:1–10, 11–14; Josh. 1:7).[7] Hereafter, obedience to the way of Yahweh according to Mosaic Torah will be righteousness (*tsdaqah*) for Israel (Deut. 6:25; cf. 9:4–6; 30:15–20).[8]

---

blessing to all nations. Its theme is introductory and basic to the entire subsequent history of redemption. See David J. A. Clines, *Theme of the Pentateuch*, JSOTSup 10 (Sheffield, UK: JSOT Press, 1978), 29.

6. This universal standard, violated by our first parents (Gen. 3), may be broadly defined as loyalty to Yahweh. After the fall (cf. Gen. 3:15), the bearers of Yahweh's worldwide redemptive mission must exhibit justice (*mishpat*) and righteousness (*tsedeqah*) as their expression of active faith in his promises (Gen. 15:6; 22:18).

7. Under Mosaic Torah, the presence of the covenant Lord is both a blessing and a threat. Yahweh's presence is a blessing to Israel, notably through the partial fulfillment of covenant prom-ises, including the activity (at times) of his Spirit in the governance of powerful mediators. In the face of these blessings, however, Israel's response, historically, manifests the power of reigning sin, exacerbated within its life by the demands of Mosaic Torah (cf. 2 Kings 17:13–15, 19). Therefore, in spite of blessing, wrath and curse threaten the nation's very existence.

8. Israel *receives* the land and blessings from Yahweh as a gift, not because of Israel's righ-teousness, but because of the wickedness of the nations already in the land (Deut. 9:4)—though Israel is also far from innocent (v. 6ff.). God's gift of the land is a fulfillment of the oath he swore to Abraham, Isaac, and Jacob (v. 5). Thus, he demonstrates loyalty to his covenant commitment. This quality of God's character, exemplified in the commandments, becomes an ethical imperative for Israel. *If Israel is to retain the land and continue to receive Yahweh's blessing,* Israel must adhere to the covenant in wholehearted devotion to him (10:16). Obedience means well-being for Israel, and righteousness is right standing in God's sight.

Even David, and each king after him, would be subject to the legal process that originated with Mosaic Torah (cf. Deut. 17:18; 2 Sam. 7:14–16; 22:21–25; 1 Kings 11:33, 38). In fact, it was the duty of both king and people[9] to seek justice and righteousness in the society (cf. Deut. 11:26; 31:27–29; 32; Josh. 24:15–19; Ps. 72:1–2). Particularly in Isaiah, the future of David's city, Zion, would be subordinated to the righteousness of the entire Israel of God, yet unrealized (cf. Isa. 1:2; 2:5; 5:7; 33:5; 52:1; 56:1; 59:12–14).

Israel's election to servanthood is based in God's purpose for creation and the claims of covenant history, beginning with Abraham, and refocused in Mosaic Torah—apart from this matrix of revelation, its calling cannot be understood. Nevertheless, the selection and vocation of servant Israel is not a concern of the Pentateuch alone; it is also the special concern of the prophetic book of Isaiah. *According to Isaiah, Yahweh selected Israel to be a servant*, a harmony of witnesses to the uniqueness of Yahweh and a mediator in his plan for worldwide rule from Zion (cf. Isa. 43:10; 44:8; 46:10–11; 57:13). As a servant, Israel was chosen to bear the divine mission to the world. To fulfill this mission, however, servant Israel must display the very justice and righteousness of God (cf. 48:18–19).

The "Story" behind Isaiah

Isaiah 40:8 reads, "The grass withers, the flower fades, but the word of our God will stand forever."[10] Given this assertion, the reader of Isaiah can appreciate Yahweh's resolute intention to realize his plan for worldwide rule (cf. Isa. 45:23; 55:10ff.). Yahweh's word goes forth from his mouth; he will accomplish all that he purposes (cf. 55:11).

The epicenter of this global purpose is Mount Zion (2:2–4; cf. 11:9; 27:13; 57:13; 65:8–9), for "from Zion will go forth *torah* and the word of Yahweh [*dvar YHWH*] from Jerusalem" (2:3, trans. author). For the promulgation of Yahweh's *torah*, Zion will be exalted above all other mountains. It will be a universal dominion—the end-of-days establishment of the kingdom of God—characterized by justice, righteousness, and peace (cf. 1:27; 9:6ff.; 48:18; 52:7; 53:5, 11; 54:10, 13–14; 55:12; 56:1; 58:2; 59:8–9, 14; 60:17; 66:12). Many nations will see its glory and make their pilgrimage there.

---

9. Consider, at the height of the united monarchy, Solomon's repeated reference to the people of Israel as Yahweh's servants (1 Kings 8:23, 32, 36, 56–61).

10. All quotations of Scripture in this chapter are from the ESV, unless otherwise indicated.

Provocatively, perhaps, Isaiah 2:5 links the destiny of Israel to the destiny of these nations, and their joint futures are tethered to the fulfillment of this central vision concerning the kingdom of God and *torah*. Consequently, in verse 5, the prophet exhorts the house of Jacob to join the nations (*haggoyim*, v. 2) in their pilgrimage to hear Yahweh's *torah*. Rather than heeding this exhortation, however, and sharing the blessing, the house of Jacob has exchanged light for darkness. Rather than walk in Yahweh's light (*'or*, v. 5), Israel has rejected the word of the Holy One of Israel:

> Assuredly,
> as stubble is devoured by a tongue of fire,
> and a flame shrivels dried grass,
> their root will become as rot,
> and their blossoms will go up like dust;
> for they have rejected the *torah* of Yahweh of Hosts,
> and spurned the word [*'imrath*] of the Holy One of Israel.
> (5:24, trans. author)

The drama that unfolds in Isaiah is dark indeed. The realization of Yahweh's purpose would require Israel's hardening (6:9ff.; 63:17), yet Israel's persistent iniquity would only inflame his wrath, bringing the arm of Yahweh against the people (5:25). By the instrumentality of two alien powers, first Assyria and then Babylonia, Israel and Judah would experience Yahweh's powerful judgment through foreign oppression and loss of land.[11] The outlook for Judah and Jerusalem was bleak. But all things are possible with God.

We have seen that in Yahweh's universal plan for creation, Israel has a special office. Israel was born to reveal God's unique image and intention (Deut. 4:32–40; Isa. 43:10; 46:10–11), and the Pentateuch underscores the mediatorial role that Abraham and his offspring would have in Yahweh's universal design (cf. Gen. 12:1–3; Ex. 19:5–6). This relationship between Israel's particular purpose and Yahweh's universal goal raises significant questions for Isaiah's readers: will Yahweh still use Israel to realize his goal? If so, after the horrors of judgment, how will he save his people and renew

11. Even during the Persian phase of Israel's history, back in the land, the Jewish people would continue to experience foreign oppression (cf. Ezra 9:9; Neh. 9:36), with no apparent end to their distress (cf. Neh. 13).

them for the fulfillment of their distinct vocation? What is the nature of the true Israel of God?

The book of Isaiah includes a vision of Yahweh's coming to rule the world from Zion by his powerful Spirit and infallible Word. Isaiah 59:21 introduces a (new) covenant, a promise of renewal and a restoration that will be permanent (cf. Deut. 10:15–16; 30:6; Isa. 51:7; Jer. 31:33; Ezek. 33:26). Hereafter, his Spirit and his words will not depart from the people (cf. Num. 11:29; Joel 2:28–29), but will stand forevermore:

> "This is my covenant with them,"
>> says Yahweh:
> "My Spirit that is upon you [*'aleyka*, masc. sg.],
> and my words that I have put in your mouth,
> shall not depart out of your mouth,
>> or out of the mouths of your offspring [*zar'aka*, lit. "your seed"],
>> or out of the mouths of your children's offspring,"
>> says Yahweh,
> "from now on and forever." (Isa. 59:21, trans. author)

These offspring belong to the Servant (cf. 42:1; 50:4; 53:10–12). The preceding promise concerns the coming of a Redeemer (*go'el*) both to Zion and to those in Jacob who turn from transgression (59:20; cf. 53:12). Zion's Savior and Redeemer (cf. 60:16) is the Mighty One of Jacob. He is coming soon, and he looks to the one who "trembles [*kharedh*] at [his] word" (66:2).

In the total vision, then, it appears that both Zion's fundamental plight and its final destiny are tethered to the orientation of Yahweh's people to his powerful word.[12] Isaiah's vision concerns the restoration of Zion according to Yahweh's *torah* and the prophetic word. Israel must keep the way of Yahweh, and Zion must be peopled with servants who truly seek the Lord. Pertinently, Christopher Seitz comments, "God's *full and complete* redemption of Israel is contingent upon the display of justice and righteousness within Zion, however bracing may have been the earlier proclamation of God's will to save and deliver."[13] Therefore, only those whose repentance demonstrates

---

12. This link between the vocation of God's people and their orientation toward his word (i.e., *torah*) is also evident in Ezra-Nehemiah (cf. Ezra 3:2; 7:6, 10; 9:4; 10:3; Neh. 8:1, 14; 10:29; 13:3).

13. Christopher R. Seitz, *The Book of Isaiah 40–66*, NIB 6 (Nashville: Abingdon, 2001), 485 (emphasis in original).

loyalty to Yahweh's Word can expect to participate in the promised blessings of the coming kingdom.

THE SERVANT AND THE SERVANTS

The key figure in Zion's redemption is, of course, the Servant figure of Isaiah 40–53.[14] Indeed, many reflections on servanthood in Isaiah never reach the servants of chapters 54–66; they contemplate only the Servant's role in the so-called Servant Songs (42:1–4; 49:1–6; 50:4–9; 52:13–53:12; cf. 61:1–3).[15] Nevertheless, the story does not end with the work of the Servant in chapter 53, for the Servant's work both impacts and involves the servants in chapters 54–66. These chapters are concerned with Yahweh's coming to deliver the Servant's offspring, who will live forever after as servants of Yahweh (*'avdhe YHWH*) on their inheritance (*nakhalah*) in Zion (54:17).

The task associated with the Servant figure of chapters 40–55 is united via 59:21 (quoted above) to the central section of chapters 56–66 (chaps. 60–62), specifically the role of the prophetic herald of 61:1–3:

> The Spirit of the Lord GOD is upon me,
>   because the LORD has anointed me
>   to bring good news to the poor;
>   he has sent me to bind up the brokenhearted,
>   to proclaim liberty to the captives,

14. The Servant's task corresponds to that of the royal figure of Isaiah 9:1–7; 11:1–5; cf. 16:4–5; 32:1–5. He is to keep the way of Yahweh in order to produce a society whose worship and life will be characterized by justice, righteousness, and peace. See H. G. M. Williamson, *Variations on a Theme: King, Messiah and Servant in the Book of Isaiah* (Carlisle, UK: Paternoster, 1998).

15. This essay does not focus on the Servant's mediatorial role, but on the imitation of that pattern of servanthood to be reproduced in the ministry of the servants; therefore, entering into debates about the Servant's identity in these "Songs" exceeds its scope. In the context of Isaiah, the question whether the Servant's identity is collective (all/ideal Israel) or individual (an ideal/representative Israelite, a prophet, a second Moses, a royal figure) is of secondary importance to the evaluation of the Servant's *task*. Suffice it to say that the Songs move easily between national and personal Israel as the Servant of Yahweh. In chapters 40–48, the Servant is national Israel; in chapters 49–54, the Servant is a personal figure with a mission to Israel and the nations analogous to the prophetic profile of Moses or Jeremiah. What is more, his mission is a God-given, guilt-bearing vocation of vicarious suffering and glory that will enable Yahweh's salvation to extend to the ends of the earth (cf. Isa. 49:6; 52:13; 53:7, 10). See, e.g., P. Wilcox and D. Patton-Williams, "The Servant Songs in Deutero-Isaiah," *JSOT* 42 (1988): 79–102, and esp. J. Alan Groves, "Atonement in Isaiah 53," in *The Glory of the Atonement: Biblical, Historical, and Practical Perspectives. Essays in Honor of Roger Nicole*, ed. Charles E. Hill and Frank A. James III (Downers Grove, IL: InterVarsity Press, 2004), 61–89.

and the opening of the prison to those who are bound;
to proclaim the year of the LORD's favor,
  and the day of vengeance of our God;
to comfort all who mourn;
  to grant to those who mourn in Zion—
      to give them a beautiful headdress instead of ashes,
      the oil of gladness instead of mourning,
      the garment of praise instead of a faint spirit;
    that they may be called oaks of righteousness, the planting of
the LORD,
  that he may be glorified.

This herald is commissioned (that is, anointed and sent) by Israel's Redeemer to proclaim "good news" (*basser*) to the poor and brokenhearted (cf. Ps. 37:18; Isa. 41:17; 49:13; 51:19). His task, in part, is to announce the consolation of Israel and Zion (cf. Isa. 40:1ff.), to proclaim words of release and restoration (*dror* = "liberty," Isa. 61:1; cf. Lev. 25:10; Jer. 34:8) to listeners who, in their distress, are captives ("bound"; cf. Isa. 42:7; 49:5–6, 8–9) and mourners as regards the situation of God's people and Zion (cf. 57:15, 18; 60:20; 66:10).[16] Moreover, God has clothed him with garments of salvation (*yesha'*) and covered him with robes of righteousness (*tsdeqah*, 61:10; cf. 59:18–20). The time is the year of Yahweh's favor, the day of vengeance of our God (61:2); that is, the herald announces the transition to the age to come. Yet apparently, the Redeemer's coming has a dual aspect. On the one hand, he promises to bring about the righteousness his people must practice,

---

16. A straight read through the book suggests that the herald's message is addressed to God's people in the postexilic setting of incipient restoration (cf. Ezra-Nehemiah). Although actual incidents in OT history suggest a background (Ezra 9:9; Neh. 5:1–5; 9:34–36; 13; cf. Isa. 59:9–16; 66:1–5, and note 11 above), Isaiah 61 (56–66) appears to transcend them, given the vision's typological use of the Jubilee-release (Lev. 25) and its interconnectivity with prophecies regarding the Servant's role in exile and return. The vision is cast in the idiom of prophetic eschatology to depict, spiritually and metaphorically, Israel's eschatological release from captivity. On this point, see Christopher J. H. Wright, *Old Testament Ethics for the People of God* (Downers Grove, IL: InterVarsity Press, 2004), 206, 210. An underlying point of this idiom is that since Isaiah 39:8 or 48:22, *no progress* regarding the establishment of justice in the society was made (cf. 57:21; 66:24). John Goldingay explains, "The fact that there are no explicit historical references in these chapters draws our attention to the fact that this is an ongoing issue, not one confined to the particular moment in the sixth or fifth century B.C." (*Isaiah*, NIBC 13 [Peabody, MA: Hendrickson, 2001], 324). In fact, the iniquity in view here is the guilt and pollution that infects every evil age. Note, however, that the front line is now drawn internally; in the place of the instrumentality of an Assyria/Babylon, Yahweh's presence threatens Israel directly (cf. 59:18–20).

that they may be called "oaks of righteousness," planted by the Lord for his glory (61:3; cf. 6:13). On the other hand, he promises to protect and defend his people, for he is coming in vengeance against his (and their) enemies.[17] Thus the herald proclaims, and he is well equipped for his commission: God has put his powerful Spirit upon him (61:1; cf. 42:1), and he has God's own words in his mouth (cf. 50:4; 51:16).

Among his audience we may recognize the servants of Yahweh. In 59:21, God informed the Servant that he would give his offspring the same Spirit and words as the blessings of a new covenant. Hence, there exists a vital, divinely ordained, Servant-servants connection: *God promises by an everlasting covenant* (brith 'olam, cf. 55:3ff.; 61:8–9) *to give to the servants what also belongs to the Servant.* What is more, the connection established is bidirectional: not only do servants benefit *from* the Servant's work, they are a considerable benefit *of* that work. They are a fruit of the Servant's labors, his blessed progeny. Yahweh promises the Servant, "He shall see offspring" (*zera'*, "seed," 53:10–12), just as he had promised a multitude to Abraham (Gen. 17:2; cf. Isa. 51:2). By his work, then, the Servant secures *both* a blessed multitude for himself *and* the blessed Spirit for his offspring. This same endowment with the Spirit connects both the Servant with the prophetic herald and the servants with the herald's audience. Intratextual connections suggest that the servants who benefit from the Servant's work are also the listeners who benefit from the herald's ministry.[18]

As the special offspring of the Servant, these servants are personally bonded in solidarity to him and equipped for a servant's mission (cf. 45:25; 53:11–12; 65:23; 66:19–21). The blessing of the Spirit and the words they receive are benefits promised not only to them but also to their descendants after them. These benefits announced by the prophetic herald are new covenant blessings (61:8; cf. 59:21), just as God promised: "I will pour my Spirit upon your offspring, and my blessing on your descendants" (44:3;

---

17. The coming of the Redeemer (*go'el*) comforts the mourners not only because he is their Liberator, but also because he is their Blood-Avenger (cf. 61:2). On this point, see Bradley Gregory, "The Postexilic Exile in Third Isaiah: Isaiah 61:1–3 in Light of Second Temple Hermeneutics," *JBL* 126 (2007): 486. In this use of *go'el*, Gregory correctly recognizes another typological use of Pentateuchal legislation in Isaiah (cf. Num. 35; Deut. 19).

18. Willem Beuken writes, "What connects the commission of this speaker with that of the Servant, are the coordinating themes of being moved by God's spirit, good tidings and consolation, and ultimately the ascent of a righteous progeny" ("Servant and Herald of Good Tidings: Isaiah 61 as an Interpretation of Isaiah 40–55," in *The Book of Isaiah*, ed. J. Vermelyn, BETL 81 [Leuven, Belgium: Leuven University, 1989], 439).

cf. 32:15–17). Willem Beuken comments, " 'The prophet', by executing his mission, transmits his own features to the afflicted. He makes them and also their descendants into bearers of God's spirit. In this way God's new people, a people with progeny, comes into being."[19]

> Their offspring shall be known among the nations,
>> and their descendants in the midst of the peoples;
>> all who see them shall acknowledge them,
>>> that they are an offspring the LORD has blessed.
>>> (Isa. 61:9; cf. 65:23)

This vision for the servants is the subject matter, expressly, of Isaiah 54–66.

Isaiah 54–66 provides a portrait of servanthood as a total vision for discipleship and life in solidarity with the Servant. Therefore, in imitation of the Servant's life of suffering, servants are called to a vocation involving self-denial (cf. 58:1–12) and self-restraint (cf. 56:2, 4, 6; 58:13–14), humiliation and hardship (66:2, 5)—a self-sacrificing service to God. Consequently, the pattern of servanthood established by the Servant is basic to their existence as his blessed offspring. *In him they receive the spiritual dynamic necessary to fulfill their vocation, and their display of servanthood becomes the criterion of their identity as servants in solidarity with him.* Since, in Isaiah's vision, they also inherit his special vocation (paraphrased by Genesis 18:19), they are charged to "keep the way of Yahweh . . . so that Yahweh may bring about for Abraham what he has promised him." Put differently, they are the Servant's disciples (*limmudim*, 50:4; cf. 8:16, 20; 30:9–21; 53:11; 54:13) in whom the Pentateuchal purpose that commenced with Abraham (refocused in the mediatorial role of Moses) and advanced through the Davidic monarchy (cf. 2 Sam. 7; 22:24–25; Isa. 55:3) is renewed[20] in Isaiah's total vision for the realization of Yahweh's aim to exercise his sovereignty over a worldwide covenant community. These servants are the righteous ones who will inhabit the holy city, Zion. They will play a key role in the reestablishment of the community.

God's final aim in granting this salvation is to create a people for his own glory, united to the Servant, and equipped by his Spirit to dwell in

---

19. Ibid., 432.

20. As regards Isaiah 55:3, Seitz is correct: "That aspect of the Davidic covenant pertaining to David's role vis-à-vis the nations has been enlarged to encompass God's people at large. . . . What would be saying too much is that the promises associated with David have now ceased" (*Isaiah 40–66*, 482).

their inheritance forever. Thus, with the fulfillment in view, in accordance with their ministry, the mourners in Zion will be comforted (61:2–3), all her inhabitants will be righteous, and Zion will become a haven of rest (cf. 52:1; 66:24). There they will worship King Yahweh, reigning with him in the permanency and security of a glorious new creation (66:22).

But here, especially in Isaiah 54–66, we must recognize that the covenant established between God and Israel as a corporate people has implications for every person under it. "The emphasis on salvation remains in all its force," explains Seitz, "but it has been directed towards those within Jacob who are obedient to the prophetic word delivered from the Servant and 'his offspring.'"[21] Put differently, only those disciples whose turning from transgression demonstrates their solidarity with the righteous Servant are true servants of Yahweh (59:20; cf. 49:23; 57:13; 64:3; 65:16). Only they are the "Redeemed of the LORD" (62:12).

SERVANTHOOD—YAHWEH'S MEASURE

Recognizing this aspect of the covenant is not to suggest that Isaiah 54–66 introduces a radical individualism into Israel's history; undeniably, the character of servanthood in these chapters tells against this. Most telling, however, is the rendering of servanthood in intercessory prayer (63:7–64:12), resembling Abraham in Genesis 18:22–33 (cf. 20:7).

Of course, the prayer's ultimate concern is Israel's relation to God. It expresses the servants' intense corporate awareness[22] in loving intercession (cf. Isa. 66:5). First, the prayer recounts Israel's collective past in the redemption of the exodus vis-à-vis the mediation of the great prophet, Moses (63:7–14). On this basis, it conveys the servants' fervent desire for Yahweh to intervene in a new saving action for the entire house of Israel (63:7; cf. 63:17). Second, Isaiah 63:7–64:12 is a penitential prayer (cf. Neh. 9): because of Israel's rebellion, these servants (as Isaiah before them; cf. Isa. 6:5, 10–13) not only acknowledge their shared guilt and pollution with all Israel, but confess the righteousness of God's judgment on them. Isaiah 64:5–6 (cf. 5:24; 40:8) reads:

21. Ibid., 502.
22. This awareness is discernible throughout the prayer in the striking repetition of the first-person plural (cf. 63:7, 16–19; 64:5–9, 11–12). Nevertheless, the phrase "for the sake of your servants" in 63:17 suggests that it was offered by a representative of this community.

> You meet him who joyfully works righteousness,
>> those who remember you in your ways.
>>> Behold, you were angry,
>>>> and we sinned;
>>>>> in our sins we have been a long time,
>> and shall *we* be saved?
>>> We have all become like one who is unclean,
>>>> and all our righteous deeds are like a polluted garment.
>>> We all fade like a leaf,
>>>> and our iniquities, like the wind, take us away.

Consequently, the servants confess the collective iniquity of the Israelite people.

Notice also that the supplication rests on their *status* as Yahweh's servants. As such they cry to him, "Return for the sake of your servants" (63:17; cf. 37:35). Conceivably, this expression identifies the target of Yahweh's response as Israel's enemies—it does not yet imply a distinction within Israel. As regards this prayer, then, the servants confess their sin together with *all* Israel, broadly conceived. The sincerity of their confession is evident in their recognition that *Israel's consolation is found in neither Abraham nor Jacob* (63:16; cf. 64:5), *but only in their coming Redeemer*:

> For you are our Father,
>> though Abraham does not know us,
>> and Israel does not acknowledge us;
> you, O LORD, are our Father,
>> our Redeemer from of old is your name. (63:16)

As regards the servants, this prayer manifests their true poverty of spirit. In remembering Yahweh's great works, they humbly confess that their need is so great that he alone can meet it. But his promises are also great—and he alone can fulfill them!

Therefore, in faith, they retell the mighty works of their Redeemer (cf. 63:7–14): "From of old no one has heard or perceived by the ear, no eye has seen a God besides you, who acts for those who wait for him" (64:4). Thus, after recalling the climactic events of the exodus, they pray for a genuinely new thing to take place: "Behold, please look, we are all your people. . . . Will you

117

keep silent, and afflict us so terribly?" (64:9, 12). And so they hold fast to the covenant, persevering and trusting that once more the mountains will quake at Yahweh's presence and the nations will tremble at his word (64:1–2).

Their answer to prayer arrives in chapter 65. Here Israel is narrowed in terms of the distinction that Yahweh intends to effect. The Redeemer comes "for my servants' sake" (*lma'an 'avaday*, v. 8):

> Thus says the LORD:
>> "As the new wine is found in the cluster,
> and they say,
>>> 'Do not destroy it,
>>>> for there is a blessing in it,'
>>>> so I will do for my servants' sake,
>>> and not destroy them all."

Thus, the criterion of servanthood becomes the standard against which all Israel is measured.[23] In accordance with this measure, the Judge of all the earth will be vindicated.

This single verse, evoking earlier passages of Isaiah (cf. 1:9–10; 5:2–3; 27:2ff.), contains a significant allusion to Abraham's intercession for Sodom (cf. Gen. 6:12; 18:22–32; 19:15). Here the Judge of all the earth announces that he is coming as a Warrior (cf. Isa. 59:17–20; 63:1–6). But his opponent is Israel, against whom he will render selective judgment—righteous and unmediated. This judgment will divide the righteous and the wicked according to Isaiah's standard of servanthood, vindicating God's true servants in Zion (61:9). Accordingly, "[he will] not destroy them all" (*lvilti hashkhith hakkol*, 65:8; cf. *lo' 'ashkhith*, 3x in Gen. 18); he will deliver the blessing in it (= "my servants"). That is, recalling Isaiah 61:2, though favorably disposed to deliver his servants, God will come with vengeance upon his enemies, who are measured according to the criterion of servanthood (cf. 52:1; 60:12; 66:2, 5). This, then (according to Isaiah), is the unpardonable sin: his servants have interceded for all Israel, just as Abraham interceded for Sodom, but

---

23. The phrase "for David's sake," shorthand for God's covenant with David, recurs in the Deuteronomic history (cf. 1 Kings 11:13, 32; 2 Kings 8:19; 19:33–34; 20:6). David's faithfulness is the standard against which the kings of Judah were measured. I owe this insight to Al Groves, and I think it applies here to the servants. Just as God's requirement for the king reflects in principle his requirement for all Israel (Deut. 17:15, 18–20), so the Servant figure's loyalty to Yahweh plays a similar role (Isa. 55:3), and servanthood becomes the standard of measure for servant-disciples.

many in Israel have refused to acknowledge the Lord and follow the way of righteousness specified for his servants (cf. 65:1). Seitz is worth quoting at length:

> God effects a distinction the supplication was not urging. . . . The supplication *cannot* hold true: for those . . . who do not seek him, and who do not reckon God's glorification to involve the ones who, ironically, are making supplication on their behalf (66:5). The irony . . . is poignant and tragic. The Holy One cannot and will not hear the cries of those who have repudiated God and who have as well rejected the righteous ones who cry out on behalf of all Israel, including their opponents.[24]

Therefore, they who forsake his way, opposing his servants, are destined to the sword (65:12); the wicked will bear *both* their iniquities *and* their fathers' iniquities (v. 7; cf. 66:14–17, 24). But Yahweh promises to restore the fortunes of his beloved servants *and* their descendants (cf. 65:9–11):

> Behold, my servants shall eat,
> but you shall be hungry;
> behold, my servants shall drink,
> but you shall be thirsty;
> behold, my servants shall rejoice,
> but you shall be put to shame . . . (65:13)

Thus, there are two kinds of offspring within Israel: (1) the blessed servants, who seek Yahweh and walk in the way of servanthood, and (2) the idolatrous wicked, who seek their own way, and expose themselves as the brood of the adulterer and the sorceress (57:3). There is narrowing: Yahweh will restrict the Israel of God to the offspring of the Servant. Only those whose servanthood indicates their solidarity with the Servant can inhabit holy Zion.

By the same standard, there are only two kinds of people in the world: (1) the righteous Israel of God and (2) the unrighteous outsiders (cf. 66:24). Thus, Yahweh enables a broadening: provocatively, perhaps (cf. 2:5), 56:1–8 states that God does not show partiality to ethnic Israelites: even the foreigner and eunuch who adhere to covenant he calls "servants" (v. 6). Indeed, the range of righteous offspring includes all flesh (*khol basar*)

24. Seitz, *Isaiah 40–66*, 541.

who fulfill God's promises to Abraham as they extend the message of God's glory to the ends of the earth (cf. Isa. 2:1–4; 56:1–8; 57:13; 60:1–2, 3–4ff.; 66:18–19).

THE ESCHATOLOGICAL HORIZON OF ISAIAH'S TEACHING AND FULFILLMENT IN CHRIST

To appreciate the context of Isaiah's teaching on servanthood, one must appreciate the eschatological horizon of Isaiah 54–66:

> Say to the daughter of Zion,
>> "Behold, your salvation comes;
>>> behold, his reward is with him,
>>>> and his recompense before him." (62:11)

> "I create new heavens and a new earth,
>> and the former things shall not be remembered or come into mind."
>> (65:17; cf. 65:25; 66:22–23)

Isaiah foretells the transition to the age to come, in which new covenant blessings (59:21; cf. Jer. 31:31, 40; Ezek. 36:26), even Zion (Isa. 54:14–17), are given to servants on account of atonement made by the Servant (53:11–12).[25] Accordingly, these gifts are offered freely, without money or price (55:1–2). They are the blessings of new creation, the age of the Spirit.

Nevertheless, before time (cf. 60:21–22; Gal. 4:4), these servants are addressed in the imperative mood: "Keep justice [*mishpat*], and do righteousness [*tsdaqah*], for soon my salvation [*yshu'athi*] will come, and my deliverance [*tsidqathi*] be revealed" (Isa. 56:1). Blessed are they who do what he commands (v. 2), for his reward is with him (62:11). Nevertheless, we should not think that a moralistic program arises here, for God's righteousness means salvation for servants! Although for Isaiah's audience the fulfillment is future, their present acts of justice and righteousness express their faith in God's future saving action. They are good works produced by servants who enjoy solidarity with the Servant and wait for the full manifestation of Yahweh's kingdom. By faith, they say "Yes" to

---

25. On this point, see Groves, "Atonement."

Isaiah's vision and bear the name of the "God of Amen" (*be'lohe 'amen*, 65:16, trans. author).[26]

It should be stressed, then, that this is *not* a legalistic program. Autonomy (reliance on one's own strength) is pride and self-deception. But servants who rely on God are nourished by their eschatological belief; resting in him, they are (with Augustine) restless to do God's will.

The all-important thing, then, is faith's object. In terms of the transition in view, it is the coming of God's righteousness: "For the LORD has a day of vengeance, a year of recompense for the cause of Zion" (34:8). He is coming soon: to resist him is madness and death (66:24); to trust him is wisdom and life (57:13; 66:22–23). So in the face of God's imminent intrusion, turning from transgression does not encourage passivity. Turning from transgression encourages active faith in God; it means observing his ways and trembling at his word, until the structures of the old covenant and *torah* pass from symbol to reality with the coming of his eschatological reign. "For thus said the Lord GOD, the Holy One of Israel, 'In returning and rest you shall be saved; in quietness and in trust shall be your strength' " (Isa. 30:15).

Therefore, servants persevere, trusting that the word of the Amen will come to pass (cf. 2 Cor. 1:17–20; Rev. 3:14). For this reason, exhortations in Isaiah 54–66 keep a particular indicative situation in view—the eschatological horizon of definitive fulfillment. This future state of affairs provides the motivation for *torah*-keeping in the present period. Until the new age dawns (60:1ff.), servants await the fulfillment of *torah* and the prophetic word; thus, present exhortations are the key to understanding the indicative: *they bring to light the situation and vocation of servants committed to Isaiah's total vision.* Their faith in the near fulfillment of Yahweh's word is their reason for keeping covenant (56:1); their trembling at his word is the reason they are the esteemed (66:2); and their active faith and servanthood demonstrate hope in the arrival of his kingdom (cf. v. 5), whence they will have rest. Their exercise of justice and righteousness, then, is appropriate to their faithful preparation for that day (cf. Matt. 3:8–10).

This vision, originally cast for an early postexilic audience,[27] acquires its full realization, stability, and permanency in the coming of the kingdom and

---

26. For a defense of this translation, see Joseph Blenkinsopp, *Isaiah 56–66*, AB 19B (New York: Doubleday, 2003), 282.

27. On the line of Israel's history, the reforms of Ezra-Nehemiah are a partial (sub-eschatological) realization of this vision, continuing the provisional, though legitimately organized, political and social community of Israel under Mosaic Torah. Yet as a provisional fulfillment, Ezra-Nehemiah

the outpoured Spirit: Jesus is the Servant of the Lord whose mediatorial role inaugurated the eschatological fulfillment of Isaiah's vision. By faith-union with him, servants follow his pattern of Servant-ministry in their ongoing ministry of reconciliation (2 Cor. 5:17–21; cf. Isa. 49:8–13; 65:17; Matt. 5–7; 28:18–20). *From Pentecost to the consummation of the age, this Isaianic vision is fulfilled in the active faith and servanthood of Jesus' disciples.* Consequently, the power to fulfill their calling comes from the redemptive accomplishment of Jesus' messianic suffering and glory, including Pentecost.[28] He is True Israel; in him, servants demonstrate that they are his mother, brothers, and sisters (Matt. 12:49–50). Like him, they do the will of their Father in heaven (cf. John 3:36; 15:10); in him, their good works are eschatological works (cf. Eph. 2:10; Phil. 2:13).

THE CHARACTER OF SERVANTHOOD

We are now positioned to survey the character of servanthood. And given our post-resurrection vantage point, we can now appreciate its character more fully; our outlook is transformed by the new covenant realities inaugurated by Jesus Christ. The Servant of the Lord is come, and in his obedient suffering unto death, he has set the pattern once and for all. In imitation of *this Servant*, servanthood continues to observe God's way, according to his word (cf. Isa. 55:8; 56:11; 65:2; 66:4, 18). According to his pattern, the exhortations reflected throughout chapters 54–66, summarized by the demand to keep covenant, are grounded on the realities that transpired in the coming of the Son and of the Holy Spirit. In union with him, servants enjoy his benefits; thus, servanthood is evidence of *whose servants they are*. Simply put, Jesus' disciples obey his commands (John 14:21). To "serve" in any other way is a contradiction of their union with Christ and identity as children of God; it is disloyalty, an imitation of the children of transgression and deceit (Isa. 58:4; cf. 1 John 2:6, 19).[29]

---

also indicates that the vision stands unfulfilled. See J. G. McConville, "Ezra-Nehemiah and the Fulfillment of Prophecy," *VT* 36 (1986): 205–24.

28. Even before Pentecost, God's Spirit was the dynamic empowering the faith and life of his servants; only he was not present then with the permanency and fullness with which he is present for Christians now, after the inauguration of the new (eschatological) age. On this point, see Richard B. Gaffin Jr., "Pentecost: Before and After," at http://www.kerux.com/documents/KeruxV10N2A1.asp.

29. These unrighteous offspring are contrasted with the servants throughout Isaiah 56–66. They are ignorant, blind, complacent, slothful, greedy, self-absorbed, and debauched children.

To illustrate, consider the Sabbath command (Isa. 56:2, 4, 6; 58:13–14). Here, "Sabbath-keeping" is shorthand for "covenant-keeping" (56:4; Ex. 31:16); it delights to glorify God and requires self-restraint. Yet, given the eschatological perspective of these chapters, by observing the Sabbath, the servants demonstrate their desire for eschatological rest (cf. Heb. 4:9). Therefore, grounded in the former creation (Ex. 20:8–11) and exodus (Deut. 5:12–15), Sabbath-keeping manifests their faith in new exodus and new creation. It displays their trust in God's word, and their identity as his servants (cf. James 2:17–18).

Next, consider fasting (Isa. 58:1–12). It does not seek its own pleasure; rather, it imitates the love and self-denial of the Servant who loosed the bonds of wickedness, freed the oppressed, shared bread with the hungry, and covered the naked (58:6–7; cf. 61:1–3). In this way, fasting follows the costly pattern of servanthood set by Christ; it is *his* pattern of self-sacrificing service to others. Thus, true disciples reflect his character, overflowing in care for the world (cf. Matt. 5:43–48; John 3:16).

JESUS' "MOTHER AND BROTHERS"

Christians know that Jesus came to serve (Mark 10:45); indeed, his whole earthly life was characterized by servanthood. But he did not come merely to serve the world; rather, he came to redeem a people for the supreme interests and glory of his heavenly Father (John 3:16; cf. Matt. 6:10; 26:39; Phil. 2:7–11). And so it must be for Christians: even in their suffering (cf. Rom. 8:17; 1 Peter 4:16ff.), they must follow his example—they must live for the glory of God. To this end, he has poured forth the blessed Spirit.

The humble Servant-King, now exalted, has inaugurated the new age (2 Cor. 5:17). In him, God's original intentions for image-bearing servants stand secure. This is good news! Yet his kingdom is not of this world, and his servants must not be like the rulers of this age (Mark 10:43; 1 Peter 5:5). As his ambassadors, they follow his pattern of servanthood in their ongoing ministry of his reconciliation, characterized by justice and righteousness, self-sacrifice and suffering.

They put themselves before God's way, pursuing drunkenness and gluttony, and following their own desires in such pagan practices as child sacrifice and cult prostitution. Their leaders, too, are selfish shepherds who put themselves before the care of God's people. Even their worship of Yahweh is false, self-serving, and manipulative (cf. 58:1–14).

Jesus has shown us the way (John 14:6), and he intercedes for us still (Heb. 8:1). In union with him, the Spirit and the gifts are ours (1 Cor. 12:4–6; Gal. 5:22), and he will come again for his elect, who are marked by repentant faith. So persevere, zealously seeking the things above, where Christ is (Col. 3:2), and abide in him (John 15:5; 1 John 4:13; Gal. 5:16–18). For in his fellowship, we are no longer servants (cf. John 15:13–15)—*we are friends*!

9

Israel's *Via Dolorosa*: Toward an Appreciation of Lamentations as Scripture

BRADLEY C. GREGORY

DURING HIS LECTURES at Westminster Seminary, Al Groves would sometimes encourage his students to ask the following question about a passage in the OT: If this passage were missing from the Bible, what would the church lack as a result? When it comes to the book of Lamentations, many of us might be tempted to answer: Not much.

Although few Christians would be interested in formally removing the book of Lamentations from the canon of Scripture, it has all too often been functionally sidelined in the practice of the Christian faith. It is difficult to find a sermon on Lamentations, and if not for the hymn "Great Is Thy Faithfulness," most Christians would be totally unfamiliar with the book. And there are some good reasons for this. It is a dark and gloomy book, filled with the horrors of a brutal siege and reminders of God's wrath toward his people. What spiritual benefit is there in contemplating mothers so desperate that they boil their own children for food (Lam. 4:10)? In comparing Lamentations with the uplifting passages of the Gospels and Epistles, it is easy to see why Christians who have read this little book so often choose not to make a return trip to it.

Historically, this attitude toward Lamentations is not new. In the life of the early church, it rarely came in for comment—and then only as part of the larger Jeremiah material. In fact, the only extant commentary on Lamentations from the patristic period is the very short one by Theodoret of Cyrus. The main use of Lamentations during this time came from a Christological reading of Lamentations 4:20, which was widely held to be a prophecy of the passion of Christ (since the fathers held that Jeremiah had written Lamentations, it was read as a prophetic text). Although excerpts of the book were treated in some works, such as Gregory the Great's *Moralia in Job*, and there were a few medieval commentaries, it was not until the Reformation, with its emphasis on *sola Scriptura*, that Lamentations was regularly commented on.

It is clear, then, that for most of the church's history, Lamentations has played a very limited role, even though it has always been held to be the Word of God. This observation is even more striking when one considers that in Judaism the book of Lamentations has had a much larger impact. In addition to being the subject of major exegetical works such as the Targum to Lamentations and *Lamentations Rabbah*, it also serves as one of the five books associated with the annual holiday cycle. The book of Lamentations is the main text to be read and considered for the fast of the Ninth of Av, which commemorates the destruction of the Solomonic temple in 586 BC (the historical event being mourned in Lamentations) and the destruction of the Herodian temple in AD 70.

The reasons behind the prominence of Lamentations in Judaism are complex, but the central thing to note is that with the fall of the second temple and the ensuing transition to rabbinic Judaism, Jews understood themselves to be a people living in exile, awaiting the future redemption of Israel by God. Because the concept of "exile" functioned as a way of understanding their current situation, there was an obvious analogy between their own lives and those who had lived in Babylon following the destruction of the Solomonic temple. Because Lamentations was written in the wake of the fall of the temple and the Babylonian exile, it was readily adaptable into the theological framework of rabbinic Judaism. The upshot of this phenomenon is that the exilic experience of suffering and the longing for redemption became theologically incorporated into the self-understanding of Judaism.

While Christians will obviously part ways with Judaism on certain aspects of interpretation, the idea that we are in some sense still in exile awaiting the final restoration by God is a theological idea that the church needs to recover for herself in how she understands her life between the first and second advents of Christ. Along these lines, the rest of this essay will try to unpack the implications of the fact that Lamentations is part of the Bible and how it relates to the gospel.

In order to begin comprehending the theological value of this book, we must understand up front that distilling a theology of Lamentations from a text that is so raw and even bewildering in its expression of suffering has proved to be a difficult task for scholars. There have been numerous proposals for how best to understand Lamentations, especially in relationship to the rest of the Bible, but for the most part there has been no consensus on a "central theme" to the book. The reason for this is that Lamentations is wholly unlike a treatise, such as Paul's Epistle to the Romans, and thus it resists attempts to systematize its theological discourse as though it were. Additionally, most scholars point out that Lamentations seems to have an "internal dialogue" as it attempts to come to grips with the tragedy of Jerusalem's fall, but noticeably absent from this dialogue are any statements by God himself, who remains agonizingly silent throughout. Those who have experienced their own deep suffering through loss or pain can immediately understand how misguided it would be to bypass their coping process with simple theological statements, for all kinds of thoughts race through their heads as they oscillate back and forth, struggling to understand God's providence (and even his silence), their own contributions (if any) to their suffering, and so forth.

Lamentations is the biblical window into the national grieving process of Israel, which, although confusing at times to the reader, is utterly realistic in this regard. Nevertheless, in its wrestling with the profundity of suffering during the destruction of Jerusalem, Lamentations does embody theological dialogues not just within itself but also, at least at the canonical level, with other biblical writings—and these dialogues are the key to understanding the contribution of Lamentations to the gospel and the rest of Scripture.

Before returning to the theology of Lamentations, we will begin unpacking its scriptural significance by surveying three ancient strategies for recontextualizing this little book in broader biblical-theological themes: the Deuteronomic-Jeremianic, the Isaianic, and the liturgical.

LAMENTATIONS AS PROPHETIC REQUIEM

The first strategy for understanding Lamentations is suggested by the Greek translation of the OT, known as the Septuagint (LXX).[1] For our purposes, the LXX of Lamentations has two striking features. First, the book is placed directly after the book of Jeremiah (as in our English Bibles today). Second, the translator prefaces the book with this statement: "And after Israel was taken into exile and Jerusalem was laid waste, Jeremiah sat down weeping and composed this lament over Jerusalem." Whereas the Hebrew version of the book neither identifies the author nor places it with the prophetic books (rather, it is placed among the Writings),[2] the Greek bears testimony that some early interpreters thought the book should be interpreted in relationship to the prophetic literature, and especially Jeremiah. Although seemingly a small thing, this has important implications for interpretation.

From this angle, the main theological themes present in Jeremiah and some of the other Prophets become highlighted in the reading of Lamentations. Foremost among these is the theme of sin and judgment as found in the book of Deuteronomy. Over and over again, Deuteronomy and prophetic books such as Amos and Jeremiah warn that if Israel continues to sin, God will send her into exile. For example, Deuteronomy 4:25, 27 says, "If you then become corrupt and make any kind of idol, doing evil in the eyes of the LORD your God and provoking him to anger, . . . the LORD will scatter you among the peoples, and only a few of you will survive among the nations to which the LORD will drive you."[3] Blessings follow from obedience, but the curse of exile and death follows from disobedience.

Jeremiah, who was heavily influenced by Deuteronomy, gives similar warnings about the consequences of disobedience, and he often characterizes Israel's unfaithfulness in terms of adultery or harlotry (see Jer. 1–4). The metaphor is quite understandable, since idolatry is the lavishing of intimate worship on a foreign god, when Israel is in covenant with the God

1. Lamentations was translated sometime during the two centuries before Jesus. See Karen H. Jobes and Moisés Silva, *Invitation to the Septuagint* (Grand Rapids: Baker Academic, 2000), 34.

2. The Hebrew OT is divided into three sections: the Torah, the Prophets, and the Writings. The Prophets include not only the prophetic books but also Joshua, Judges, Samuel, and Kings. The Writings include the remaining OT books: Psalms, Job, Proverbs, Ruth, Song, Ecclesiastes, Lamentations, Esther, Daniel, Ezra, Nehemiah, and Chronicles.

3. All quotations of Scripture in this chapter are from the NIV.

of Israel. Important in this regard is the imagery used in Jeremiah 13:19–27. After prophesying that Judah will be exiled for her sins, Jeremiah says that her skirts will be torn off and she will be sexually abused (v. 22). He goes on in verses 24–27 to deliver a threat from God that includes this promise: "Because you have forgotten me and trusted in false gods, I will pull up your skirts over your face that your shame may be seen—your adulteries and lustful neighings, your shameless prostitution!"

When one comes to the book of Lamentations with this Deuteronomic-Jeremianic lens in mind, one easily sees a number of correspondences. Foremost, Israel's sins are presented as the reason for the calamity (Lam. 1:5, 8, 14, 18, 22; 2:14; 3:39, 42; 4:13; 5:7, 16). In addition, throughout the book there are connections to the covenant curses in Deuteronomy 28, where God detailed the horrors that would come upon Israel if she broke the covenant (see Lam. 1:3, 5, 9; 2:20; 3:45; 4:10, 16; 5:12). Lamentations even states that what has happened is a fulfillment of God's word that he decreed long ago (2:17). Finally, the prophetic use of the metaphor of the unfaithful woman for covenant disobedience finds vivid correspondence in Lamentations. Jerusalem is personified as "Daughter of Zion" and is pictured as a shamed, abused woman. In imagery similar to that in Jeremiah 13, Zion is portrayed as naked, exposed, sexually violated, and impure (Lam. 1:8–9, 17). Therefore, throughout the fabric of Lamentations are interwoven connections to the Deuteronomic-Jeremianic idea that the exile and destruction of Israel, and especially Jerusalem, result directly from Israel's sin.

From this vantage point, then, Lamentations functions as a disheartening confirmation of the prophetic warnings. This perspective is the dominant one found in many commentaries both ancient and modern. Because most of those in the early church worked from the LXX of the OT, it is not surprising that the sin/judgment perspective is frequently employed. For example, Theodoret of Cyrus repeatedly connects the tragedy reflected in Lamentations with the warnings from Deuteronomy as well as the Prophets. He makes the theological point that God gave the Israelites fair warning, so the fall of Jerusalem was both just and to be expected. From this point naturally flows the homiletic conclusion that sin will not go unpunished and that repentance is urgent.[4]

4. The clearest modern example of this approach is in F. B. Huey Jr., *Jeremiah, Lamentations,* NAC 16 (Nashville: Broadman Press), 446–47.

But although the linking of Jerusalem's fall with Israel's sin (an unusual feature of ancient Near Eastern city laments) is an important component in Lamentations, the book presents a more subtle and complicated view. While Theodoret is emphatic throughout his interpretation that the judgment was equitable considering Israel's sin, recent interpreters are increasingly pointing out that Lamentations presents a mixed picture. Through a sophisticated use of imagery, the poet seeks to elicit sympathy and compassion for Zion.[5] For example, in chapter 1, Daughter of Zion is presented both as a harlot and as a rape victim. In fact, there is an imbalance in both the quantity and the quality of the descriptions such that the descriptions of Zion's suffering far outweigh the affirmations of her sin, which is mentioned in only the most generic of terms.

Along a similar line, in a number of places in Lamentations the poet seems to question the equity of the punishment. It is not so much that God is charged with injustice, but that once one goes beyond the corporate level of the punishment, the distribution of suffering does not correspond well to the guilt of individual parties. There are frequent references to the suffering of children and infants as well as the implication that those who are gloating over Jerusalem's destruction are no less guilty than Israel. Barry Webb captures it well: "[Lamentations is] as much about the *experience* of suffering as about its causes, and the element of protest running through them shows a struggle between heart and head, between theological acceptance and moral outrage. At one level the divine anger is acknowledged to be right. But at another it remains simply unendurable."[6] For this reason, the Deuteronomic-Jeremianic lens, which views Lamentations as reflecting the fatal consequences of sin, is both important and helpful but is not totally sufficient for an appreciation of Lamentations' contribution to biblical theology. The book is a sort of prophetic requiem—but it is also more than that, for the death of Israel is not the end of the story.

5. The most sensitive readings in this regard are the commentaries of Adele Berlin, *Lamentations: A Commentary*, OTL (Louisville: Westminster John Knox, 2002); F. W. Dobbs-Allsopp, *Lamentations*, Interpretation (Louisville: Westminster John Knox, 2002); and Kathleen O'Connor, "Lamentations," NIB (Nashville: Abingdon Press, 2001), 1011–72. Also see Elizabeth Boase, *The Fulfilment of Doom? The Dialogic Interaction between the Book of Lamentations and the Pre-Exilic/Early Exilic Prophetic Literature*, LHBOTS 437 (London: T&T Clark, 2006).

6. Barry G. Webb, *Five Festal Garments: Christian Reflections on The Song of Songs, Ruth, Lamentations, Ecclesiastes and Esther*, NSBT 10 (Downers Grove, IL: InterVarsity Press, 2000), 78. Also note Isaiah 40:2 in this regard (see below).

LAMENTATIONS AS REDEMPTIVE-HISTORICAL HINGE

A second lens that has proved helpful is that of reading Lamentations alongside the book of Isaiah. This approach can best be seen in the lectionary system of early Judaism, in which the reading of Lamentations is preceded by the reading of Isaiah 1:1–27 and followed by seven passages of consolation selected from chapters 40–63. But the connections with Isaiah have been developed by contemporary scholars as well.

As the rabbis noticed, the similarities in both language and themes between Isaiah and Lamentations are numerous enough as to be more than mere coincidence. Rather, the two books seem intended to be read in light of each other. In some cases they share nearly identical phrases. For example, Isaiah 52:11 and Lamentations 4:15 both contain similar references to turning away and to avoiding touching anything impure. In fact, there are at least thirty of these connections between Lamentations and Isaiah, especially chapters 49–55 (which address the situation of the restoration from exile).[7] But more importantly, the connections in phraseology are part of a larger thematic connection between the two books concerning the story of Zion and the Suffering Servant.

As mentioned above, in Lamentations Zion is pictured as a mourning woman who is like both a widow (1:1) and a mother bereaved of her children (1:5). She is afflicted, abandoned, desolate, and empty both of God's people and of her former glory. Five times in the first chapter it is repeated that there is no one to comfort Zion despite her pleas (1:2, 9, 16–17, 21; cf. 2:13).[8]

While Zion is the main character for most of Lamentations, however, in chapter 3 the main character switches to a suffering man. A careful reading of Lamentations reveals that there is a close relationship between the experiences of this singular man and of Zion. Both cry out for help or consolation; both dwell in darkness; both are desolate and bitter; both are a laughingstock; both feel hunted by God; but both also petition God and confess their sins. Yet the struggle of this man in Lamentations 3 has an

7. See the catalogue in Norman Gottwald, *Studies in the Book of Lamentations*, SBT 14 (London: SCM Press, 1954), 44–45.

8. Another important aspect of Lamentations' portrayal of Zion is that it reverses descriptions of Zion found in Psalms 46–48. The contrast between Zion in the Psalter and in Lamentations is an important component, but space does not permit an exploration of it here. See J. Andrew Dearman, *Jeremiah/Lamentations*, NIVAC (Grand Rapids: Zondervan, 2002), 452–53; Sheri L. Klouda, "Zion," in *Dictionary of the Old Testament: Wisdom, Poetry, and Writings*, ed. Tremper Longman III and Peter Enns (Downers Grove, IL: InterVarsity Press, 2008), 938–43.

added component: slivers of hope begin to intrude into his pain (vv. 21–23). Although it would be a mistake to overemphasize this element in order to blunt the uncomfortable pictures of agony that surround it, it is nevertheless true that the poet does begin to move out from his pain to affirm a hopeful future. In addition to the similarities between the experience of this man and those of the community of Zion, he also seems to represent the larger community in some way. Remarkably, through the first twenty-one verses he always uses "I," "me," and "my" and pictures himself as both afflicted by God and mocked by his own people. But at the beginning of the confession of hope, a change occurs. Now he begins speaking of "we" and "us" both in the confession of hope and in the subsequent verses where he both acknowledges their sin and calls on his people to repent and turn to the Lord.

In Isaiah there is a similar dynamic between Zion and the Suffering Servant. Whereas Zion is judged for her sin early in the book (Isaiah 1–5), chapters 40–55 concern the restoration of Zion. Just as Zion's plea for comfort was a dominant theme of Lamentations 1, Isaiah 40 begins with: "Comfort, comfort my people, says your God. Speak tenderly to Jerusalem, and proclaim to her that her hard service has been completed, that her sin has been paid for, that she has received from the LORD's hand double for all her sins" (Isa. 40:1–2). This theme of comfort will continue through the rest of the book. In Lamentations 5:20 Zion questions why she has been abandoned, but in Isaiah 49:14–15 God responds: "But Zion said, 'The LORD has forsaken me, the Lord has forgotten me.' 'Can a mother forget the baby at her breast and have no compassion on the child she has borne? Though she may forget, I will not forget you!' " Although Lamentations mourns the loss of her children, Isaiah 49:17–21 promises that she will have so many children that they will complain of being cramped. All the precious things that were lost in the exile (Lam. 1:7) will come flowing back into her (Isa. 60–62).

Likewise, when one considers the Suffering Servant, there are parallels as well. In Isaiah there are some indications that the Servant is Israel (41:8; 44:1–2, 21; 45:4; 48:20), but there are other indications that the Servant is someone who is part of Israel and has a mission to Israel (Isa. 49:1–6; cf. 42:1–7; 50:4–9; 52:13–53:12; 61:1–3). It is noteworthy that Isaiah 50:4–9 and 52:13–53:12 contain several connections to Lamentations 3, especially verses 25–30. In both, the Servants are silent while being afflicted by God and offer their cheeks to be struck (a phrase that appears in the OT in only these two places). Both are mocked and rejected by others and are the victims of

132

injustice. Both men go into darkness and plead with the Lord to vindicate them. Both intercede for their fellow Israelites, but whereas the speaker in Lamentations had included himself in Israel's guilt (3:42), the Servant in Isaiah is described as someone who has not rebelled (50:5; 53:9–12) and his bearing the sins of others is more pronounced (53:5–12). Finally, just as the man in Lamentations is inclined toward hope in God's future mercy and restoration, so the Suffering Servant of Isaiah will be exalted (52:13–15) and experience restoration (53:10–12).

One could multiply connections almost endlessly, but the point to be considered here is that the death and destruction of Zion pictured in Lamentations is not the end of the story when read in light of Isaiah. Rather, it is only a hinge in the story. Out of judgment and death will spring new life. In fact, Ezekiel is even more vivid. He describes the effect of the exile on Israel not just as a death, but as a desolation so complete that there are only dry bones with absolutely no life in them. But when the word of the Lord comes upon them, a miraculous resurrection occurs (Ezek. 37). Because of God's covenant with his people, the death of Israel must give way to the resurrection of Israel. In addition, reading Lamentations alongside of Isaiah suggests that the suffering man in Lamentations 3 and the Suffering Servant in Isaiah are in some way connected. This figure is ambiguous insofar as he is in some sense the embodiment of Israel and in another sense a representative person within Israel who suffers on behalf of Israel. The suffering, death, and restoration of this mysterious Servant, then, is deeply bound up with the destiny of Israel as God's people.

This Isaianic perspective on Lamentations, of course, builds on the Deuteronomic-Jeremianic perspective, which saw in Lamentations the fatal consequences of sin. It does so by fleshing out what was already latent there because the Deuteronomic-Jeremianic understanding of God as sovereign over the events of the destruction and exile implies that God is also able to restore, something promised in Deuteronomy itself (see 4:30–31; 30:1–10). Likewise, just as the prophetic predictions of destruction came true, so one can trust their predictions of restoration as well. Therefore, by layering the Isaianic perspective on top of the Deuteronomic-Jeremianic perspective, we come to a fuller understanding of the role of Lamentations in a biblical theology.

Yet these two lenses for reading Lamentations still do not exhaust the book's canonical significance. In this regard, it is important to note that

Lamentations is not rendered dispensable once one arrives at the larger narratives concerning Israel and Zion in the Prophets. The situating of Lamentations within a conversation with Deuteronomy, Jeremiah, and Isaiah cannot be allowed to detract from the expressive power of Lamentations by absorbing it into these larger prophetic understandings, however helpful they might be. As Adele Berlin says, "the book is not an explanation of suffering but a re-creation of it and a commemoration of it."[9] It is not as though we can simply leave Lamentations aside once we have made these larger biblical-theological connections. It does not just play a supporting role for other biblical books, but has a voice of its own alongside these other books—and this point leads us to the final lens we will consider.

LAMENTATIONS AS LIVING LITURGY

Up until this point we have not made much of the fact that Lamentations is poetry intended to be recited by the worshiping community. But this aspect is reflected in the location of Lamentations in the Hebrew arrangement of the Bible, where it is placed not among the Prophets but among the Writings. This ordering of the books reflects the fact that Lamentations is read as part of the liturgical cycle in Judaism. It is one of five books known as the *Megillot* (Song of Songs, Ruth, Lamentations, Ecclesiastes, and Esther) that are still read annually at the five major festivals in the Jewish calendar (respectively, Passover, Pentecost, Ninth of Av, Tabernacles, and Purim).

In some Christian lectionaries, Lamentations is featured once a year, on Holy Saturday. Just as this book is read on the most significant fast day in Judaism, it is read on the "darkest" day of the Christian calendar, the day between Good Friday and Easter when Jesus was dead but not yet resurrected. In other words, the liturgical understanding of Lamentations reflected in the Hebrew arrangement gives striking testimony to an understanding of Lamentations as having ongoing significance in the life and worship of God's people. Although the historical event of Jerusalem's destruction has passed, the mourning voices in Lamentations continue to have relevance because of the book's status as sacred Scripture.

Despite the role of Lamentations in Christian lectionaries, however, the church has in general done a poorer job than the synagogue in appropriating the book into its self-understanding as an exiled and suffering community.

---

9. Berlin, *Lamentations*, 18.

While the circumstances in late antiquity (notably the destruction of the temple in AD 70 and the eventual rise of the Christian empire) contributed greatly to this neglect, a deeper understanding of the theological relationship between Lamentations and the gospel should help Christians to reclaim this book as having spiritual significance in their own lives and in the life of the church.

LAMENTATIONS AND THE GOSPEL

At first glance, the contribution of Lamentations to the NT appears to be meager, since there are no actual quotations and only one allusion. In Matthew 5:39 Jesus evokes the image of the suffering man being struck on the cheek in Isaiah 50:6 and Lamentations 3:30 as an exhortation to abstain from revenge.[10] But a number of deep connections can be made between Lamentations and the gospel when considered from the three wider biblical-theological themes explored above.

First, we noted in reading Lamentations alongside Jeremiah that one prominent theme is that the destruction of Jerusalem came as a result of sin. The city, including the temple, was destroyed because of the people's rebellion, and so God, true to his word, brought judgment on them. Likewise, throughout the NT we are told that Jesus' death was to pay for sin (e.g., Rom. 6:10; 1 John 1:7). And yet there is a deeper connection. The destruction of the temple in 586 BC becomes a picture of Jesus' death insofar as Jesus' body is understood to be a new temple and the crucifixion to be the destruction of that temple (John 2:18–21; cf. the lectionary reading above). Along this line of thought, a contemplation of the book of Lamentations does not just give us an appreciation for the agony of the people at the time, or even the horrors of warfare in general, but also provides an analogy for understanding the passion of Jesus, who also experienced a rupture in his relationship with the Father in his death on the cross (cf. Mark 15:34). In addition, in our discussion of this Deuteronomic-Jeremianic perspective we noted that Lamentations complicated the prophetic picture by accenting the tension between the justice of the destruction because of the people's sin and also

---

10. Other NT passages contain elements that are found in Lamentations but also in other parts of the OT such that it would be difficult to know that Lamentations was the specific text in mind. Cf. Lam. 1:15 and Rev. 14:19; Lam. 2:1 and Matt. 5:35; Lam. 2:15 and Matt. 27:39; Lam. 3:15 and Acts 8:23; and Lam. 4:2 and 2 Cor. 4:7.

the way that some innocents were suffering because of the sins of others. Although not exactly analogous, the death of Jesus is both an injustice, insofar as he suffered despite being innocent of any wrongdoing, and at a deeper level a making of satisfaction for God's justice.

The second lens viewed Lamentations in relation to Isaiah and found the suffering expressed there to be part of a redemptive-historical hinge. Here we noted that the suffering of Zion and the Servant was not the end of the story but instead was a prelude to eventual restoration. In fact, the exilic prophets such as Ezekiel vividly portrayed this exile and restoration as a *death and resurrection of Israel*. We also saw that the Suffering Servant was mysterious because he seemed to embody Israel but also to be an individual within Israel with a ministry to Israel. In the person of Jesus, we can see these prophetic conceptions converge and find their resolution. On the one hand, Jesus was a Jew who understood himself to have a ministry to Israel proclaiming restoration and the kingdom of God. But on the other hand, Jesus himself embodied Israel, and he lived out Israel's story in miniature. Israel had been called God's "firstborn son" (Ex. 4:22), had come out of Egypt, had gone through the wilderness, had lived in the land, had been exiled, and was still awaiting restoration. Likewise, the Gospel writers, especially Matthew, are at pains to show that Jesus is the firstborn Son of the Father, who was called out of Egypt, overcame temptation in the wilderness, engaged in ministry in the land of Israel, then died, spent three days in the grave, and was finally resurrected on the third day.[11] From this angle, then, the passion and death of Jesus connect not just to the destruction of the temple, but to the "death of Israel" that occurred with the fall of Jerusalem and subsequent exile. In this way, the anguished voices of Lamentations resonate with Jesus' cry on the cross, "My God, my God, why have you forsaken me?" (Mark 15:34). Jesus' *Via Dolorosa* recapitulates Israel's *Via Dolorosa*.

In coming to the third lens, that of the liturgical use of Lamentations, we observed that an appreciation for how Lamentations fits into these biblical-theological themes does not exhaust its relevance. It is not as though, having made these connections, one can then leave the book of Lamentations aside, because as Scripture it continues to give a voice to suffering and anguish. The same could be said of the themes in the book that point toward the person of Christ. Understanding their relationship to the life, death, and resurrec-

---

11. For a fuller treatment see N. T. Wright, *Jesus and the Victory of God* (Minneapolis: Fortress, 1996), esp. 198–368, 540–611.

tion of Jesus becomes the foundation for the church's use of the book. On the one hand, the book finds its fulfillment in the passion of Jesus, and the church looks back with gratitude and worship. On the other hand, it has continuing relevance because God's work of redemption in the world is not yet complete. We live between the first and second advents of Christ, and this means that as members of the body of Christ we, too, will have to take up our crosses. Sometimes suffering will come as the consequences of our own sins. Other times it will come as a result of the sins of others. And still other times it will come from the brokenness of a creation that still groans for its redemption (Rom. 8:22–23).

It is the bewildering complexity of suffering in a fallen world, a complexity that resists simple theological models, that finds ultimate expression in the book of Lamentations. The simple *expression* of suffering apart from attempts at wholly adequate theological explanations is canonically validated as a constitutive aspect of the church's ongoing life. The church must learn to see her own life as one that exists between the beginnings of restoration in the first advent and the aspects of exile that continue until the second advent. This realization infuses the topic of suffering with a solemnity—one might even say a sacramentality—that must be honored as in some sense inexplicable, at least from the human perspective of limited understanding. It affirms that just as we can never fully comprehend the profundity of Christ's passion, even if we can theologize about it and its salvific effects, so the suffering of his pilgrim church should never be reduced only to simple explanations of sin/judgment or eschatological deferral. While suffering is not wholly incomprehensible, neither is it fully explainable.

Lamentations resists Christian triumphalism that downplays the necessity of humbly sharing in the sufferings of Christ and impresses upon the church that until Christ returns she is a community that is in some real sense a community who suffers in exile, albeit one in which the light of restoration has begun to dawn (cf. Phil. 3:10; 2 Cor. 1:5). The path of the church is the way of the cross, and as long as she sojourns toward the return of her King, suffering in all its bewildering complexity will be part of her calling and refinement as the body of Christ (2 Cor. 4:8–10). From this vantage point we can begin to understand how a book such as Lamentations that is haunted by God's silence can function as God's Word for the church today.

It is my great pleasure and honor to offer this essay in memory of Al Groves, who was my teacher, mentor, and church elder during my years at Westminster Seminary, but who also continued to be a dear friend and confidant well after I had left. His uncommon blend of scholarly acuteness with pastoral and devotional warmth has impacted me in ways I am still discovering. It was during one of our conversations in his living room that we discovered a shared interest in Lamentations, and we both agreed that this tiny book had much from which the church could benefit. It is my hope that this essay will aid in that endeavor.

10

Jonah and Janus: Character Hermeneutics and the Two Faces of Jonah in the History of Interpretation

SAMUEL L. BOYD

IN A FALLEN WORLD, how do we know when someone is a "good guy"? Correspondingly, how do we know when someone is a "bad guy"? This process of evaluation forms the foundation for character hermeneutics, or the interpretive process whereby we make decisions about the integrity, or lack thereof, of people we encounter in the various contexts of our lives. This decision process and the questions involved in evaluating our relationships are not easy in a world of total depravity. Our ability to distinguish good character from bad is hampered by our own sin, which in turn qualifies what we mean by "good" and "bad." We must ask these questions, however, since they are the foundation of discernment and wisdom as we seek both to address the reality of sin in our lives and to find the work of Christ's redemption in our relationships.

In much the same way as we ask these questions in our interactions with other people, we also ask them when we encounter an individual in a narrative. As the sequence of a story's plot unfolds, the interactions between the characters described therein cause us to evaluate their integrity. This evaluation process also entails a vertical component when reading the Bible. One should consider how an individual's relationship with God is portrayed, since this relationship often determines how individuals in the Bible act toward one another.

Such an evaluation is important when reading the book of Jonah. This little book contains many elements that excite the reader's imagination as it tells of the prophet's call to deliver a message from the Lord to Nineveh. These elements often force the reader to think about the meaning of the various events of the prophet's life portrayed therein. It is the prophet himself, however, who is perhaps the greatest cause for deliberation in the book. According to some scholars, the narrator is telling Jonah's story in a manner that makes him a comic figure, and an example teaching us what not to do. According to others, however, the prophet is depicted as an individual who struggled with the call he received from God and how to reconcile his call with God's character.

This essay will explore these varying views concerning the integrity of Jonah. It will describe the reasons why some scholars in the history of interpretation have understood Jonah as an individual worthy of our sympathies, and why some scholars read Jonah's character as one of uncertain, if not blatantly poor, integrity. We will then compare these two ways of understanding the character of Jonah with how Matthew and Luke evaluate the importance of this prophet. Finally, we will consider how an awareness of our decisions to interpret individuals in the Bible can provide models for our interactions with one another. More specifically, we will examine how Matthew and Luke's use of Jonah should serve as the norm for how we, in turn, apply character hermeneutics to other people in our communities.

THE TWO FACES OF JONAH IN CHRISTIAN INTERPRETATION

Although containing only four chapters, the book of Jonah has produced an enduring legacy in modern culture. The dramatic events described in the book catch the reader's attention, and the miraculous components often serve as the focal point for preaching and teaching the book. Given the central role of the prophet in these events, much attention has also been directed toward interpreting Jonah as a character throughout his narrative. This section will discuss the theological importance of the prophet in the early church and the two ways in which Christian interpreters subsequently struggled to read his character: Jonah as a flawed but sympathetic prophet on the one hand, and Jonah as an individual of uncertain, if not explicitly poor, character on the other. We will then be in a better position to understand how other traditions, such as Jewish interpretation, also handled this issue, how Matthew and Luke employ the prophet in relationship to Jesus, and how we can use his character to develop a reading strategy that lends itself to practical application.

In the generations following the ministry of the apostles, the image of Jonah being spewed forth from the fish reminded believers of the certainty of resurrection and victory over death. This image is visible much later in stained glass at Lincoln College, Oxford, as well as in other medieval representations.[1] With an exegetical imagination often lost on modern interpreters, these early Christians, such as Pseudo-Chrysostom, Ambrose of Milan, the Venerable Bede, and the Egyptian monk John Cassian, employed the text in a variety of teaching and preaching contexts. In much of this work, one reads of Jonah as a positive type of Christ: Jonah's flight from the Lord represents Jesus' incarnation as the second person of the Trinity left his heavenly dwelling to take on flesh (Jerome), Jonah's slumber in the ship is understood in light of Christ's body in the tomb (Cyril of Alexandria), the psalm in chapter 2 of the book of Jonah is correlated with the last days of Christ (Hesychius of Jerusalem), and so forth.

Jerome's commentary, *In Ionam*, is an excellent example of this positive interpretation of Jonah's character. While not glib about the sin involved in Jonah's rebellion against God's initial call, Jerome grounds Jonah's character in his understanding of Christ's person and work.[2] The patent faults of the stubborn prophet, once correlated with specific examples in Jesus' life and ministry, are thus placed in a redemptive context. In other words, the events in Jonah's life are occasions to see how his character prefigures Christ. According to Jerome, Jonah's reluctance to travel to Nineveh is not driven

1. Yvonne Sherwood, *A Biblical Text and Its Afterlives: The Survival of Jonah in Western Culture* (Cambridge: Cambridge University Press, 2000), 18. This book contains a fuller discussion of some of the sources mentioned in this section of the essay, as well as many other attempts to interpret the book of Jonah in the Christian tradition (11–48).

2. Ibid., 14, 20. While an accessible translation of Jerome's commentary in English is not yet available to this author's knowledge, one can find editions in Latin and French, as well as quotations in translated English in Sherwood's work. See also Barbara Green, who cites a forthcoming, though currently unavailable, translation (Barbara Green, ed., *Jonah's Journeys* [Collegeville, MN: Liturgical Press, 2005], 55–62).

so much by xenophobia as by nationalistic zeal. It is not that Jonah wants to see Nineveh destroyed, but instead Jerome claims that Jonah feared that Nineveh's positive reaction to his message would be, by contrast, condemnation on his own stubborn people. In this manner, Jerome likens Jonah positively to Paul, who displays his zeal for Israel in Romans 9:4, as well as Christ, who in Matthew 10:5–6 commands that the twelve disciples go "to the lost sheep of the house of Israel" and not to the Gentiles.[3] In addition, Jonah's moments of doubt, from Jerome's point of view, resemble Jesus' plea that the cup might pass from him in Matthew 26:39.

While Jerome considered Jonah's character to be flawed but redeemed, emphasizing positive points of comparison between Jonah and Jesus, Augustine took a different approach. Augustine did not write a commentary on the book of Jonah, but one can collect his thoughts on the book scattered throughout his works.[4] While he acknowledged the importance of Jonah as a sign and prefiguration of Christ in his writings, he nonetheless focused on many elements in which Jonah's character was a counterexample of the gospel. No more explicit is this negative portrayal of Jonah than in the prophet's apparent resistance to preaching to Nineveh, which Augustine compares to an attitude that is opposed to the extension of the gospel beyond the borders of Israel. Interestingly, Augustine and Jerome communicated their thoughts with each other concerning the book of Jonah, most famously in a letter in which Augustine reprimanded Jerome regarding his translation of the vine in Jonah 4 as "ivy," a translation that Augustine thought to be egregiously erroneous. In this manner, these contemporaries displayed differences of opinions in small matters, and also differed in their understanding of the character of Jonah. Jerome opted for a sympathetically flawed character while Augustine preferred a mixed characterization, though both gave due consideration to the typological use of Jonah in Matthew and Luke.

Martin Luther, in researching for his lectures on the book of Jonah, consulted Augustine's thoughts concerning the prophet.[5] In doing so, Luther adopted the mixed portrayal of Jonah's character found in some of Augustine's works. Jonah is not without sympathy in Luther's lectures. Rather, Luther comments, at times, compassionately on the difficulties of the prophet

---

3. All quotations of Scripture in this chapter are from the ESV.

4. Green, *Jonah's Journeys*, 17–18; Sherwood, *A Biblical Text and Its Afterlives*, 22.

5. Sherwood, *A Biblical Text and Its Afterlives*, 22. See also Martin Luther, "Lectures on Jonah," in *Lectures on the Minor Prophets II: Jonah, Habakkuk*, ed. Hilton C. Oswald and Jaroslav Pelikan, Luther's Works 19 (St. Louis: Concordia, 1974).

as one who suffered many pains and a torn conscience in his struggle with God's call. Indeed, in many of Luther's works on Jonah, including sermons, commentaries, and the aforementioned lectures, one finds many positive descriptions of Jonah and his prefiguration of Christ. At the same time, the Ninevites, representative of the Gentiles, are portrayed saintly, and by comparison Jonah becomes the referent of his own statement in Jonah 2:8 as one whose obsession with his national identity makes him "regard . . . vain idols" and thereby forsake the "hope of steadfast love."

Although one finds strokes of Christological readings of Jonah's character, Luther also connected Jonah with narrow nationalism and hatred of foreigners evident in Psalm 79:6. One author states Luther's approach to the character of Jonah as follows: "In Luther's reading Jonah no longer orbits the realm of Christological superlatives but is emphatically grounded in the realm of the 'weakness of the flesh.'"[6] While such a comment is perhaps an overstatement, it is accurate to view Luther as a departure from earlier commentators such as Jerome in his understanding of Jonah's character. Luther wrote that these early-church exegetes displayed a "silly deference" in their assessment of the Prophets, wounding the obvious words of Scripture and attempting to "force it and stretch it, before they would admit that those sinners were saints."[7] Later, John Calvin would take a similar stance, claiming in his commentary on Jonah 4:10–11 that Jerome had been much too soft in interpreting Jonah's integrity.

This negative appraisal of Jonah's character appears even in popular retellings and references to the book of Jonah. For example, the VeggieTales movie *Jonah* also interprets the prophet as a xenophobe who despises the fish-slapping Ninevites and whose reluctance to deliver his "message from the Lord" is matched only by his unremitting recalcitrance at the end of the movie. Yet little, if any, time is devoted to how Christ fulfills the prophetic call of Jonah, and so the movie exists primarily as an entertaining character study on the prophet as a negative exemplar.

This survey of the interpretation of Jonah's character in the Christian tradition is not meant to favor one interpretive strategy over another. Rather, we have observed the struggle involved in interpreting the character of Jonah: should he be examined primarily for his positive role in redemptive history, in light of how his prefigurement of Christ transforms the use of his person

6. Sherwood, *A Biblical Text and Its Afterlives*, 23.
7. Luther, *Lectures on the Minor Prophets II*, 45.

in the sign of Jonah appearing in Matthew and Luke (discussed later in this study), or should we concentrate on his failings and many attendant trials as a result of his struggles to understand God's call? Both interpretations have their merits and insights. A one-sided approach is bound to miss many of the intricacies and complexities that have fascinated exegetes for centuries. This tension in evaluating how Jonah's character functioned also appears in Jewish literature. Before considering how Matthew and Luke employ Jonah, we will briefly examine three examples of how Jewish exegetes also struggled with this question.

THE TWO FACES OF JONAH IN JEWISH INTERPRETATION

Christian interpretive tradition concerning the character of Jonah reveals the complexities involved in making sense of how one should under-stand the prophet's actions. Jewish interpretation also shows a diverse array of opinions about Jonah. In this tradition, one finds both positive assess-ments (Jonah as a penitent prophet) and more tragically flawed portrayals as well. We will consider three Jewish sources that discuss Jonah, and then move on to discuss what the NT has to say about this prophet.

The first Jewish source we will examine is the *Midrash Jonah*, a rab-binic commentary on the book of Jonah. Although the four versions of this work come from a later date, from the ninth to the thirteenth centuries, the details contained therein, especially in the *De Rossi* version of this midrash, likely originated much earlier, given the similar interpretive characteristics as those in the Gospels and other early rabbinic sources.[8] While in many instances the Ninevites come off morally superior to Jonah, who is said in this commentary to be swallowed by two fish and to be afflicted by snakes and scorpions as extra punishment for his sin, nonetheless in many cases Jonah was associated with messianic expectation. For example, the *Midrash Jonah* claims that Jonah was the son of the widow of Zarephath and that, in his resurrection to life from death by Elijah (1 Kings 17:17–23), Jonah, both as a youth and as an adult in Jonah 2, prefigured the resurrection and promise of the Messiah.[9]

Another example of the midrash taking a positive view of Jonah is found in the commentary on Jonah 4:11, the last verse of the book, which

---

8. Bezalel Narkiss, "The Sign of Jonah," *Gesta* 18 (1979): 63–64.

9. A similar interpretation is found in the *Lives of the Prophets* 10:6.

ends with God's question to Jonah. Is Jonah recalcitrant and hardened in his ways? Or is Jonah's silence before God similar to Job's silence before God (Job 40:3–5), evidence that Jonah has yielded to God's perspective? The *Midrash Jonah* interpreted the end of the book in line with the latter perspective. To make this image of the penitent prophet explicit, the commentary claims that Jonah quoted a selection of the prayer in Daniel 9:9, "to the Lord our God belong mercy and forgiveness." This partial quotation is even more appropriate when one reads the rest of Daniel 9:9–10: "for we have rebelled against him and have not obeyed the voice of the LORD our God by walking in his laws, which he set before us by his servants the prophets."[10]

This notion of the penitent prophet may also be seen in Jewish liturgy. On Yom Kippur, or the Day of Atonement (Lev. 16), the book of Jonah is read in its entirety in the synagogue as the Haftorah reading (a non-Pentateuchal selection of the Bible that is read to accompany the theme of the Pentateuch passage). The theme of repentance and atonement in the book of Jonah is emphasized by the sudden and dramatic conversion of the Ninevites, and is fitting as a liturgical reading on this day.

It is interesting, however, to observe the context of the reading of Jonah, which may elucidate another perspective on the prophet. The reading that follows the book of Jonah is Micah 7:18–20, a passage focusing specifically on the forgiveness and atonement of Israel. The preceding verses (Mic. 7:16–17) focus on the destruction of the nations. If these two readings are juxtaposed and set in context of the Day of Atonement, then, given the strong emphasis on specifically Israelite repentance in Micah 7:18–20, this setting for the reading of the book of Jonah gives a thematic link in Jewish liturgy through which one can interpret not only the Ninevites as penitent, but Jonah as well.[11] Such a reading with Micah 7:18–20 creates a pleasing reversal of Jonah chapter 2: the sinful Jonah was cast into the depths of the sea as a cosmic judgment from God, but the penitent Jonah, connected with all Israel in Micah 7:19, has his sins cast into the depths of the sea by God. The book of Jonah does not overtly state that the prophet was penitent, nor does the liturgy on Yom Kippur explicitly interpret the object of repentance

10. Jack Sasson, *Jonah*, AB 24B (New York: Doubleday, 1990), 320. For other intrabiblical exegetical trajectories, see Uriel Simon, *Jonah: The Traditional Hebrew Text with the New JPS Translation*, trans. Lenn J. Schramm (Philadelphia: JPS, 1999), xxxvi–xxxix. See also the discussion concerning whether Jonah is satirized in the book, or whether the book evokes compassion for the prophet (xxi–xxii).

11. Simon, *Jonah*, xiii.

and atonement in the book of Jonah as the prophet himself. Instead, the thematic context and association of readings in this tradition opens avenues through which one can examine how the association with the penitent Jonah, a positive picture of his character evident in the midrash, developed hermeneutical legitimacy.

A positive assessment of Jonah's character, as a prefiguration of resurrection and example of repentance, is not the only interpretation of the prophet in Jewish literature. We have already examined the complex nature of the *Midrash Jonah*, which also describes in detail the cost of divine retribution for rebelling against God's initial call. Another midrash, known as the *Mekhilta de Rabbi Ishmael*, which dates to the second century AD, also known as the Tannaitic period in rabbinical thought, developed a darker picture of Jonah.[12] In this rabbinical work, which is actually a commentary on the book of Exodus, the criteria for a good and bad prophet emerge as a topic for discussion. A good prophet is defined as one whose prophetic message contains words of zeal for both God and the nation of Israel. By this standard, Jeremiah was the exemplar because in Lamentations 3:42, traditionally thought to be penned by Jeremiah, the prophet represents both God's perspective to the people ("we have transgressed and rebelled") and the people's perspective to God ("you have not forgiven").[13] Jonah, however, showed disregard for God by fleeing his call, an action that revealed only his zeal for the nation of Israel. According to the rabbis in this source, if the Gentiles repent, this act of contrition might bring condemnation against Israel, and so Jonah attempts to divert this possibility. Thus, while nonetheless considered a prophet, Jonah in the *Mekhilta de Rabbi Ishmael* becomes a second-class prophet on the level of Elijah, who had zeal for God but not Israel (1 Kings 19:10), and was not considered to have the prophetic flair and purity of Jeremiah.

The issue of Jonah's character was complex for Jewish interpreters as well as Christian exegetes. In the Jewish tradition, one finds both positive and negative appraisals of the prophet. Given the struggle to discern the nature of the prophet, whether he was a figure of redemption and model of penitence or stubborn rebel and subpar prophet, we can better appreciate the hermeneutical difficulties involved in understanding how Jonah's

12. Jacob Neusner, trans., *Mekhilta according to Rabbi Ishmael: An Analytical Translation*, 2 vols., Brown Judaic Studies 148, 154 (Atlanta: Scholars Press, 1988).
13. Ibid., 1:8–9; Sherwood, *A Biblical Text and Its Afterlives*, 121.

character functions in this book. We will now consider how Matthew and Luke portray the character of Jonah, and then how we can seek to apply this apostolic interpretation of the prophet to our own ministries.

THE TWO FACES OF JONAH IN THE NT

In the previous sections, we discussed some representative examples of the struggle in both the Christian and Jewish traditions of exegesis, resulting in a mixed evaluation of Jonah's character. He is at times understood to be a flawed prophet who ultimately found his significance as a positive prefiguration of the resurrection of Christ, while at other times he is viewed as an example of a prophet whose stubbornness showed a persistent unwillingness to heed God's word. We will now consider how Matthew and Luke employ Jonah. One scholar considers the varied interpretations of his character in the Christian tradition to be the result of the perception that even in the Gospels "the interpretation splits, bifurcates, multiplies, and mutates."[14] This observation raises the question whether one can find theological coherence in Matthew and Luke's use of Jonah. We will first consider the sign of Jonah in Matthew and Luke, and then examine the theological unity contained in Matthew and Luke's utilization of the prophet as a foreshadowing of both the person and the work of Jesus.

Jonah is mentioned in Matthew 12:38–42 as a response to the scribes and Pharisees, who desire to see a sign from Jesus.[15] Jesus then claims that his generation will see the sign of Jonah and explains why the prophet serves as a meaningful basis for a rejoinder. In the same way that Jonah was in the fish for three days and nights, so also Christ will undergo a similar experience in the grave. In addition, Jesus finds Jonah's preaching ministry relevant in this manner and compares Jonah's preaching ministry to his own, highlighting the efficiency of Jonah's preaching and emphasizing the irony of Jesus' own intransigent generation when it refused to repent after hearing his words. While Jesus strengthens this theme of his word ministry when mentioning Solomon's wisdom in Matthew 12:42, the logic for using the sign of Jonah, signaled by the comparative conjunction (*hosper* resolved with *houtos*) and

14. Sherwood, *A Biblical Text and Its Afterlives*, 12.

15. In Matthew 16:4, Jesus also refers to the sign of Jonah. But this verse does not contain the theological explanation that appears in Matthew 12:38–42 and Luke 11:29–32, and therefore is not considered in this examination. For similar reasons, Mark 8:12 is also not the focus of this study.

coordinating conjunction (*gar*), seems to be in reference to Jonah in the belly of the whale (Jonah 1 and 2). Thus, the death and resurrection appear to be the primary referent of this sign in Matthew 12:38–42.

Luke's version of the sign of Jonah contains both similarities and differences. This account appears in Luke 11:29–32. Perhaps most striking is the lack of explanation of the sign based on the events of Jonah 1 and 2, namely, the prophet's encounter with the fish, which in this context would augur Jesus' death and resurrection. Instead, immediately after announcing the sign in Luke 11:29, Jesus begins his explanation with a comparative conjunction (*kathos* completed by *houtos*) and postpositive coordinating conjunction (*gar*), a similar construction to that in Matthew 12:40, in reference to Jonah as a sign to the Ninevites. Since the book of Jonah does not claim that the Ninevites saw Jonah's ordeal with the fish (which would be impossible because of geographic constraints), Jonah's preaching ministry seems to be in view, which is further clarified in Luke 11:31–32. But instead of addressing the conversion of Nineveh at Jonah's preaching followed by the comparison with Solomon's wisdom, as is the arrangement in Matthew 12:41–42, Luke places the comparison with Solomon's wisdom between Jesus' initial statement about the sign of Jonah and Nineveh's conversion in 11:30–32. This arrangement in Luke effectively highlights the word ministry of Jesus, embedding Solomon's wisdom in the middle of his argument concerning how Jesus is the better Jonah.

Is Luke saying something different from Matthew? The difficulty in harmonizing the two passages is evident in a fifth-century codex, known as Bezae Catabrignsis, where the phrase from Matthew 12:40 is inserted at the end of Luke 11:30. This variation is rightly rejected, however, since it neither fits the context nor is found in other manuscripts. Again, Jonah's adventure in the fish was not a sign to the people of Nineveh, since the book of Jonah does not indicate that they witnessed the event. Geographical proximity would have prevented them from seeing the fish regurgitate Jonah (Nineveh was nowhere near a large body of water). Moreover, Luke never uses the word for *sign* (*semeion*) as employed in Luke 11:29 to refer to a miraculous event, much less Jesus' death and resurrection.[16] Rather, if Luke 11:32 is a

---

16. George M. Landes, "Jonah in Luke," in *A Gift of God in Due Season: Essays on Scripture and Community in Honor of James A. Sanders*, ed. Richard D. Weis, Library of Hebrew Bible/Old Testament Studies (Sheffield, UK: Sheffield Academic Press, 1996), 139. In Acts, however, Luke uses the same word approximately thirteen times to refer to miracles (139n15).

continuation of the logic of Luke 11:30, the sign in view is the preaching ministry of Jesus, rooted in reference to the conversion of the Ninevites and fulfilled in Jesus' ministry through the preaching of the apostles in Acts. This raises a question: Are we presented in the Gospels with another pair of conflicting views about Jonah, with Matthew interpreting Jonah as a type of the death and resurrection while Luke interprets Jonah as a type of Jesus' preaching ministry?

Theological coherence between Matthew 12:38–42 and Luke 11:29–32 is not found in conflating the two passages. Rather, both passages contain complementary theological categories. Matthew focuses on the deed ministry of Jesus, expressed ultimately in the death and resurrection of Christ, whereas Luke uses Jonah to convey the word ministry of Jesus. If we read Matthew and Luke in this manner, allowing each to bring its theological perspective to the table, our picture of Jesus' ministry is enriched because both theological categories are necessary to understand the significance of Jesus' person and work. If we permit Matthew's emphasis on the sign as found in Jonah 1 and 2 and Luke's presentation of the sign as found in Jonah 3 and 4 to coexist, then, following the examples of the Gospels, we have a rich exegetical framework in which to read Christ as the fulfillment of every verse of the book of Jonah. In this manner, Matthew and Luke present Jonah neither as a xenophobic prophet[17] nor as a negative exemplar. Instead, they portray Jonah as a prophet whose narrative is redeemed in the blood of the greater Prophet, Jesus Christ. Matthew and Luke's presentation of Christ's words reveals how a flawed character such as Jonah finds resolve in redemptive history in the life and work of Christ.[18]

We also find in Matthew and Luke the basis to resolve the struggle of interpretation concerning the character of Jonah in the Christian tradition.

17. It should be noted that neither Assyria nor Nineveh, which would eventually become the capital of Assyria under Sennacherib (705–681 BC), is explicitly portrayed as an enemy against Israel or Judah at any point in the history of these nations preceding 2 Kings 14:25, the passage that describes Jonah's service under Jeroboam II. Whatever the historical backdrop, according to the canonical presentation it remains an inference that Jonah rebels against his call out of a hatred for the Ninevites as foreigners who eventually conquer Israel. This inference is due either to proximity of explicit antagonism of Assyria against Israel (which begins in 2 Kings 15) or to prophetic insight. Neither scenario, however, is explicitly described in 2 Kings 14:25 or the book of Jonah.

18. See also Samson in Hebrews 11. My thanks to Brad Gregory, who has pointed out a similar phenomenon in 2 Peter 2:7, where Lot, a character of dubious integrity who selfishly takes for himself the better choice of land when he separates from Abram in Genesis 13:10–12 and is perhaps willing to get drunk, leading to the birth of Moab and Ammon in Genesis 19:33–38, is nonetheless called "righteous."

The sympathetic reading of Jerome finds fulfillment in Matthew and Luke's treatment of Jonah as a prophet whose message is described in the same context as Solomon's wisdom. Exegetes such as Augustine, Luther, and Calvin were also correct to address the sin involved in Jonah's reluctance to obey God's word.

REFLECTIONS ON AL GROVES, CHARACTER HERMENEUTICS, AND JONAH

As we have seen, when someone reads a text, that person is not passive. Rather, reading texts requires engagement. When one reads a text, whether history or fiction, he or she invokes certain faculties, such as the ability to trace various themes in a book and the ability to discern when symbolism and metaphor are being used. We should remember that we also bring ourselves to a text—all the implications of being people who sin and people against whom others sin. But sin is not the final word. We also bring our stories of redemption in Christ and seek to persuade others not just that the Bible's account of sin and redemption is one coherent account of reality, but that it *is* reality. Thus, Al Groves was fond of reminding his students that "there are no free motifs." In other words, when interpreting Scripture, every theme is attached to a larger development of the plan of salvation wherein God reconciled himself to the world in Christ.

Such an awareness of reading strategies and the connection between reader, text, and God is especially relevant for the interpretation of the character of Jonah. This essay has examined various understandings of the character of Jonah in the history of interpretation, and how Matthew and Luke perceived the person of Jonah in light of Christ's word and deed ministries. We have assessed various interpretive opinions concerning Jonah's integrity, seeking to be sympathetic as to why certain interpreters viewed the character of Jonah as they did. Thus, the two faces of Jonah in the history of interpretation are resolved in the one plan of salvation through the two faces of Jonah in Matthew and Luke as auguring the death and resurrection and preaching ministry of Christ.

If we follow Matthew and Luke's use of Jonah, we will put ourselves in a position to make our exegesis consistent with our ministry practice. To begin this brief reflection, a quote from a famous philosopher seems appropriate: "There is nothing outside the text."[19] While intricate qualifica-

---

19. Jacques Derrida, *Of Grammatology*, trans. Gayatri Chakravorty Spivak (Baltimore: Johns Hopkins University, 1998), 158.

tion of this quote would be appropriate, if nothing else than to make it clear that this philosopher was not operating from a Christian worldview, there is something enticing about this idea for Christians when set in the context of the authority of Scripture. We live in and under a text.

In other words, when we read Israel's story and Jonah's story through Christ, we are also reading the church's story and our story. So we live *in* this text. We also live *under* the authority of Scripture, as people who proclaim the Bible to be the ultimate rule for how we live our lives and make the decisions that we make. Our lives are not lived in a vacuum, and therefore our interactions with other people reflect functional theologies derived from our sense of either being held accountable to scriptural teaching or being in rebellion against it. Therefore, just as Matthew and Luke viewed Jonah through the lens of Christ's death and resurrection and preaching ministry, thereby emphasizing redemption in an otherwise uncertain character, so also we should be compelled to approach all our relationships in the same manner. If we are consistent in applying our theology to our ministry, then this Christological reworking of Jonah in Matthew and Luke should encourage us also to place those to whom we are ministering in the same redemptive context.

It is my honor to contribute to this festschrift in honor of Al. He understood the value of story better than anyone else I know. He appreciated how a narrative is not simply something to be analyzed but also an influence on how we live. Al read the Bible as history and as narrative, and for the same reasons urged his students to connect their own histories with God's narrative of redemption. If we disconnect Jonah from redemptive history, there is little about him that is redeemable, and what we are left with are character studies that focus on his rebellion and God's attendant punishment. Al greatly discouraged this approach. If we read Jonah by grounding our interpretive practice in Christ's person and work, then we practice character hermeneutics, attaching individuals in redemptive history to a greater purpose interpreted in light of redemption and grace. Interpreting Jonah in this manner is not glib toward the reality of sin. Rather, it allows us to call attention to the egregious nature of rebellion against God without losing hope. For those who call on the name of Christ as Savior and Redeemer, sin and the accompanying injustices of this world are realities that can be seen for the monstrous aberrations that they are. In light of Christ, however, sin and injustice are not the ultimate reality. For Jonah, as for Christians, mercy wins in the end, transforming us from characters who deserve wrath into characters who are granted life.

II

Beauty in an iPod Culture: Reflections on Mediation and Christian Ethics

WILLIAM EDGAR

THE QUEST FOR UNIVERSALS

Much of the history of philosophy is about the search for universals. A universal can be a property or a relation that has particular instances. For example, a square is the universal of which tiles on a floor or card tables are instances. Philosophers have wanted to know whether universals exist in reality or whether they are inventions of ours. If something has no spatial position, how can it be exampled in several places and across time?

The two classical answers from ancient Greece are these: (1) universals exist independently of things, or *ante rem* (Plato's idealism), and (2) universals exist in things, or *in re*, although not independently of them (Aristotle's realism). A variety of other answers exist. (3) Conceptualism says that universals exist independently of things, or *post rem*, because the mind groups things together upon reflection. (4) Nominalism says that universals are in the word, or *flatus vocis* (the breath of the voice). (5) Although we think of universals as most often rational concepts, the irrational can also become a kind of antirational universal. Mysticism, the absurd—these are types of absolutes despite their discomfort with such a label.

The quest for universals far exceeds the bounds of philosophy. Surely it is one of the basic characteristics of human life. When the Creator, the triune God of revelation, is left out of the quandary, we will look for universals somewhere within the limited one world of an eternal universe. The consequence of this omission is a thinning out of our world and its order. There can no longer be proper distinctions or proper boundaries between things. As universals are proposed within this only-one-kind-of-being that is presupposed when there is no Creator, things tend to lump together; they collapse. There is no elbow room, nor are there "joints" between things, as it were.[1]

If the Enlightenment generally tried to replace, or at best complement, a theologically grounded metanarrative with a more rationalistic one, its failures set into motion a vast, complex search for universals that could be believed. The late nineteenth and early twentieth centuries exhibited a particularly poignant quest, or series of quests, in the wake of that failure, which were experienced across the board—and not only in philosophy. A particularly instructive place to observe this search is in the evolution of modern art.

A PATH TO MODERN ART

The hinge figure in the development of modern art is Paul Cézanne (1839–1906). He represented the culmination, if not the exhaustion, of the Western approach originating in the Renaissance, but also the need to revitalize fine art altogether. His struggles can be understood as the search for unity and diversity, absolute truth and concrete particulars. He thus longed to find structural universals, yet without losing the robustness of individuation. As for many other artists, his paintings were not copies of nature, but interpretations of reality. Put more strongly, a painting is a parallel of a part of the world, creating its own authentic reality. We can illustrate what this meant for Cézanne by looking at one of his most important subjects, *Le Mont Sainte-Victoire*, which he painted over and over again throughout his life.

1. For a fascinating study on distance and relation see Wayne L. Roosa, "A Meditation on the Joint and Its Holy Ornaments," *Books and Culture* 14, 1 (January–February 2008): 16.

This series is a useful measure of the particular artistic search in which Cézanne engaged. In the earlier renditions, colors are blended, and there are fluid definitions between motifs: the ground, the trees, the mountain, the sky. In the later ones, we have delineated blocks of color, and the boundaries are strongly defined. And what we especially notice are the geometric shapes that form the basic units of the composition. In *Mont Sainte-Victoire* (1902–4, Philadelphia Museum of Art), we notice on the left side of the mountain three distinct "steps" defined by the colors brown, green, and then tan. Each step is self-contained, with no apparent mediation or flow between them. Though a bit less distinctively, the section on the right flank of the mountain has squares going from light blue to purple and brown, again with no transition.

In *Mont Sainte-Victoire vu des Lauves* (1902–4, Kunstmuseum, Basel), perhaps the most radical in the series, the entire painting is made up of small geometric shapes, using shades of tan, green, pink, and blue. There is no real mingling, but only a feeling of being collected in the same space. Although there is no blending, Cézanne manages to hold everything together. It is one scene, and a clearly recognizable one, that "studies" the mountain and the surrounding landscape.

According to H. R. Rookmaaker, Cézanne, along with several other contemporaries (particularly Vincent Van Gogh), was on a quest to find reality.[2] The Enlightenment trust in reason was not fully abandoned, yet reason alone could not fully account for ultimate truth. Specifically, Cézanne was reacting to Impressionism, whose basic principle was to capture a fleeting slice of life, by a sort of recording of what the retina perceived. Without denying the importance of the eye's gaze, Cézanne wanted to move visual art further, to keep it in the classical tradition of great art, yet without any simple nostalgic return to the past. As he dedicated himself to discovering the basic structures of reality, he needed to do so without losing the particulars: "This led him to his slow, laborious method: by looking, looking, looking again and again he tried to *see* the structures, the rationalistic principles 'behind' the thing seen, the universal ideas that ordered what he saw."[3] He was remarkably successful.

What Cézanne was able to keep in a delicate balance, his successors could not. There has been a long debate among art historians about whether,

---

2. H. R. Rookmaaker, *Modern Art and the Death of a Culture*, 2nd ed. (Downers Grove, IL: Inter-Varsity Press, 1973), 93–96.

3. Ibid., 95.

and how, Cézanne influenced the successive styles of modern art. My own conviction is that much of what followed owed more to what artists thought they were learning from the master than necessarily to the master's intended legacy.[4] In any case, the style known as Cubism came fast on the heels of Cézanne's late oeuvre. Certainly Pablo Picasso (1881–1973) moved things in a radical direction, and changed the face of modern art forever. In his Cubist period, unlike Cézanne, Picasso sought to abandon the humanism of Western tradition, and to forge ahead by discovering the reality behind appearances, without the support of the European metanarrative. Not unlike Plato, but with a more rebellious purpose, he looked for universals in geometrical shapes and mathematical configurations.

Les Demoiselles d'Avignon (1907, Museum of Modern Art, New York) is a violent painting, one that depicts five nude women, standing in what looks like the seductive poses of prostitutes. The way the painting is rendered makes these figures anything but alluring. Their shapes are abstract and quite geometrical, and there is the suggestion of African masks for the faces. Purposely reminiscent of Cézanne's *Les Grandes Baigneuses* (1900, The Barnes Foundation, Merion, Pennsylvania), instead, these are not real women, but objects, set in a conceptual space. The work is at once a transgression of classical art and a manifesto for Cubism. Leo Steinberg called it a "philosophical brothel."[5] No wonder Picasso drew scores of sketches and studies before composing the main work. It was a sea change in the history of art.

Continuing the quest, Picasso become more and more attached to geometrical forms, culminating in "analytical Cubism," in which the actual subject matter is very difficult to discern. Consider *Man with Violin* (1912, Philadelphia Art Museum), which requires an archaeologist's instinct to find clues of the person and the instrument. Rookmaaker calls this "the decisive step," by which he means that Picasso gave up on the very possibility of universals, and concluded that this world is absurd, without meaning.[6] He notes that the term is anachronistic, since one would have to wait for Albert Camus or the theater of the absurd before it would be used intentionally. But the idea of the absurd was in the air, expressed in such works as the poetry of Arthur Rimbaud, Edward Lear's nursery rhymes, and Lewis Carroll's *Alice*

4. See Denis Coutagne, *Cézanne en vérité(s)* (Paris: Actes Sud, 2006), 559ff.
5. See Patricia Leighten, "Revising Cubism," *Art Journal* 47, 4 (Winter 1988): 269–76.
6. Rookmaaker, *Modern Art*, 120.

in Wonderland. Picasso was one of only a very small group who could think this way. I am not altogether certain that Picasso really was committed to absurdity. His quest for absolutes can still be felt, even in his rebellion. But the point is, painting from this time on was "free" to sever the connections between visible nature and the work on the canvas.

There was plenty of opposition to what Picasso was doing. He himself would later come back to styles more akin to the depiction of real subjects. But once this "decisive step" had been taken, the door was open to further quests, some of which were radical indeed. We may think of Piet Mondrian (1872–1944), who reduced all pictorial elements to their most basic forms, right angles and primary colors. His works are strongly intellectual, with titles such as *Composition 10*. Importantly, Mondrian insisted that there be no frames for his paintings, since they were merely focal points, a slice within the larger life around.

We may think of Mondrian's artistic "opposite," Paul Klee (1879–1940), whose strange works are ghostlike and depict a kind of mysticism, one that looks for universals in the irrational, not the rational. Much of modern art went in this sort of mystical direction. Viewers were considered less and less outside participants or critics, and more and more partakers in the work, or even the artistic process. As modern art continued to go down this path, it developed forms that encouraged a melting together of viewer and object. Events, constructions, the increasing use of technology and video—all of these serve to join everything together. Diana Lynn Thompson is a contemporary installation artist who works with ephemeral moments, accumulated objects, collected stories, and insertion/intervention strategies, which she documents in video and photographs. As an environmental installationist, she will pull pine needles off a tree and carefully paste them on a wall, or she will place four thousand blue marbles on a secluded beach and wait for the high summer tides to rearrange the marbles each day and document them. One of her favorite lines is by Ursula K. Le Guin: "Our world goes through and through us and we through it, there's no boundary."[7]

To be sure, modern art is not monolithic. Neither is there a single story or a single threat of those who accepted the "decisive step," and then moved on in ever more radical directions. Many other trends, some of them specifically inspired by the Christian faith, asserted themselves alongside the more avant-garde art. Here is the simple point we want to make: whether in

7. Quoted at http://dianathompson.net.

the arts or in philosophy, and beyond, when we have no grounding in the view that a triune Creator, One who made the world but is not confused with it, in whom there is equal ultimacy of unity and diversity, then we will have to look for universals within a single realm, a single kind of being. Without a beginning point at which there is unity and diversity at the same time, a beginning point that is outside of our world, yet intimately related to it, substitute beginning points will be imagined, ones that will be either reductionist or chaotic, faces of the same coin.

THE SERVICE OF METAPHOR

In the arts, or even in social life, the result is the impossibility of finding either the proper structures or the proper space. Tellingly, this will become a world without the possibility of metaphor. A painting is a parallel world to the subject being painted. It is a metaphor. But when that distance and similarity cannot be comfortably placed in the same world, both are lost.

Professor Groves was fascinated by metaphor. Typically he focused on the parallel term, *motif*. As he defined it, "A motif is a recurring image, signaled by figurative language, that says something about one person, place or event in terms of another person, place or event. . . . It has both a rhetorical and revelatory (cognitive) dimension."[8] A favorite aphorism of his was: "There are no free motifs." Like the author of *The Rule of Metaphor*, Professor Groves sought to show that "metaphor is the rhetorical process by which discourse unleashes the power that certain fictions have to redescribe reality."[9] But more particularly, he desired to apply this power to the way in which biblical texts function.

In a memorable exercise to help students become better able to recognize the power of motifs, he would ask them to rewrite Psalm 23 without any metaphor! The result was as comical as it was instructive: "The higher feudal authority is the one who directs me; I shall have no basic needs. . . ." The psalm and its teaching have been ruined! When metaphor is eliminated—if that can ever really happen—one of the greatest losses is the ability to work through a motif in order to widen and deepen one's understanding. Put

8. J. Alan Groves, *Syllabus: Old Testament Motifs (OT 791)* (Westminster Theological Seminary, 1997), 1.

9. Paul Ricœur, *The Rule of Metaphor: The Creation of Meaning in Language* (Boston: Routledge, 2003), 7.

differently, motifs provide heuristic opportunities, and thus draw us in as more than machines who absorb facts.

Paul Ricœur often underscored the heuristic function of metaphor.[10] Accordingly, the similarity and dissimilarity between the two or more instances tell us something true, but also set us to discover something new and pertinent. Thus, comparisons between the object and a motif are more than simply an illustration. Consider, for example, how we might say of someone who shows kindness to an unlovely person, "He is such a saint." A poetic truth is expressed that conjures up images of religious heroes, persons without guile, medieval pictures of figures with halos, and so forth. Yet also in the exercise of making the comparison, we learn more about the world, we grow in our ability to make judgments, and we may even enhance our understanding of medieval art! Or consider how we might say of someone who got the better of an argument: "He buried him." Here again, we learn that some arguments are like mortal combat. Someone has to win. Compare this to saying, "He dazzled them with his rhetoric." Here, argument is compared to radiance, to a shining light. It is a display of brilliance, rather than a duel. We learn about the world, and not only a thin slice of it, through metaphor.

I well remember sitting with Francis Schaeffer as he engaged in discussion with interlocutors. His points were often underscored with game metaphors. "As we move the pieces across the chess board," he would say while trying to advance an argument. Or, "Let's go to the mat on that one," he would say, more provocatively. One sensed the atmosphere of engagement with rules, scorecards, and even conventions of combat. There were diplomatic norms to shape the way in which each person could enter the discussion. We tend not to notice those rules until someone breaks them. When arguments degenerate, the participants might throw things at each other, or put their dukes up. The point here is simply to notice how a world with these "joints" is a world that is comfortable with unity and diversity. When the space is diminished, we are jammed into each other and cannot properly function.

The same goes for warfare itself. Winston Churchill famously said, "The wars of peoples will be more terrible than those of kings."[11] What he meant was that when noble conventions give way to raw, industrial conflict, death

10. Ibid., 239–56.
11. Winston Churchill, "The 'Tattered Flag'" (speech, House of Commons, London, May 13, 1901).

and cruelty will be unprecedented. Whether it be Napoleon's strategies or the American Civil War, the shift from the more polite, humane conventions of killing the enemy to treating them as objects is clearly observed in the large-scale carnage of the twentieth century's total wars.[12] Once again, the mediating space is reduced—certainly one of the more sordid results of leaving God out of the equation. What has happened in its place is an attempt to create new space without recourse to religion, to find some meaning in military death despite God's absence. Perhaps such things as the declarations of human rights during warfare are a part of this compensatory picture. Again, the metaphor teaches us much about who we think we are.

Professor Groves liked to teach about this heuristic, "discovery" quality of the metaphor. He regularly used film clips in his courses, many of which illustrated the principle of cross-referencing motifs as heuristic tools. He often used the parallels between the opening scene of Ian McKellen's *Richard III* (1995) and that of an earlier film, *Brazil*, written by Terry Gilliam (1985). *Brazil* is a story about dystopia. Filmed in a combination of Baron Munchausen bizarreness and dreamlike romance, it represents a powerful central government that uses cumbersome technology to control all things. Full of ironies, the music includes the original version of Ary Barroso's "Aquarela do Brasil," eliciting a faux nostalgia, a different but equally imaginary world where things are sweetness and light. Near the beginning, the innocent Mr. Buttle, by a computer error involving a swatted fly, is confused for the suspected terrorist, Mr. Tuttle. At night the internal security police surprise Buttle in his home by drilling a large hole in the ceiling, and crashing into the room. These masked men throw a leather hood and a chain over him and drag him away—all of this before his terrified mother.

A decade later, the film *Richard III*, while very different in certain ways, nevertheless exhibits several parallels to *Brazil*, whether intentionally or not. Set in an imagined fascist England of the 1930s where there is a civil war, it follows the rise to power of Richard, a Nazi-like tyrant who proceeds by murdering and betraying all his rivals. This time the music is from swing bands of the era, again exhibiting a kind of saccharine wistfulness in contrast to the violence of the times. The opening scene shows the heir to the throne

12. Drew Gilpin Faust has given us a remarkable study on how the conventions for life and death changed during the American Civil War (*This Republic of Suffering: Death in the American Civil War* [New York: Knopf, 2008]). She paints a disturbing picture of how all the rules for treating the dead were changed, with bodies unburied, tombs unmarked, carnage inconceivable.

sitting down to dine in an office. After receiving a disturbing telegram about the oncoming army of Richard, a tank bursts in through the wall, and masked guerrillas shoot the young man and his aged father, King Henry.

While quite different on the surface, these two scenes are strongly related cross-textually. However unlikely it may be that McKellen or director Richard Loncraine was unaware of relating the intrusion scene in *Brazil*, what matters is the resulting fact of their obvious parallels. When Professor Groves suggested that there are no free motifs, he meant that whether consciously or not, the author, filmmaker, or poet is constrained by artistic purposes, and perhaps by something deeper, to make allusions of various kinds. Accordingly, in the universe of discourse of human language or image, all things are profoundly interconnected.

AN ATMOSPHERE FOR LEARNING

To make motifs stand out with particular significance requires the proper respect for context. What surrounds these two intrusions is the setting. Without contrasting yet complementary settings, the motif cannot work. The success of a motif or a metaphor, then, depends on a world in which there is both unity and diversity. In a word, for metaphor to work there must be mediation. Mediation has always been around—indeed, we cannot live without it—but in our advanced technological societies we are presented with particular challenges, ones perhaps unforeseen by the breathless producers of our technological devices.

Let us think for a moment about learning. An important, though simplistic, observation can be made: that for purposes of intake, we have moved from the pencil and eraser to word processing. Today so much is transmitted digitally that we scarcely remember how to use a notepad, do a mental calculation, or spell a word. This is true across the sociological board. Instead of actually going to the bank, we pay online. We order online. We read texts, even classic books, online.

Many of us contributing to this festschrift work in an academic setting. We are well aware of how learning has changed dramatically just in the last few years. In a recent rather amusing study on YouTube, about 150 students are sitting in a nineteenth-century-style lecture hall, in semicircles facing the front. As the camera roves around the room, each student holds up a sign. Here is a sampling:

- "I will read 8 books this year, 2,300 Web pages & 1,281 Facebook profiles."
- "I will write 48 pages this semester, and over 500 pages of e-mails."
- "I spend 3½ hours a day online; 2½ hours on my cell phone."
- "I am a multitasker; I have to be."

And a couple with a social conscience add items such as this one:

- "This laptop costs more than most people make in a year."[13]

Several features emerge. The most obvious, as we just stated, is the shift from the printed page (known, revealingly, as hard copy) to electronic media. The phenomenon is widespread. For the news, the daily or weekly paper is being replaced by the Internet. Television itself is under threat because of the Internet. We may now even go to Web TV! All the major newspapers as well as the news channels are available on the Internet, so that we do not need to actually open the paper at breakfast or sit down in the evening in front of the family television to watch the news, although many still do so for cultural or traditional reasons. Typically, younger people are far more likely to learn from the Internet than older folks. This trend brings opportunities and challenges.

The same is true for the entertainment industry. Consider the iPod. Everybody who's anybody has one: the President of the United States, the Queen of England, and people such as Karl Lagerfeld, the designer, who claims to have seventy of them, able to play over sixty thousand CDs. It is not just young people, but many different kinds of people, from clergy to CEOs to rappers. They are international. Stand in line, sit at a café, and you'll see people walking by, smiling or waving to the invisible orchestra in their ear. It would be rare to walk into a subway or train and not see a majority of people with little wires attached to their ears.

This product was launched in October 2001. Today it has sold well over 130 million units. It is easily the best-selling digital audio player ever. There are a number of forms, including the *iPod classic*, which is drive-based, the *iPod touch*, which is used by touching the screen, the video-capable *iPod nano*, and the *iPod shuffle*, which has no screen. While the iPod classic stores different media onto a hard drive, the other models use flash memory, a

13. http://mediatedcultures.net/mediatedculture.htm.

nonvolatile computer memory that can be erased and reprogrammed.[14] The technology and the new models change almost weekly.

The iPod can transfer photographs, games, videos, calendars, and any number of other materials, as long as there is support for those features. Think about how we now listen to music. From such places as iTunes large numbers of musical selections may be downloaded. And this brings with it many features. The iPod has an enormous capacity to store. You can put a lifetime's listening on there. You may listen to things you didn't know you had, or had forgotten. How about Sinead O'Connor's rap album, or Louis Armstrong's *Hot Five*?

The product makes several boasts. For example, your choice of music can become more informed. As with the "find" function on a computer, you can request titles by composer, year, or even keyword, such as *heaven* or *blue*. And you can use the random function, called *shuffle*, for the iPod to be your DJ, and introduce you to things from all kinds of genres. You can also share tunes over a network and build resources with friends, say college friends or egghead friends. You can now go to a party where the DJ uses the MP3J to give a group the program of choice. A character called Johnny Rocket has sponsored iParties in places such as Philadelphia and London, by promoting a *Playlist Club*, which empowers the partygoer to be active in musical choice. Many companies exist that will help you create a repertoire, and make sure you are up on the latest in your taste-field.

THE IPOD CULTURE

The iPod culture has some fascinating aspects. It used to be that you could walk into someone's home and look at his bookshelves in order to know the character of that person. For example, if you enter my living room and look at the bookshelves, you will find volumes on history, particularly European history, lots on music, from classical to jazz, and many art books. Downstairs, in the study, there are reams of books on theology, sociology, culture studies, and so forth. Obviously, I read to relax or enjoy in the living room, and do my study and writing downstairs. I am a lover of the arts,

---

14. It is a specific type of Electrically Erasable Programmable Read-Only Memory (EEPROM) that is erased and programmed in large blocks, avoiding the need to erase the entire chip in order to start again. Recently, Apple added the iPad, a cross between the iPod and a computer, to their product line.

especially of music, but I am a student of world history. I am a professional theologian, with a special concern for sociology.

Today one can do a similar profile based on the selections in my iPod or my network preferences: large amounts of sacred music, from medieval chant through Bach to Tavener, lots of African-American music, and classic rock from the early years. Music has always been an important way to access a society's mores, hidden assumptions, and customs. But the iPod medium tells us much more than just what kind of music, and therefore views of the world, one may have. The medium itself speaks volumes.

Some consequences of the iPod are quite amusing. New psychological conditions are being identified in the iPod world. For example, *playlistism* means the snobbish way in which someone can examine his neighbor's oh-so-boorish collection of disco or show tunes instead of highbrow music, say Gregorian chant! The opposite is *PAS*, or *playlist anxiety syndrome*, which means that you fear your musical image will make you look bad. As a result, many people manage their lists in a way that shows a surface sophistication, but hides the music that is preferred.

We live in a media-saturated culture. The question before us, then, is how much of it is good, and how much of it is negative. The deeper question is whether we have left space for metaphor. Or are we on the same desperate quest for universals?

ADVANTAGES

Many positives must be noticed. Walks on the beach are quieter, since few people still listen to music with their boom boxes. You can be far more discreet with your musical pleasure. Earphones have improved so that your neighbor does not need to hear the thumping sound of a drum, or the high-strung melodies of the violin. My brother loves the *Lieder* of Hugo Wolf, and his wife can't stand them; so he can tune in and phase out, listening to Wolf without disturbing the family.

Of course, access to knowledge has become extraordinarily enhanced because of tools such as the Internet. Although some of us older folks have endured a steep learning curve, what is available online, especially if you know how to use the right search engines, is astonishing. We can be in contact with many parts of the world in an instant. Globalization occurs not only through information but also by being able to take ourselves to a certain place rather easily. Being interdependent with people and cultures from around the planet is a biblical ideal! Max Stackhouse, always a thoughtful commentator on globalization, puts it this way:

> We face a new international interdependency that invites us into new relationships with our neighbors near and far in spite of the resurgence of ethnic and tribal violence in troubled, bloody corners of the globe. Now, enjoying each other's cuisine, sharing each other's customs, singing each other's songs, producing and buying each other's goods, and even thinking each other's thoughts is more widely possible than ever before. However superficial most of this seems most of the time, the multicultural reality of pluralism is a fact of life as well as an educational slogan. Global is what we are and do.[15]

And while there are certainly dangers with globalization, particularly when dominant economic powers seek hegemony over the weaker ones, it is not a foregone conclusion that local cultures will be steamrolled into conformity. One feature tied in to globalization is known as *glocalization*, which means that a particular cultural tradition may travel the world, but it will always take on local color. Other voices besides those from the West can be better heard.

Mediation is providing a way to hear the good news of the gospel far and wide. It is providing a way in which the ideals described in Psalm 87 can be fulfilled: citizenship in Zion is granted to people from every nation, even the former enemies of Israel, such as Rahab, Babylon, and Philistia (Ps. 87:4). Many countries officially closed to the influence of the Christian message hear it anyway because of communications that devices such as the Internet provide. I have traveled a number of times into China, and there the church has moved from surviving to thriving, greatly aided by the ability to go under the radar and hear the good news. Historians argue that one significant force in the demise of the Communist world is the Internet.

CAUTIONS

From Cézanne to the iPod would seem worlds apart, but the epistemological issues are really the same. Before we become utopian about mediated culture, though, let us consider the downsides. One of them is in the way

---

15. Max Stackhouse, *Christian Social Ethics in a Global Era* (Nashville: Abingdon, 1995), 18–19.

in which music is delivered (e.g., via iTunes). I grew up on 78 and 33 rpms, or vinyls. The great advance of the 33 was its size. Just as important was the record jacket, which allowed us to have liner notes, biographies, pictures, and so forth. Then came the CD, with even greater recording capacity. The notes were squeezed into little booklets, full of information, but with minuscule type. Now we have simply songs. The data on the computer is minimal. We have content without context. Despite the advantages of having so much music available, this is also a negative, in that it encourages us to listen to mere sound bytes, mere isolated sound phenomena. We don't know how to situate them into the larger world of music or of experience. No "joints"!

Another negative, the opposite side of the coin of its positive, is the creation of personal isolation. Is it good that hundreds of people walking down Fifth Avenue or the Champs Elysées, most of them wearing earphones, can live in their own universe, without much regard to the surroundings? Perhaps so; perhaps not. We don't want to nurture the illusion that a large city street is a communion of the saints. Yet there is a certain neighborhood on the sidewalk, nevertheless. Being aware of my fellow walkers, peering into the shop windows, giving money to a homeless person, getting out of the way of a large dog—these are part of the fabric of human community in a city setting.

A recent report by a woman who commutes on foot to work every day explains. She has about a ten-minute walk in central Boston. She acquired an iPod shuffle, which allowed her to listen to her favorite rock songs, instead of the urban noise. Trees, dogs, cars, sirens—everything disappeared during her walk. All was like being underwater, she decided. And then she thought she was really missing these things. Parents pushing toddlers in strollers, people shoveling snow off the sidewalks, kids waiting for a bus—all were replaced by a screaming 1979 track from The Police. She concluded that instead of escaping to musical paradise, it was like putting herself in a hall of mirrors, and suddenly she felt very, very small, even adrift, isolated, alone. So she decided not to listen while she walked, and to hear the world, with its cacophony and its harmony alike.[16]

Of course, such anecdotes cannot substitute for hard evidence. Numerous studies are emerging that point to both the dangers and the advantages of the iPod culture. While somewhat one-sided, the recent book *Mediated*, by Thomas de Zengotita, helpfully shows the connection between a culture

16. From a radio testimony: http://www.onpointradio.org/shows/2005/03/20050314_a_main.asp.

that flatters the individual and the narcissism promoted by everything from iPods to blogging to self-help guides.[17] The author is particularly sensitive to the impression that we all live in Times Square, making us into "the ultimate Cartesians" who cannot be sensitive to the suffering world around.

The sociological term for this phenomenon is *privatization*, which has been well analyzed but not so well opposed. Peter Berger has often alluded to privatized religion as belonging to a society that respects everyone's right to hold personal convictions as long as they do not disturb or violate anyone else's space, which renders them mostly impotent. To be sure, one of the enduring problems of modernity is how to promote not only religious freedom but the capacity to benefit the public square, without at the same time coercing our neighbors. Berger advocates a middle way in which respectful pluralism can live alongside faith-based initiatives for amelioration.[18] Once again, all depends on "joints" that hold things both together and at a distance.

One more negative to consider, and not the least, is what we might call indiscretion. We are not just talking of pornography here, which, of course, is a terrible blight. It takes indiscretion to new levels of abuse. But the same holds for more ordinary levels. A recent article in the fascinating book *Everyday Theology* describes the problem. In "Welcome to the Blogosphere," youth minister Justin Bailey explains that he had very little idea of what was going on in the lives of his young people until he discovered Xanga, a series of Web diaries by adolescents.[19] To his astonishment, he found out that these youths would share things—both bad and good—on blogs that they would never tell him or their parents. In addition to critiquing the obviously narcissistic side of blogging, Bailey points out the shift in the location of authority that is going on. Instead of a restrained group of experts, now everyone controls the information. One result is the fascination with scandal. Another, however, is an increasing suspicion of spin, hence a greater distrust in authority. Further, there is a shift in ecclesiology, from the traditional church to an amorphous planetary community of spiritual people, who by definition are interested in just about anything and everything that qualifies as spiritual.

17. Thomas de Zengotita, *Mediated: How the Media Shapes Our World and the Way We Live in It* (New York: Bloomsbury, 2006).

18. Peter L. Berger, foreword to Charles L. Glenn, *The Ambiguous Embrace: Government and Faith-Based Schools and Social Agencies* (Princeton, NJ: Princeton University Press, 2002).

19. Justin A. Bailey, "Welcome to the Blogosphere," in *Everyday Theology*, ed. Kevin J. Vanhoozer et al. (Grand Rapids: Baker Academic, 2007), 173–89.

Our wise youth pastor does not pan all of this but calls for a discerning use of these technologies.

Many of us who now must use e-mail for our work lament similar problems. People allow themselves to say things electronically that they never would offline. Memos rather than letters, "Bill" rather than "Dear Bill," lazy language rather than good English, and especially tones that would not pass when speaking live—all of these are permitted, so it would seem, because of this rapid form of "messaging." Not to speak of the sheer quantity of messages every day, and every hour. I don't believe I am saying these things because of my age, but because of the reality of these most convenient, most frustrating forms of communication. We are now on an electronic leash. Oh, that we could be blessedly out of touch sometimes!

One more facet of this indiscretion to note. Do we want to live in a society without secrets? Not an easy question. Some hidden facts need to come to the surface. Had the cooking of the books at Enron and other large companies been revealed sooner, the mess might have been far less. But there is another side to it. Some secrets are worth keeping. Pastors know that. At a recent luncheon for ministers, one of the guests had been a counselor for President Clinton after the scandal of his affair with a young intern. We asked him whether the President's repentance was genuine. He rightly answered that it was a pastoral secret. We do not really need to know about this matter, which is between a man and his God.

Is it possible to find beauty in an iPod culture? Surely it is. But that can be achieved only when we clothe our communications, our listening, our downloading with ethical norms full of grace. Only when we fight hard to claim the right to metaphor, to context, and to rules of engagement can we expect beauty to emerge. Otherwise, we will become like the machines we've invented.

CONCLUSION

What we are left with is the need for great wisdom in discerning how to use these technologies. While true, it does not spell out the specifics to be told that we are in the world but not of it (John 17:15–16). Nor does it tell us much to be reminded to "test everything; hold fast what is good. Abstain from every form of evil" (1 Thess. 5:21–22 ESV). These are the right principles. But in the trenches, as we make use of these technologies, we will want to grow in our discernment "by constant practice to distinguish good from evil" (Heb. 5:14).

No success in these subtle matters will greet us unless we begin at the beginning, with a God who is outside the creation, yet intimately related to it, a God who is both one and many, and who therefore has given us a world with both universals and particulars. If we are too squeezed together by the overconnections of electronics, we will have no space, no freedom to move about. Cézanne and Picasso clearly sensed this. But do we? If we are too disjointed because of the isolation of an iPod culture, we will have no community—neither with one another nor with the Creator, who is our Redeemer and Friend.

12

The Legacy of J. Alan Groves:
An Oral History

KIRK E. LOWERY

IT IS WELL KNOWN that the published work of researchers in any discipline tells only part of the story. Sometimes the rest of the story is told by others, or in memoirs and biographies. More often, the untold story is lost. Because I was a participant in and eyewitness to Professor Groves' scientific research—especially his most original and creative work—I desire here to document the context of that published research.

In 1980 I was deep into the research for my doctorate at the University of California, Los Angeles. Professor Groves heard of my research agenda and found that it nearly duplicated his own, so he telephoned me. We discovered that we had a common vision: using information technology to leverage biblical studies. Our goals were similar: an electronic version of the Hebrew Bible, with each word associated with linguistic information that could then be used in further research. That "further" research we also held in common: the study of the linguistic structures of not just individual words or individual sentences, but whole groups of sentences. In the jargon, we both were interested in the "text linguistics" or "discourse analysis" of the Hebrew Bible, a grammar not just of words or clauses, but of the text. We saw the computer as a means of reaching that goal. My dissertation[1] was a pilot project intended to innovate and validate methods for using the computer and linguistics to reach these research goals. As for Professor Groves, he embarked on the task of providing for the entire Hebrew Bible what I was doing for just one canonical book, Judges.

During the next eighteen years we had frequent contact, although I was living in Europe. I used his developing databases in my own work and sent him many suggestions and corrections. We met often at academic conferences; when I was on the North American continent I often visited him at the Westminster Seminary campus and sometimes lectured there for his students. When in 1998 Professor Groves heard that I was considering a major career move, he offered me a position at Westminster to work directly on our mutual concern: the *Westminster Hebrew Bible Morphology Database*. Given our history together, the reader should not be surprised that I accepted his offer with alacrity. At his initiative, Professor Groves asked me to adopt and care for the growth and development of his "baby," as he called it, the then-known Westminster Hebrew Institute,[2] and I became director in January 2002. In 2009, the Groves Center was spun off from Westminster Theological Seminary as an independent nonprofit corporation. What began as the work of an individual scholar has now taken on a life of its own.

THE PYRAMID'S BASE: THE TEXT

As an engineering undergraduate at Dartmouth College, Professor Groves was exposed to the number-crunching mainframe computers used in engineering during the 1970s. He came to understand that computers could crunch not just numbers, but text as well. His faith led him to envision the computer as becoming what I call a "prosthesis" for the mind as it studies the sacred text. He knew that the human mind, wonderful information processor though it is, has serious limitations: it can get tired, make mistakes, overlook important facts, fail to see significant patterns. The computer, although prone to mindless interpretation of instructions, is ruthlessly consistent and

1. Kirk E. Lowery, "Toward a Discourse Grammar of Biblical Hebrew" (Ph.D. diss., University of California, Los Angeles, 1985).

2. The faculty of Westminster Theological Seminary renamed the Institute the J. Alan Groves Center for Advanced Biblical Research on December 15, 2006, just six weeks before Al's death on February 5, 2007.

overlooks nothing. The computer plus the human mind is a very powerful observer of any data, including the Bible.

Where to start to realize this vision? With the text itself, obviously. The first step was to create an electronic version of the Hebrew Bible. Professor Groves looked around and discovered that he was not alone in needing such a text.[3] Although there were several electronic texts in existence, none of them were publicly available for scholars. And there were problems to solve.

- Computers did not have the ability to represent the Hebrew text, which consists of consonants, vowels, accents, and other marks combined together in complex ways.
- There was no direct access to the primary manuscript used for the printed Hebrew Bibles. The Leningrad Codex was unavailable for direct study.
- The process of manual input of the text inevitably brings typographical errors.[4]

These problems were eventually solved, sometimes by "brute force" manual methods, but also by using automated comparison of the text with other electronic texts. Professor Groves came to realize that, in most aspects, the goal of an accurate electronic text and the problems of producing and transmitting copies of that text were exactly the same as the goal and problems of the ancient scribes and copyists of the Hebrew Bible:

3. The text began as an electronic transcription by Richard Whitaker (Princeton Seminary, New Jersey) and H. Van Parunak (then at the University of Michigan, Ann Arbor) of the 1983 printed edition of Biblia Hebraica Stuttgartensia (BHS). It was continued with the cooperation of Robert Kraft (University of Pennsylvania) and Emanuel Tov (Hebrew University, Jerusalem), and completed by Professor Groves. The transcription was called the *Michigan-Claremont-Westminster Electronic Hebrew Bible* and was archived at the Oxford Text Archive (OTA) in 1987. It has been variously known as the "CCAT" and the "eBHS" text. Since that time, the text has been modified in many hundreds of places to conform to the photo-facsimile of the Leningrad Codex, Firkovich B19A, residing at the Russian National Library, St. Petersburg—hence the change of name. The Groves Center has continued to scrutinize and correct this electronic text as a part of its continuing work of building morphology and syntax databases of the Hebrew Bible, since correct linguistic analysis requires an accurate text.

4. J. Alan Groves, "Correction of Machine-Readable Texts by Means of Automatic Comparison: Help with Method," in *Bible and Computer: Methods, Tools, Results: Proceedings of the Second International Colloquium*, Association Internationale Bible et Informatique, Jerusalem, June 9–13, 1988 (Paris: Champion-Slatkine, 1989), 275.

> For me, one positive result of trying to sanitize machine readable texts has been a new appreciation for that masoretic methodological madness by which those earlier copyists preserved the accuracy of the texts that they were copying! Possibly what we need today is a strong dose of masoretic methodological medicine for machines.[5]

Professor Groves often remarked to me that "we're just 3rd millennium masoretic scribes." He had a deep sense of standing in that grand and venerable tradition of Bible preservation and transmission. One of the great differences, however, is the advantage that information technology gives us: 100 percent accurate copying of a text file. When an error is discovered and corrected, that correction is automatically preserved in every succeeding generation of copies of that file. Visual comparison of versions of files is no longer necessary. It is accomplished in milliseconds by computer. All one has to worry about are the differences between files.[6] In the years since 1987, when the first version of the text was released, many errors have since been discovered and corrected. In the past five years, we have corrected hardly a single consonant, one or two vowels per year, and a few more accents. We can have a high degree of confidence that the present condition of the text is "essentially perfect." What remains is how different individuals interpret ambiguities in the physical manuscript itself.

It is important to understand that the goal was not to preserve the *original* text of the Hebrew Bible. Nor was it to create a text that is "correct" according to the rules of orthography and cantillation as taught in Judaism. Rather, the goal was to create, as exactly as humanly possible, a *representation* or "mirror image" of the manuscript *Codex Leningradensis* (Firkovich B19A), with all its warts and blemishes. The interpretation and "correction" of the perceived mistakes of the scribe were deliberately left to a later stage of interpretation. We have the physical manuscript; all else is interpretation of one kind or another. Since the text would become the basis of all later data processing, the integrity of that text overrode all other considerations.

The first version of the electronic Hebrew Bible was released to the public in 1987. It has been the basis for the Hebrew text in all the Bible software products, for many Web sites, and even for printed editions of the text.[7]

5. Ibid., 276.
6. Ibid., 278.
7. Cf. recently A. Philip Brown II and Bryan W. Smith, eds., *A Reader's Hebrew Bible* (Grand Rapids: Zondervan, 2008).

ERECTING THE FIRST FLOOR: A MORPHOLOGY OF BIBLICAL HEBREW

With the completion[8] of the text on which all other analysis would be based, Professor Groves proceeded with the next step:[9] splitting the text into the smallest units of meaning (morphemes)[10] and attaching labels or "tags" that indicate information about that tiny unit: the part of speech (noun, verb, etc.), the lemma (i.e., the dictionary form of the word), its language (Hebrew or Aramaic), gender, number, verbal stem, verbal conjugation, and so on. One of the problems with automating the labeling of the text is that computers do not understand natural language very well. Since human beings use language very flexibly and computers are very rigid in their understanding of language, writing programs to automate the process of linguistic analysis is very difficult (some say impossible). So one must compromise.[11] Professor Groves used a combination of computer programs and manual checking to "bootstrap" the first pass to create the database.[12]

Morphemes mean what they mean in a context. But "context-bound" parsing is computationally very difficult. That is because a component of interpretation is needed. It is far easier to parse morphemes by giving every uniquely spelled unit its own lemma and parsing and creating a dictionary. Then one simply has the computer look up the parsing in the dictionary as it examines each morpheme in the text. But morphemes can be ambiguous in their analysis depending on their context. For example, the Hebrew word *melek*, "king," can be in either the absolute or construct state. By itself, we simply cannot say. It is both and neither. The word *mlakim*, "kings," can be only in the absolute state, and *malkey*, "kings of," can be only in the construct

---

8. I am speaking here of the logical process. In actual fact, Professor Groves had already begun this second stage of analysis concurrently with the final stages of completing the biblical text.

9. The complete description of the process of creating the morphology database is found in J. Alan Groves, "On Computers and Hebrew Morphology," in *Computer Assisted Analysis of Biblical Texts: Papers Read at the Workshop on the Occasion of the Tenth Anniversary of the "Werkgroep Informatica" Faculty of Theology Vrije Universiteit, Amsterdam, November 5–6, 1987*, ed. E. Talstra (Amsterdam: Free University Press, 1989), 45–86.

10. It turns out that version 1.0 (1991) contained 425,889 morphemes. Today, version 4.12 contains 480,494.

11. This is a matter of continuing debate among computational linguists, with the consensus swinging back and forth every few years. Cf. Ivan A. Sag and Thomas Wasow, *Syntactic Theory: A Formal Introduction*, CSLI Lecture Notes no. 92 (Stanford, CA: CSLI Publications, 1999), 33. Professor Groves used the equivalent of what is known today as a context-free grammar (CFG) to parse the text and verify it. The need for manual checking is consonant with the known limitations of CFG models of grammar.

12. Ibid., 51–52.

state. We don't need to see the context. Writing programs to handle words such as *melek* is very difficult and complex. And it gets worse: sometimes the analysis depends on which lemma you say it comes from. And what do you do with words that are clearly nouns in their form, but are used like adverbs in some sentences? If you have only one "box" to fill in the label, which is it, noun or adverb?

The question is not an academic one. In modern Bible software, one can search and make complex queries of patterns of morphological information. The result of those queries can be statistically summarized. If the database is inconsistent or wrong, to that extent the user's results are also wrong, perhaps without the user's being aware of it. If scholars are basing their published results on conclusions based on flawed results from the database, everyone suffers. Hence, from the very beginning, Professor Groves was very painfully aware of the need for precision, consistency, and accuracy.

The first version of the morphology (released in 1991) represented the opinion of Professor Groves on every word in the Hebrew Bible. If he had published his opinions in the traditional fashion, the resulting publication would have been hundreds of pages in length. As just one example, let us consider how the database treats the *ketiv-qere* phenomenon.[13] In approximately nineteen hundred places in the Leningrad manuscript, the scribes noted in the margin that one should ignore the spelling of the main text, the *ketiv* (that which is written), and instead read (aloud) the form that is noted in the margin, the *qere* (that which is read [aloud]). The *qere* uses the vowels found in the main text. The *ketiv* remains unvocalized. Since consonants with different vowels can mean different things in Hebrew words, many times the linguistic analysis of the *ketiv* is much less clear than the *qere*. Professor Groves wanted to provide a lemma, part of speech, and parsing to all of the *ketiv*, which meant that he must first add the vowels—that is, he had to figure out what the intended vocalization of the *ketiv* might be.

In the end he reconstructed all nineteen hundred vocalizations and added a lemma, part of speech, and parsing to each *ketiv*. This was a major research project, with important observations and conclusions as to how the variance might have originated—all bound up and implied by the vocalization and analysis. This also has implications for our understanding of the history of the transmission of the text. Professor Groves lamented to me on

---

13. For the standard treatment of this subject with bibliography, see Emanuel Tov, *Textual Criticism of the Bible*, 2nd rev. ed. (Minneapolis: Fortress, 2001), 58–63.

several occasions that he had not published the results of his work, using all the notes he made during the course of his reconstructing the *ketiv*. Yet the results abide and are available to the interested user.

CONCLUSION

Professor Groves' death prevented him from accomplishing all that he envisioned.[14] Nevertheless, his vision continues to inspire us. The Hebrew syntax database he spoke of is now nearing completion, and plans are already underway for new possibilities, including other ancient Near Eastern languages and texts. The pyramid, the foundations of which he laid, is growing. Tens of thousands of users of all descriptions are making use of the text and data that he created. Unlike ordinary academic publications, Professor Groves' databases are not static, but are living, growing collections of knowledge and experience in understanding the text and message of the Hebrew Bible. Since Professor Groves' work forms the foundation of the Hebrew Bible digital pyramid of knowledge, it is difficult to overstate the significance and impact of his legacy for the next century of biblical studies.

---

14. His stated plan existed in four stages: the text, the morphology, a syntax, and a semantic extension to the database. Cf. Groves, "On Computers and Hebrew Morphology," 46–48.

13

"Has Anything So Great as This Ever Happened?" The Role of Deuteronomy 4:32–35 in Redemptive History[1]

J. ALAN GROVES

BEFORE WE TURN our attention to the book of Deuteronomy and the role of chapter 4 for the book, let me offer a few personal words.

It is a great honor to be here before you today, and I am very mindful of the role that many of you in this auditorium have had in my formation and development. Some of you will even hear explicit echoes of your influence in the address this morning. Let me acknowledge that it is impossible anymore for me to know where your voices leave off and mine begins. I do, however, feel I must acknowledge a special indebtedness to Professors Gaffin, Green, and Poythress. They have provided me the particular language and framework to help me express those things I have been seeing in the book of Deuteronomy for so many years, but had found so hard to articulate.

1. This is the inaugural address for Professor Groves, delivered March 24, 1999, here belatedly published. The oral nature and tone of the address have been largely preserved in this article, which was produced from Professor Groves' full manuscript. Only a few stylistic and formatting matters have been changed.

STRUCTURE OF DEUTERONOMY AND ROLE OF DEUTERONOMY 4

Given the scholarly attention paid to Deuteronomy and given its undisputed use by other books in the OT canon, understanding Deuteronomy is essential to our interpretation of the entire OT. Virtually everyone agrees that the Former Prophets (Joshua, Judges, Samuel, and Kings) were shaped by Deuteronomy's theology. Most concur that the Latter Prophets (Isaiah, Jeremiah, Ezekiel, and the Twelve) argued their case from its tenets.[2] Even Psalm 1 invites us to see that the entire Psalter is a reflection on *torah*, that is, Deuteronomy. Yet few books have been so debated concerning their structure, occasion, and purpose.

Deuteronomy consists of three final speeches by Moses. These speeches tell a story, give law, and introduce covenant.[3] Followed by a closing song of covenant lawsuit and blessings to the tribes—and spiced with exhortations to remember, to be courageous, and to obey—Deuteronomy was Moses' last will and testament. He was profoundly concerned for the generations that would follow and for their faith. In his speeches in Deuteronomy, Moses looked back to explain what had gone before and anticipated what would come to pass.

To understand Deuteronomy we need to understand the role of chapters 1–4, and within chapters 1–4 the role of chapter 4 itself. I would argue that Deuteronomy 4 is the conclusion to Moses' first speech in Deuteronomy and that chapter 4 is integral to the text, not some later insertion to bridge between the historical introduction (1:6–3:29) and the lengthy section of laws and commands that follow (5:1–28:68).[4] Syntactical markers and content provide overwhelming evidence of its essential role in its present position.[5]

---

2. I believe that the argument of Isaiah 40–48, a covenant lawsuit in form, comes from the concluding verses of Deuteronomy 4. In this lawsuit, the prophet argues against idols and for Yahweh, on the foundation that Yahweh has spoken in the past of a judgment that has come to pass. Isaiah several times uses the language of Deuteronomy 4:35, 39 that "Yahweh is God; besides him there is no other" (Isa. 43:11; 44:6; 45:5–6, 14, 18, 21–22; 46:9). Therefore, he is able to do what yet remains, the hope of a glorious salvation in Zion. He has spoken in the past. He is Yahweh; besides him there is no other. He can and will bring to pass his redemptive work.

3. Dennis T. Olson, *Deuteronomy and the Death of Moses: A Theological Reading* (Minneapolis: Fortress, 1994), 11.

4. Jon Douglas Levenson, "Who Inserted the Book of the Torah?" *HTR* 68 (1975): 203–33.

5. The initial *v'attah* plus vocative ("And now, O Israel . . .") is a macro-syntactic marker—that is, it controls the larger context, and not simply the clause that it most immediately precedes. The imperative clauses that follow are each understood as being under the force of this opening

Deuteronomy 4 begins with a clear syntactical signal—*v'attah* followed by a vocative and a series of imperatives—that Moses had come to the conclusion of his speech. Moses began this conclusion with a series of exhortations to keep the commandments, because they would reveal that Israel was a wise[6] nation. Moses recalled the fiery revelation at Horeb[7] and argued its present and future implications for worshiping Yahweh instead of idols. Finally, Moses pulled all the rhetorical stops and let loose with that extraordinary series of rhetorical questions we heard read earlier in the OT reading—extraordinary in their number and length and in Moses' explicit exhortation to "ask now about the former days . . . from one end of heaven to the other" (Deut. 4:32).[8]

Finally, I am going to make the claim, perhaps an extravagant claim, that in chapter 4 Moses was not only providing his interpretive key for his speeches in Deuteronomy, but also showing his understanding of the rationale for the entire Pentateuch, his understanding of the climax and purpose of redemptive history.

"MOSES BEGAN TO EXPOUND THIS TORAH"

We tend to think of Moses primarily as mediator of God's words to Israel. Perhaps our view is almost that of inspired ventriloquist: God spoke to Moses; he repeated the words to the people. But the opening of the book of Deuteronomy challenges the audience to augment their understanding of Moses' role in Israel with the words in 1:5 that "Moses began to expound[9] this torah, this teaching . . ."[10] Moses was not simply spokesman and mediator, but

---

syntax. *V'attah* often marks the conclusion or main point of an argument within a larger speech, usually an imperative or series of imperatives to which the speaker is calling special attention (cf. Gen. 27:8; Deut. 10:12; 1 Kings 3:7).

6. Note that wisdom language is the language of a father-son relationship.

7. Per the usage in Deuteronomy, *Horeb* is used throughout the paper instead of its equivalent, *Sinai*.

8. Unless otherwise noted, the translation of the English text is my own translation of the Hebrew.

9. The verb *b'r* occurs only in Deuteronomy 1:5, 27:8, and Habakkuk 2:2. While its connotation may vary in each context, it seems to have a sense of "doing something clearly" (Jeffrey H. Tigay, *Deuteronomy: The Traditional Hebrew Text with the New JPS Translation*, JPS Torah Commentary [Philadelphia: JPS, 1996], 5). The meaning of *hatorah hazo't* ("this torah") is debated. Recently scholars are suggesting more frequently that "law" is inadequate or misleading. "A program of catechesis" has been suggested by Olson (*Deuteronomy*, 10–11).

10. *B'ever* is translated by the NIV as "east of the Jordan," begging the question of the position of the one writing the comments. *Torah* is translated "teaching" by the JPS translation and several other commentators.

also *interpreter* of Yahweh's word—an interpreter not only of the words of God, but of his actions and deeds as well. By identifying the climax to the story and making plain its purpose, Moses provided Israel a hermeneutic, an interpretive framework within which to understand and interpret revelation.

Beginning in 1:6, Moses began to interpret this *torah*, this teaching, not by giving exhortations and commands, but by tracing the experience and events of the people of Israel since leaving Horeb. He reminded them of the story they had all experienced or heard about. Moses placed the commandments, decrees, and laws into a broader history, an all-encompassing story. This story's author was Yahweh, an Author able to write with events as well as words.

I have purposely and advisedly chosen *story* as the operative genre to describe what Moses was telling. For some, the term *story* may connote fiction, something made up, nonfactual, and nonhistorical. I mean nothing of the sort. Moses was accurately recounting actual events. But I choose to describe Israel's experiences as *story*, rather than *history*, because *story* more clearly communicates what Moses understood about God's actions from the beginning.

For us in the modern age, history as a record of events too often leaves the impression of bare, almost journalistic reporting, beginning at any arbitrary point on a timeline and not necessarily going anywhere in particular. Story, on the other hand, is understood as a genre that has unity, direction, and purpose. Stories have plots with beginning, middle, and end, climax and denouement. Under the hand of the author they go somewhere. The history of Israel was such a story. That story had a climax. And it had a purpose. God was taking it someplace.

History with a Goal: The Story Has a Climax

When Moses comes to the pileup of rhetorical questions at the end of chapter 4, beginning at verse 32, he gives his interpretation of the climax of the story. The exodus was *the event* that made sense of what God had been disclosing since he made man on the earth. Inspired by the Spirit, Moses had come to understand that the exodus was the climactic event in the story. Not just Israel's history, but all human history. Israel's fiery birth in the exodus was rooted in earlier history, even the earliest of history. When Moses said in 4:32, "Ask now about the former days, long before your time, from the day God created man on the earth," it was a hook to the well-known events recounted in Genesis 1. From the beginning, when God created man, the story had a goal. God was taking it someplace.

Through the lens of the exodus, Moses was telling his generation to reread the story from creation to their day afresh, to see that promises to Adam, Abraham, Isaac, and Jacob had all been fulfilled in God's exodus deliverance. It's like coming to the end of a murder mystery where all is revealed. A reader goes back to reconsider everything in the light of the final revelation of the murderer. Words, events, and evidence take on new significance. Suddenly that which was prominent fades into the background and seemingly insignificant details and ambiguities become salient. So it is with Moses and his story. The promise after the fall, the calling of and promises to Abraham—all pointed somewhere. The exodus did not occur in a vacuum. It was no accident in history. God had spoken beforehand concerning what he would do. And now he had done it. Everything served this great salvation that God had wrought. It was this insight that shaped the writing and presentation of the events for the whole Pentateuch.

YAHWEH'S SELF-DISCLOSURE: THE PURPOSE OF THE STORY

Just as Moses finally grasped the significance of the exodus event as the *climax* to the story of humanity, he apprehended the *purpose* of the story as well. In Deuteronomy 4:35 and 39, Moses said that "Yahweh did these things so that Israel might know that Yahweh was God; besides him there was no other." The events of the exodus, God's deliverance of the people he had chosen, revealed God and his purpose for all to see—a salvation of one nation that would ultimately be a blessing to all nations. It was Yahweh's noisy, highly visible declaration to the world, and especially to his people, that he was the Lord, that there was none besides him. It was his deafening statement of self-disclosure.

GOD REVEALS AND CONCEALS HIMSELF: PARADOX IN THE STORY

Reveals

According to Moses in chapters 1–4, Yahweh made himself known in three distinct ways: (1) through the great and mighty deeds he performed,

(2) through the Ten Commandments, his *torah*, his word through Moses, and (3) through the nation[11] that he had chosen out from among all the other nations to be his holy possession.

We have already talked about how God's mighty act of saving his people Israel out of slavery in Egypt revealed him mightily to the nations. This is obvious. God's *torah* also revealed his character, his attributes, his heart, and his holiness. In Deuteronomy 4:6–8, Moses said that the wisdom displayed in God's *torah* would so impress the other nations that they would marvel at Israel's God. This is also obvious. I don't think I need to elaborate further on these points, but I will spend some time with the next point.

What does not jump so quickly to the minds of the audience, nor to our minds, is the notion that Israel itself was to be a revelation of Yahweh to the world. God created Adam in his image, to be his son (Gen. 1:26–27; 5:1–3). Adam disobeyed God and distorted the image of God in him, distancing himself from his Father. But God preserved Adam's seed by means of promise and deed, through all manner of tribulations—flood, famine, barren wives, cruel servitude, and much more. By choosing Adam's descendant Abraham, Yahweh began the creation of a new son, a new people, a new humanity. God faithfully preserved the seed of Abraham, the line of the promise, caring for and nurturing his descendants patiently through the years, blessing and multiplying them against all odds, building to the appointed time when he would take this one chosen nation out from among another nation for his own treasured possession. The climax toward which the story had been building arrived, and God dramatically drew forth his people from the womb of Egypt, a newborn nation, his nation, his newborn son (cf. Ex. 4:22–23; Deut. 1:29–30; 32:6).

The picture of Israel as firstborn son, as Adam was God's son, is a primary theme in the Pentateuch. In Deuteronomy 4 Moses picked up this sonship language in three ways. First, when he spoke in 4:6ff. of how the nations would see Israel's obedience to the law, he used wisdom language, which is most often used to signify the goal of the parent-child relationship. Second, when he spoke of how God had disciplined them with his voice from the fire (4:36), he used the Hebrew verb *ysr*, which most often connotes the kind of instruction and teaching that a father gives his son.[12] Finally, when

11. Olson, *Deuteronomy*, 34.
12. Deut. 8:4; Ps. 2:10; Prov. 19:18.

he asked his rhetorical questions in verses 32–40, he was employing a time-honored device used by parents to drive home their points to their children (e.g., Rebekah to Jacob in Genesis 27:43–45, Proverbs, etc.).

Moses was reminding Israel that they were Yahweh's son. The exhortation to acknowledge Yahweh became an exhortation to fear and honor him as Father. As God's son, Israel was to be like him. Like Adam, they were made in his image, and called to be holy as he is holy. Israel was shown who Yahweh was so that they might honor him. They were given his law so that they would see the heart and character of their Father and know how to behave, think, and view the world as his children. Israel was a son who was to bear the name of his Father with honor. Behavior that was not appropriate to the image of the Father profaned his name, and exhibited a disregard for the salvation he had wrought, the unique election of that people from among all the peoples in the earth.

Not only was Yahweh revealed by what he had done *for* Israel, but he was also revealed *in* Israel, the son born to bear his image. Israel was the new humanity that had been anticipated from the beginning of Genesis forward. Moses saw the climax of the story in Israel's election and saw that God's purpose was to disclose himself through his deeds on behalf of Israel and through his birthing Israel in his image, as his son.

Indicative to Imperative

In Deuteronomy 4:39, Moses finished his speech with an exhortation (and I paraphrase): "Acknowledge, know in your inmost being, that Yahweh is God over the whole universe. There is no other. Therefore, keep his commands. Live in a manner appropriate to your position as son of the Holy One."

Moses moved from the indicative to the imperative. A quick grammar review for those of us who have been out of junior high for more than two years: An indicative statement communicates factual information. An imperative gives a command.

The order is essential here. The structure of Moses' opening speech in chapters 1–4 adheres to this order: indicative to imperative. First the indicative: who God is, what he has done. *Then* the imperative: the responsibility incumbent on a son. Too often the imperative, the "therefore do this," is seen as having priority and the indicative is viewed merely as the grounds for the command, and almost ancillary.

Yahweh's self-disclosure in his actions and presence is often overlooked, as evidenced by the fact that most scholars view these first four chapters as mere prologue to the legal material that follows. Even when these deeds of Yahweh are given some prominence, they are seen merely as the servants to the commands, for which they are the background. Many view the imperative as primary, the indicative as secondary.[13]

But I believe Moses argued differently.

Moses put a primacy on God's self-disclosure, a self-disclosure that surely included his words and will, but first and foremost was found in his miraculous actions on behalf of Israel. Moses had been teaching the people what God had done. On that basis he called Israel to wholehearted obedience and worship of Yahweh, an obedience best summed up in his interpretation of the Ten Commandments in 6:4–5—love the Lord your God with all your heart, soul, mind, and being.

Moses interpreted the commands as being a response to Yahweh's self-disclosure. He did not present the self-disclosure as serving the commands. This point that the indicative is primary cannot be overstressed.

In 4:9 Moses exhorted Israel to remember what they had seen and to teach that to the next generations. This is the program, the agenda. The great indicative, these great acts of God, his great deliverance, was not to be kept to themselves. The fear of the Lord comes from an encounter with the living God. Moses exhorted Israel to learn to fear the Lord and to teach the next generation. How would they pass on their faith and teach the next generation to fear Yahweh? The first step was to pass on the great and wondrous deeds they had seen with their own eyes (Deut. 4:9).

Moses argued from indicative to imperative throughout Deuteronomy. In 6:20–25, for example, he raised the future situation: "When your son asks you, 'What do these stipulations, decrees and laws mean?' tell him, 'We were slaves of Pharaoh in Egypt, but Yahweh brought us out of Egypt with a mighty hand. Before our eyes Yahweh sent miraculous signs and wonders—great and terrible—upon Egypt and Pharaoh and his whole household.'" So what did these laws mean? They meant that God had saved Israel. He made them his people, loved them, made them his children. Had anything as great as this ever happened?

13. The scholarly world has so focused on the imperative as to say *the sign* of Deuteronomic theology is retribution theology—history seen as explained in terms of blessing for obedience, cursing for disobedience. Olson rightly critiques this position (*Deuteronomy*, 175).

Not only is Deuteronomy shaped by this movement from indicative to imperative, but so is the entire Pentateuch. The extended narrative of Genesis and Exodus functions as a lengthy indicative, that is, foundation, to the Ten Commandments such that the Ten Commandments begin *not* with imperatives, but with the evocative words, "I am Yahweh, your God, who brought you out of Egypt, out of the land of slavery" (5:6; cf. Ex. 20:2). One clause, yet pregnant with associations for those who had experienced the exodus. The imperative, the command, comes second in the self-disclosure of God. It does reveal God, particularly his character and attribute of holiness. But the imperative is always grounded in Yahweh's actions, deeds, and person. This indicative-to-imperative pattern is picked up in subsequent books of the canon.

The book of Joshua finishes with an editorial remark that Israel served Yahweh during the lifetime of Joshua and the elders who outlived him, who had known everything the Lord had done for Israel.

Judges 2:6–11 quotes this same editorial remark and even emphasizes that the people had *seen* the great things the Lord had done. But Judges further says that there came a generation who knew neither the Lord nor what he had done for Israel and that this generation did evil in the eyes of the Lord. The people lost sight of the indicative, and so they abandoned the imperative.

When Samuel addressed the people for the sin of the manner in which they had asked for a king, he confronted them with the evidence before the Lord as to all the righteous acts performed by the Lord for them in Egypt (1 Sam. 12:7–8).

To Isaiah he showed himself as the Holy One. Then came a commission for a lifetime.

In Psalm 78 the psalmist opens his psalm with the lessons learned late in time from history past: "I will teach the things that seem to have become hidden, things that our fathers told us, but have not had impact in our lives. We will tell the next generation the great and praiseworthy things he has done." So the psalmist recites a history—Israel disobeyed; they forgot what God had done, the wonders he had shown them. Wonder upon wonder was recounted, but they did not believe. They flattered him with their lips, but their hearts were not loyal. Their heart was the problem. They had seen the gospel and heard it, but they failed to combine it with faith (Heb. 4:1–2).

The psalms, as a day-and-night meditation on the *torah*, reveal a focus not on the commands of the Lord but rather on a declaration and acknowledgment, even in the many laments, that Yahweh was God; besides him there was no other. The psalms invite the reader, therefore, to join in the praise. There was exhortation to proclaim the great and mighty deeds from one generation to the next. There was faith that the generations would proclaim the wonders he had done.

Indicative to imperative: first, what God did in making Israel a son in his image; then what response was appropriate. This is the movement of Deuteronomy. This is the movement that those first generations of interpreters of Yahweh's self-disclosure understood.

Conceals

But there is a paradox or a strange tension in God's self-disclosure. In Deuteronomy 4:10, immediately on the heels of exhorting Israel to remember what they had seen with their own eyes and to teach this to the succeeding generations, in language and syntax that shows he was still awestruck after all these years, Moses reminded them of something they had *not seen* at Horeb:

> The day you stood before Yahweh your God at Horeb, when Yahweh said to me, "Gather the people to me, and I will make known my words to them, so that they may learn to fear me all the days they live on the earth and teach their children," you gathered and you stood at the base of the mountain—the mountain was blazing with fire to the very heart of the heavens, there was thick darkness and dense clouds. And Yahweh spoke to you from the midst of the fire—the sound of words you heard, but a form you did not see; only a voice. (Deut. 4:10–12)

Moses was telling them to remember what they had seen with their eyes and then remember what they had *not* seen with their eyes! They had seen his great and mighty deeds in Egypt and for forty years in the wilderness. At Horeb they had seen Yahweh's fiery, threatening presence, but they had *not seen him*, only the evidence of his presence. He had concealed himself—"they saw no form"[14] (4:12, 14). They had seen the *evidence* of his presence, but not Yahweh himself. In 4:36, within the concluding section of chapter 4, Moses again mentioned the hide-and-seek experience at Horeb,

14. Tigay makes the noteworthy suggestion that they were being reminded that he had seen that certain things were invisible (*Deuteronomy*, 46).

how Yahweh "had made them hear his voice to discipline them," that is, to teach them the fear of the Lord. Yahweh was the Holy One. His holiness was a genuine threat to the lives of those who had not been made holy. He could not reveal himself fully to an unholy people without destroying them. In the larger context of his other theophanic appearances, Yahweh's keeping himself out of sight was actually an act of gracious preservation! The people would have died if they had had this contact with God. At that time Israel rightly recognized this (5:24–27) and begged God to have Moses be the one who mediated between themselves and Yahweh. By concealing himself, Yahweh actually revealed himself in the glory of his holiness.

Isaiah the prophet will later exclaim in praise of Yahweh over against idolatry: "Truly you are a God who hides himself, O God and Savior of Israel" (Isa. 45:15).[15]

THE PROBLEM OF ISRAEL'S HEART: TENSION IN THE DENOUEMENT

But there was a problem. Israel's lack of holiness and their inability to keep covenant with Yahweh, their Father, created a tension in the denouement of the redemptive story. In Moses' third speech wherein he was leading the new generation in making covenant with Yahweh, he began by reminding the Israelites once again: "You have seen, with your own eyes, everything that Yahweh has done in the land of Egypt to Pharaoh, all his servants and his land. Great trials you have seen with your own eyes, those awesome signs and wonders. But Yahweh has not given you a heart to understand, or eyes to see or ears to hear to this day" (Deut. 29:2–4). It was not enough to see the great deeds of the Lord. The Israelites had to have the heart to respond. The problem, as Moses was quick to remind them, was in fact that they were stiff-necked (9:6, 13; 10:16; 31:27) and hard-hearted, prone to worship of false gods.

This is not the behavior of one called to be a son. A son obeys his father out of love for the father and for the honor of the family name. This

---

15. See also Isaiah 42:14 and 57:11 concerning the silence of God. Three significant details about the Isaiah passage: (1) Isaiah rarely speaks directly to God. (2) The context is one in which those from Egypt are bowing down and proclaiming Moses' message—"Surely God is with you, and there is no other; there is no other god" (45:14). Just as Moses said, the nations would recognize God through Israel. Moreover, it is the language of Moses' finale in Deuteronomy 4:35 that is on the lips of Egyptians. (3) The passage immediately leads to Isaiah's condemning idolatry, much like the context of concealment in Deuteronomy 4.

is a fairly foreign concept to us modern Westerners, but still very much a part of the culture in other parts of the world. Yet even we can understand that the obedience of a slave—begrudging, minimal, extracted by fear and force—is different from the obedience of a son, who loves his father and obeys from the heart. In 10:12–16 Moses said that they needed to circumcise their hearts if they were to fear Yahweh and serve him as sons. But Moses recognized that they could not. The further word of the Lord in 30:6 was that Yahweh would one day circumcise the hearts of Israel so that they might love him with their whole beings—with heart, soul, mind, and body. Only a new humanity could approach him, one with a circumcised heart.

"HAS ANYTHING SO GREAT AS THIS EVER HAPPENED?" YAHWEH WAS NOT FINISHED

By using a rhetorical question, a speaker assumes that his audience knows its answer without the answer's needing to be spoken. In fact, a rhetorical question functions as an emphatic statement about something on which the speaker assumes he and his audience agree.[16] As we have noted, Moses closed his opening speech in chapters 1–4 with a string of rhetorical questions:

> Has anything so great as this ever happened? Or has anything like it been heard of? Has any people heard the voice of God speaking from the midst of the fire as you have heard and lived? Or has any god tried to come to take for himself a nation out of the midst of another nation . . . ? (Deut. 4:32–34)

Moses knew the answer, and the audience did as well. Nothing so great as this had ever happened.[17] The exodus was the climax to all of human history. These concluding questions, significant in their introduction, number, length, and connection to the very beginning of time, make it clear not only that Moses believed that the exodus was the greatest event that had ever happened, but that he did not expect any greater thing ever to follow. Nothing so great as the exodus could possibly happen again.

---

16. L. J. de Regt, *Literary Structure and Rhetorical Strategies in the Hebrew Bible* (Winona Lake, IN: Eisenbrauns, 1996), 52, 55.

17. Ibid., 71.

Imagine how shocked Moses would have been to learn that something even much greater lay ahead! In the exodus, the story of mankind had reached a climax. But not yet *the* climax.

We must remember that Moses' own words about the need for a new heart cried out for something to come. The story wasn't finished. But the ending that came would have surprised Moses. The resurrection changed everything. In its light, Moses' rhetorical questions must be answered differently than he and his audience assumed. For in Christ, God *did do* an even greater thing. The story of God's people had a greater, unexpected climax.

The exodus events revealed God's glorious plan and ability to choose and save a people for himself. Yet in Jesus' death on the cross and in his resurrection, Yahweh accomplished an even greater salvation for his people, a salvation to which the exodus pointed. In the death and resurrection of Christ, God set his people free—not from a hostile nation, but from the very grip of sin and the power of death itself. He rolled back not the oppression of four hundred years, but the curse on man from the time of Adam. The exodus, for all its climactic reality and significance, was only a shadow pointing ahead to *the* deliverance, the new exodus that Jesus would lead through the cross and out from the tomb. The choosing and redeeming of God's people in the exodus was not the final note in the symphony. But it was the key theme, introduced sketchily at the beginning, carried forward with greater clarity in the call of Abraham, seeming to climax in the clash of cymbals that was the exodus, but then building again, growing, strengthening until it reached a deafening crescendo in the surprising coda of the cross and resurrection.

As Moses rightly reread history through the lens of the exodus, understanding it anew, so we are to look back over the story of the human race through the lens of Jesus' resurrection. To pick up our murder-mystery analogy again, we know the climax of the story, and everything that has happened is transformed in the light of its end. The promise to Adam has been fulfilled in Christ. Jesus became the sacrifice, once for all—and so much more.

In Hebrews 2:1–4, the writer of Hebrews took his cue from Moses. On the basis of the great indicative of Christ revealed as the Son of God, which he had explained in chapter 1, the writer of Hebrews argued from the indicative to the imperative, used rhetorical questions, and employed a similar kind of argument to persuade his audience that the resurrection was the greater climax of the story.

Just as the exodus from Egypt was accompanied by mighty signs and wonders, so too Jesus' life and ministry were attested to by signs and wonders: "How shall we escape if we ignore such a great salvation? This salvation, which was first announced by the Lord, was confirmed to us by those who heard him. God also testified to it by signs, wonders and various miracles, and gifts of the Holy Spirit distributed according to his will" (Heb. 2:3–4).[18]

Just as Israel was to reveal the glorious character of their Father Yahweh by being his image, by being his son, by obeying their Father, so too Jesus, the true Israelite, revealed his Father by being in his image, by being the True Son, and by obeying his Father with all his heart. But Jesus was the firstborn of many sons. It is the church, the new Israel, the new humanity, the sons of God in Christ, through whom God is revealing himself today.

Moses saw the need for new hearts, for circumcised hearts, in order for Israel to become the true son imaging the Father. The writer of Hebrews said that the wilderness generation had had the gospel preached to them, just as his generation had, but the message to that former generation, according to Hebrews 4:2, "was of no value to them, because those who heard did not combine it with faith." In Christ, Yahweh did the impossible. He circumcised the hearts of his people so that they might believe and become true sons in his image, holy as their Father is holy. Christ has come, died, and been raised from the dead. This good news carries with it a call to respond: to repent and believe. The flow is still from indicative to imperative. In response to the staggering gift of sonship through Christ's death and resurrection, we are called to live our lives in joyful obedience and service to him, gladly following in his footsteps, imitating our heavenly Father, and bearing his image. Ours should be the obedience of sons who love their Father and willingly serve him to honor the family name that he has so graciously shared with us.

Through the words of the writer of Hebrews, we have been highlighting the parallels between what Moses saw and what was seen in greater glory in Jesus. But one difference in the two climaxes to the story stands out by its contrast. At Horeb, Yahweh concealed his form from the people in fire and dark clouds lest he destroy them by his holiness. But at the time to which the exodus pointed, the ultimate climax of history, God revealed himself to the world in the person of his Son.

---

18. Quotations from the book of Hebrews in this chapter are from the NIV.

> In the past God spoke to our forefathers through the prophets at many times and in various ways, but in these last days he has spoken to us by his Son, whom he appointed heir of all things, and through whom he made the universe. The Son is the radiance of God's glory and the exact representation of his being, sustaining all things by his powerful word. After he had provided purification for sins, he sat down at the right hand of the Majesty in heaven. (Heb. 1:1–3)

In Christ, we have seen God! Throughout the OT, the Israelites had to be careful to maintain a "safe" distance from the presence of a holy God because of their sin. Their hearts were unable to keep the covenant that God had made with them. Yahweh could not be seen by them. But now in Christ he has given us new hearts, hearts that can in fact obey him as sons should. He can dwell among us and even in us. What was obscured at Horeb he has revealed on Zion.

In conclusion, hear Hebrews 12:18–24:

> You have not come to a mountain that can be touched and that is burning with fire; to darkness, gloom and storm; to a trumpet blast or to such a voice speaking words, so that those who heard it begged that no further word be spoken to them, because they could not bear what was commanded: "If even an animal touches the mountain, it must be stoned." The sight was so terrifying that Moses said, "I am trembling with fear."
>
> But you have come to Mount Zion, to the heavenly Jerusalem, the city of the living God. You have come to thousands upon thousands of angels in joyful assembly, to the church of the firstborn, whose names are written in heaven. You have come to God, the judge of all men, to the spirits of righteous men made perfect, to Jesus the mediator of a new covenant, and to the sprinkled blood that speaks a better word than the blood of Abel.

Therefore, we ourselves can now say:

> Ask now about the former days, long before our time, from the day God created man on the earth;
> Ask from one end of the heavens to the other: Has anything so great as this ever happened, or has anything like it ever been heard of?
> Has any other people seen their God revealed before their eyes and lived?

Has any god ever tried to take for himself people from every nation, by
    living among his people, by dying for his people and by being
    raised from the dead in the power of the Spirit, like all the things
    the Lord our God has done for us in Christ?
We have been shown these things so that we might know that Jesus, the
    Son of God, is Lord; besides him there is no other.
Because he loved his people Jesus suffered and was raised from the dead.
Acknowledge and take to heart this day
that Jesus is the Lord in heaven above and on the earth below.
There is no other.

14

Curriculum Vitae

J. ALAN GROVES

EDUCATION

Dartmouth College, B.A., 1975.

Dartmouth College, B.E., 1976. Thesis: "Ground Treatment of Wastewater."

Westminster Theological Seminary, M.A.R., 1981.

Westminster Theological Seminary, Th.M., 1983. Thesis: "Chiasm as a Structuring Device in Old Testament Narrative."

Dropsie College of Hebrew and Cognate Learning, Graduate Studies, 1981–82.

Vrije Universiteit, Amsterdam, Ph.D. Candidate.

ACADEMIC POSITIONS

Lecturer in Old Testament, Westminster Theological Seminary, 1982–85.

Assistant Professor of Old Testament, Westminster Theological Seminary, 1985–89.

Director of Academic Computing, Westminster Theological Seminary, 1988–2007.

Associate Professor of Old Testament, Westminster Theological Seminary, 1989–98.

Professor of Old Testament, Westminster Theological Seminary, 1998–2007.

ADMINISTRATIVE POSITIONS

Assistant Dean of Students, Westminster Theological Seminary, 1982–85.

Dean of Students, Westminster Theological Seminary, 1985–87.

Chairman, Department of Old Testament, Westminster Theological Seminary, 1998–2005.

Vice President for Academic Affairs, Westminster Theological Seminary, 2005–6.

PUBLICATIONS

Electronic

Michigan-Claremont-Westminster Electronic Text of Biblia Hebraica Stuttgartensia (coeditor with Emanuel Tov). 1987.

Westminster Electronic Hebrew Morphology of Biblia Hebraica Stuttgartensia (editor). 1991, 1994, 1997.

QUEST: A Grammatical-Syntactical Concordancing Program (contributor). 1991, 1999.

Biblia Hebraica Quinta (technical editor, electronic and hard-copy publications). Stuttgart: Deutsche Bibelgesellschaft, 2004, 2006, 2007.

Hard Copy

Contributor, New International Version Cross-Reference Bible. Grand Rapids: Zondervan, 1984.

"Correction of Machine-Readable Texts by Means of Automatic Comparison: Help with Method." In *Bible and Computer: Methods, Tools, Results: Proceedings of the Second International Colloquium*, 271–98. Paris: Champion-Slatkine, 1989.

193

"On Computers and Hebrew Morphology." In *Computer Assisted Analysis of Biblical Texts*, Applicatio 7, edited by E. Talstra, 45–86. Amsterdam: Free University Press, 1989.

Review of "A Computerized Data Base for Septuagint Studies: The Parallel Aligned Text of the Greek and Hebrew Bible" in *Journal of Northwest Semitic Languages*. Supplement Series 1. Computer Assisted Tools for Septuagint Studies (CATSS) 2, by Emanuel Tov. *Jewish Quarterly Review* 81 (1989): 166–68.

Technology and the Seminary: The 90's and Beyond (coeditor). Philadelphia: Westminster Theological Seminary, 1990.

Review of Wissensbasierte Analyse althebraischer Morphosyntax: Das Expertensystem AMOS, by G. Specht. CBQ 54 (1992): 771–72.

Review of Verbs and Numbers: A Study of the Frequencies of the Hebrew Verbal Tense Forms in the Books of Samuel, Kings and Chronicles, by A. J. C. Verheij. CBQ 54 (1992): 771–72.

Study notes on "Judges." *New Geneva Study Bible*. Nashville: Thomas Nelson, 1995.

Old Testament Abstracts (contributor). 1992–96.

Dictionary of Biblical Imagery (contributor). Grand Rapids: Zondervan, 1998.

Translator, "Judges." *The Holman Christian Standard Bible*. Nashville: Broadman and Holman, 2004.

"Atonement in Isaiah 53." In *The Glory of the Atonement: Biblical, Historical & Practical Perspectives: Essays in Honor of Roger R. Nicole*, edited by C. E. Hill, F. A. James, and R. R. Nicole, 61–89. Downers Grove, IL: InterVarsity Press, 2004.

The Gospel According to the Old Testament Series (coeditor). Phillipsburg, NJ: P&R Publishing, 1999–2007.

"Judges, Book of" in *Dictionary for Theological Interpretation of the Bible*, edited by Kevin Vanhoozer, 410–15. Grand Rapids: Baker Academic, 2005.

"Deuteronomistic History." In *The Zondervan Encyclopedia of the Bible*. Revised edition, edited by Moisés Silva and Merrill Tenney, 2:113–21. Grand Rapids: Zondervan, 2009.

INVITED LECTURES

Vrije Universiteit (Amsterdam, November 1987).

Association Internationale Bible et Informatique, Second International Colloquium (Jerusalem, June 1988).

Georgetown University (Washington, DC, October 1988).

Centre d'Analyse et de Traitement Automatique de la Bible, Université Jean Moulin (Lyon, France, April 1989).

Eberhard Karls Universität Tübingen (Tübingen, Germany, July 1993).

Universität Greifswald (Greifswald, Germany, June 1995).

Universität Greifswald (Greifswald, Germany, November 1998).

GRANTS RECEIVED

National Endowment for the Humanities (1983–87).

Jewish Publication Society (1986).

Packard Humanities Institute (1987–88).

MAJOR CONSULTING AND PROFESSIONAL PROJECTS

Cochair, Computer Assisted Research Group, Society of Biblical Literature, 1987–90.

Co-organizer and chair, Evangelical Theological Society, "Literary Approaches to Judges Group," 1997–2003.

Consultant to Electronic Standards Group for Society of Biblical Literature.

International Board for Association Internationale Bible et Informatique (1994–2006).

Organizing committee for Third and Fourth International Conferences of the Association Internationale Bible et Informatique (1991, 1994).

Grant referee for National Endowment for the Humanities and the Stichting theologisch en godsdienstwetenschappelijk onderzoek in Nederland (Netherlands).

COLLABORATIVE COMPUTING AND HEBREW PROJECTS

University of Pennsylvania (Hebrew text project, 1983–87).

Hebrew University (Hebrew text project, 1983–87).

The Centre Informatique et Bible (Belgium) (Hebrew text project, 1983–87; Hebrew morphology project, 1987–91).

Vrije Universiteit, Universität Greifswald and the German Bible Society (QUEST program, 1989–99).

Capitol Seminary (Hebrew morphology project, 1987–91).

The United Bible Society (Biblia Hebraica Quinta, new critical edition of the Hebrew Bible, 1992–2007).

Contributors

Samuel L. Boyd (B.A., University of North Carolina, Chapel Hill; M.Div., Westminster Theological Seminary; M.A., University of Chicago) is a Ph.D. student at the University of Chicago, studying the Bible in the ancient Near East. He has done archaeological fieldwork in Turkey, and his interests range from Semitic philology to the reception history of the OT. He has taught at Westminster Theological Seminary and the University of Chicago.

Despite living on the south side of Chicago, he favors the Cubs and has an undying obsession with all things related to UNC basketball.

William Edgar (Honors B.A., Harvard University; M.Div., Westminster Theological Seminary; D.Théol., Université de Genève) is professor of apologetics at Westminster Theological Seminary in Philadelphia, where he has been for over twenty years.

Previously, he taught apologetics and missions at the Reformed Seminary in Aix-en-Provence, France, where he is still *Professeur Associé*. He has published widely in such areas as cultural apologetics, ethics, music, Huguenot history, and theology. He is an ordained Presbyterian minister, and a regular speaker in various venues. He is a Senior Fellow at the Trinity Forum, and serves on numerous boards. He plays piano for the gospel-jazz band Renewal.

He and his wife, Barbara, have two children and three grandchildren.

Peter Enns (B.A., Messiah College; M.Div., Westminster Theological Seminary; M.A. and Ph.D., Harvard University) is Senior Fellow in Biblical

Studies at The BioLogos Foundation. Previously, he was Professor of Old Testament and Biblical Hermeneutics at Westminster Theological Seminary for fourteen years. He has written and edited numerous volumes, including *Inspiration and Incarnation: Evangelicals and the Problem of the Old Testament* (Baker Academic, 2005), *Exodus*, NIVAC (Zondervan, 2000), and *Dictionary of the Old Testament: Wisdom, Poetry, and Writings* (InterVarsity Press, 2008). His scholarly interests include wisdom literature, biblical theology, the NT's use of the OT, the ancient Near Eastern context of the OT, and the dialogue between ancient Scripture and contemporary thought.

He is married to Susan and has three nearly all adult children, Erich, Elizabeth, and Sophia. His interests include baseball (manifest primarily in a fierce, predestined commitment to the New York Yankees), reading historical novels, and watching good movies.

Christopher J. Fantuzzo (M.Div., Westminster Theological Seminary; Ph.D. candidate, University of Gloucestershire) is lecturer in Old Testament at Westminster Theological Seminary in Philadelphia. He and his wife, Emily, have two children, Catherine and Thomas.

Sinclair B. Ferguson has been a faculty member at Westminster Theological Seminary, Philadelphia and Dallas (now Redeemer Seminary, Dallas), since 1982. He currently serves as senior minister of The First Presbyterian Church of Columbia, South Carolina. He and his wife Dorothy have four children and five grandchildren.

Douglas J. Green (M.Div., Westminster Theological Seminary; Ph.D., Yale University) is Professor of Old Testament and Biblical Theology at Westminster Theological Seminary, where he has taught since 1992. He was formerly an environmental lawyer in Sydney, Australia. His current research interests range from ancient Near Eastern royal ideology to Christian interpretation of the Psalter. Dr. Green is a ruling elder at New Life Presbyterian Church in Glenside, Pennsylvania. He and his wife, Rosemarie, have two children, Mitchell and Adelaide.

Bradley C. Gregory (M.A.R., Westminster Theological Seminary; Ph.D., University of Notre Dame) is Assistant Professor at the University of Scranton. He has also taught at St. John's School of Theology in Collegeville, Minnesota, and at the University of Notre Dame in South Bend, Indiana. He is the author of *Like an Everlasting Signet Ring: Generosity in the Book of Sirach* and various articles on the OT and second-temple Judaism.

He and his wife, Mendy, live in Scranton, Pennsylvania, with their two children, Benjamin and Adelaide.

J. Alan Groves (Th.M., Westminster Theological Seminary; Ph.D. candidate, Vrieje Universiteit) was at the time of his death in 2007 Vice President for Academic Affairs and Professor of Old Testament at Westminster Theological Seminary, where he had taught since 1982. In 1983 he became the director of the Westminster Hebrew Institute (subsequently renamed the J. Alan Groves Center for Advanced Biblical Research). Best known as a pioneer in the application of computer technology to the study of biblical Hebrew, Professor Groves had as his research interests the Deuteronomistic history and Isaiah. In the 1970s he served as a pastor in Vermont and for a number of years was a ruling elder at New Life Presbyterian Church (PCA) in Glenside, Pennsylvania. Professor Groves is survived by his wife, Elizabeth (Libbie), and four children, Alasdair, Rebeckah, Éowyn, and Alden.

Karen H. Jobes (M.A. and Ph.D., Westminster Theological Seminary) is the Gerald F. Hawthorne Professor of New Testament Greek and Exegesis at Wheaton College and Graduate School, where she has taught for five years. Before joining the faculty at Wheaton, she was Associate Professor of New Testament at Westmont College in Santa Barbara, California. She has also taught at Regent College (Vancouver), Eastern College (Philadelphia), and the Center for Urban Theological Studies (Philadelphia).

Dr. Jobes is the author of several books, including *1 Peter*, BECNT (Baker Academic, 2005), *Invitation to the Septuagint*, with Moisés Silva (Baker Academic, 2000), and *Esther*, NIVAC (Zondervan, 2000). She and her husband, Forrest, are members of Immanuel Presbyterian Church.

Michael B. Kelly (M.Div. and Ph.D. candidate, Westminster Theological Seminary) is Assistant Professor of Old Testament at Westminster Theological Seminary. Before coming to Westminster, he served in church planting and theological education in Latin America. For seven years he worked with Alan Groves in the Westminster Hebrew Institute, where he developed a passion for the Hebrew language, biblical theology, and a desire to teach both. His current research interests are in the books of Jeremiah and Judges, and in the field of text linguistics.

He and his wife, Shareen, have three children, Matthew, Joel, and Leah.

Samuel T. Logan Jr., (B.A. Princeton University, M.Div. Westminster Theological Seminary, Ph.D. Emory University) is International Director of the World Reformed Fellowship and Special Counsel to the President at Biblical Theological Seminary. He is also President Emeritus and Professor of Church History Emeritus at Westminster Theological Seminary. He has written articles on American and British Puritanism, the theology of Jonathan Edwards, and Christianity and Literature. He edited *The Preacher and Preaching, Confronting Kingdom Challenges*, and, with William S. Barker, *Sermons That Shaped America*.

Dr. Logan is an ordained minister of the Orthodox Presbyterian Church, and he serves on the boards of numerous Reformed and evangelical educational institutions. He is married to Susan, and they have two sons and two grandsons.

Tremper Longman III (B.A., Ohio Wesleyan University; M.Div., Westminster Theological Seminary; M.Phil. and Ph.D., Yale University) is the Robert H. Gundry Professor of Biblical Studies at Westmont College. He has written more than twenty books, including commentaries on Proverbs, Ecclesiastes, Song of Songs, Jeremiah, Lamentations, Daniel, and Nahum. In addition, he is one of the main translators of the popular New Living Translation and has served as a consultant on other popular translations of the Bible, including The Message, the New Century Version, and the Holman Standard Bible. He and Alice have three sons and two granddaughters.

Kirk E. Lowery (M.Div., Talbot Graduate School of Theology; M.A. and Ph.D., University of California, Los Angeles) is President and Senior Research Fellow of the J. Alan Groves Center for Advanced Biblical Research. He is also Adjunct Professor of Old Testament at Westminster Theological Seminary, teaching doctoral seminars in advanced Hebrew syntax, text linguistics of biblical Hebrew, and ancient Near Eastern languages such as Aramaic and Ugaritic.

His research interests include the intersection of information technology with biblical studies, as well as general and computational linguistics. He is a former chair and current member of the Computer Assisted Research Group of the Society of Biblical Literature and one of the moderators of the B-Hebrew Internet discussion group.

Dr. Lowery taught and lived in eastern Europe for fifteen years, including eight years as Professor of Old Testament for the Baptist Theological Seminary in Budapest. He is fluent in German and Hungarian. In 1998 he joined the staff of Westminster Theological Seminary as Associate Director of the Westminster Hebrew Institute, working together with Professor Alan Groves. In 2002 he assumed responsibilities as Director of the Institute until the Groves Center was incorporated as an independent nonprofit corporation in 2009.

Dr. Lowery is married to Jean, and they have one son, Kevin, who is a music performance major (violoncello) at the University of North Carolina, Greensboro. Dr. Lowery's personal interests include the active study of the oboe, and he is a licensed amateur radio operator.

Moisés Silva (M.Div. and Th.M., Westminster Theological Seminary; Ph.D., University of Manchester) has taught biblical studies at Westmont College, Westminster Theological Seminary, and Gordon-Conwell Theological Seminary. In recent years he has worked as an independent scholar on various projects, including the revision of the *Zondervan Encyclopedia of the Bible*. His special interests include Pauline exegesis and textual criticism, the Septuagint, the Semitic background of the NT, and the application of linguistic semantics to the biblical vocabulary. He and his wife, Pat, have four children and eight grandchildren.

Adrian T. Smith (B.Sc., University of London; Dip. Theol., Free Church of Scotland College; Th.M. and Ph.D., Westminster Theological Seminary) is Associate Professor of New Testament and Hermeneutics at Redeemer Seminary (Dallas). He is an ordained minister in the Associate Reformed Presbyterian Church.

Previously, he taught at Westminster Theological Seminary in Philadelphia (1998–2003), Reformed Theological Seminary (2000), and Erskine Theological Seminary (2003–6). In 2006, he joined the faculty of Westminster Theological Seminary in Dallas. In 2009, this campus became Redeemer Seminary, and Dr. Smith became a founding faculty member there.

He is married to Dawn, and they have one daughter, Emma. His spare time is devoted to watching and playing soccer.

Ebele (Eep) Talstra (B.A. and M.A. Vrije Universiteit of Amsterdam, Ph.D. University of Leiden) is Professor of Old Testament and Director of the "Werkgroep Informatica," a research group in Bible and Computing at the Faculty of Theology, Vrije Universiteit of Amsterdam. He has published many books and articles on classical Hebrew syntax, on Old Testament literary analysis (Solomon's Prayer), and on topics of Old Testament theology and exegesis (Oude en Nieuwe Lezers ["Old and New Readers"]). He is actively involved in the work of the Protestant Church of the Netherlands, and for many years has been active in a Dutch organization that works to include young people with special needs into regular education.

With his first wife, Lies, who died in January 2006, Dr. Talstra has two sons. In 2010 he will marry his new love, Saskia.

Bruce K. Waltke (Th.D. [Greek and New Testament], Dallas Theological Seminary; Ph.D. [Ancient Near Eastern Languages and Literatures], Harvard University) is Distinguished Professor of Old Testament at Knox Theological Seminary. He began his teaching career at Dallas Theological Seminary (1958–76), where he became Professor of Semitics and Old Testament and Dean of Doctoral Studies (1974). He joined the faculty of Regent College, an affiliate of the University of British Columbia, as Professor of Old Testament (1976–85) and then became Professor of Old Testament at Westminster Theological Seminary (1985–91). He returned to Regent College (1991–97), where he is now Professor Emeritus of Biblical Studies, teaching courses there annually. He was Professor of Old Testament at Reformed Theological Seminary in Orlando from 1997–2010. He has been a guest lecturer at numerous other seminaries. He served as President of the Evangelical Theological Society in 1976 and is currently on the editorial board of the Institute of Biblical Research.

While a student at Dallas, he pastored a Baptist church for two years. He has spoken at numerous Bible conferences.

His books include *An Introduction to Biblical Hebrew Syntax* (Eisenbrauns, 1990); commentaries on Micah (1987, 2007), on Genesis (2001), and on Proverbs 1–15 (2004) and Proverbs 15–31 (2005); and *An Old Testament Theology* (Zondervan, 2007). His book coauthored with Professor James Houston, *The Psalms as Christian Worship*, will be published by Eerdmans in 2010. Eerdmans is also currently preparing for publication a selection of his numerous miscellaneous articles.

Edward T. Welch (B.A., University of Delaware; M.Div., Biblical Theological Seminary; Ph.D., University of Utah) serves as a counselor and faculty member at The Christian Counseling and Educational Foundation (CCEF), and is adjunct professor of practical theology at Westminster Theological Seminary. He is the author of over a dozen books on biblical counseling, including, *Depression: A Stubborn Darkness*, and *Addiction: A Banquet in the Grave*. He is a ruling elder at Bridge Community Church (PCA). He and is wife Sheri have two married daughters and a growing number of nearly perfect grandchildren.

Index of Scripture and Related Works

Index of Names

Index of Subjects

Abrahamic covenant
  narrative of the Pentateuch, 81
  solution to humanity's condition, 80
atonement
  crucifixion at the heart of, 104
  Hebrew Bible, 92–93
  Isaiah, 93–95

biblical theology
  centered on Jesus Christ, 64
  and Christotelic hermeneutics, 62
  definition, 62–63
  influence of Geerhardus Vos, 62–64

Christotelic interpretation
  contrasted with Christocen-
    tric interpretation, 64, 66
  definition, 62
  generating mission, 72
  unfolding of redemptive history, 65
covenant, 3
  Ancient Near Eastern vassal treaty, 3
  curses for disobedience, 129
  grounded in God's promises
    to Abraham, 108
  land as symbol, 82
  prophets, 5

David
  worship at Zion, 22
death
  Ecclesiastes, 51–52
  Israel, 133
Deuteronomic history, 4–5

Ecclesiastes
  Christian reading, 57–60
  theological message, 57
ethics
  fear of I AM, 28
  speech and actions connected, 25–26
exile
  Babylonian, 84
  from Eden, 80
  ongoing condition for Jews, 85–86, 126
  theological paradigm for the church, 127

faith
  connected to worship of God, 20–21
  related to ethics, 21

globalization
  cautions against, 164–67
  positive aspects of, 163–64

Hebrew Bible
  Biblia Hebraica Quinta Project, xvi
  Codex Leningradensis, 172
  computational linguistics, 173n11
  electronic data, xiv–xv, xxvi–xxvii, 171
  electronic text, xi, xv, 171, 172
  morphology, xvi, 173–74, 173n10
heremenutics
  character, 140, 151
  missional, 62, 63, 67–72
  transformed by the Gospel, 58
history
  revelation, 63
  story, 179